Alcohol in Popular Culture

Alcohol in Popular Culture

AN ENCYCLOPEDIA

Rachel Black, Editor

AN IMPRINT OF ABC-CLIO, LLC
Santa Barbara, California • Denver, Colorado • Oxford, England

Library of Congress Cataloging-in-Publication Data

Alcohol in popular culture : an encyclopedia / Rachel Black, editor.
   p. cm.
Includes bibliographical references and index.
ISBN 978–0–313–38048–8 (hbk. : alk. paper) — ISBN 978–0–313–38049–5 (ebook)
1. Alcoholic beverages—Social aspects—United States—Encyclopedias. 2. Drinking of
alcoholic beverages—United States. 3. Alcoholic beverage industry—Social aspects—
United States. I. Black, Rachel, 1975–
HV5017.A435   2010
362.2920973—dc22   2010019892

ISBN: 978–0–313–38048–8
EISBN: 978–0–313–38049–5

14 13 12 11 10   1 2 3 4 5

This book is also available on the World Wide Web as an eBook.
Visit www.abc-clio.com for details.

Greenwood
An Imprint of ABC-CLIO, LLC

ABC-CLIO, LLC
130 Cremona Drive, P.O. Box 1911
Santa Barbara, California 93116-1911

This book is printed on acid-free paper (∞)

Manufactured in the United States of America

For my husband, Doug Cook, who offered me
support and encouragement from beginning to end.

Contents

Preface   ix

Acknowledgments   xi

Introduction   xiii

Timeline   xxi

List of Entries   xxv

Guide to Related Topics   xxvii

The Encyclopedia   1

Selected Bibliography   211

Index   219

About the Editor and Contributors   227

Preface

Alcohol production and consumption is a contentious topic in the United States. In the debates surrounding alcohol, the cultural context is often lost and over-shadowed by a focus on the health and social issues associated with alcoholism. These are serious issues that certainly require further study and debate. However, in this encyclopedia we have tried to focus on the often-marginalized and pop-culture aspects of alcohol use and misuse. Entries illuminate the favorite alcoholic beverages in the United States, how they are made, how they are incorporated in everyday life and special events, their role in history, their impacts on society and health, their role in the arts, and much more. This encyclopedia covers a broad time period: primarily from the Colonial era to the present day. A chronology helps to put the topic of alcohol in historical context. The geographic scope is largely limited to the United States, while in some instances going beyond the boundaries of this country to consider the connections and influences from outside. This encyclopedia should be seen as a starting point for further investigation. We hope that it will inspire and stimulate further consideration of the topics presented here.

More than 100 entries are arranged alphabetically from A to Z and largely focus on drinks themselves, concepts, business aspects, entertainment, ephemera, regulations, social aspects, movements, organizations, and important events that have played a part in creating the cultures of alcohol that are now part of the greater American culture and history. Sidebars throughout the work further illuminate the entries.

The contributors to this volume have a wide variety of backgrounds. Scholars from the fields of sociology, anthropology, history, and literature have lent their expertise to this work. In addition, journalists and professional writers have helped to give this encyclopedia a richer voice that speaks beyond academia. This volume has the rigor of an academic study, but the reader-friendly tone and approach will hopefully help this reach a wider audience that is interested in the popular culture aspects of alcohol in the United States.

Whether the reader is doing research on a specific subject or looking for general information on the culture of alcohol in the United States, this encyclopedia provides an excellent overview. Each entry is followed by a selection of suggested items for further reading. In addition, the selected bibliography is a solid resource for further research. It includes a section with reliable online resources, which include government agency sites, online museums, and primary sources.

Acknowledgments

This encyclopedia would not have been possible without all of the incredible contributors whose work is featured here. I would like to give particular thanks to Rémy Charest, who picked up some of the slack at the end and offered invaluable feedback, editorial support, and encouragement. I would also like to thank Pam Sezgin for her major contribution and for being such a lovely person to work with even while she faced a flooded home and the pressures of a demanding academic position. Thank you to Karen Saenz, who swooped in at the last minute with her anthropological and alcohol expertise. It was a pleasure and honor to work with friends and colleagues who are distinguished scholars and writers.

I also need to acknowledge that it was Ken Albala who was the person who first got me involved in this project and it was Wendi Schnaufer at Greenwood/ABC-CLIO who originally believed Ken when he said I was the right person for the job. Wendi, thank you for helping develop this project and for your patience and support. This has been an invaluable experience and I have learned all kinds of things about alcohol, big projects, and people while working on this book.

Introduction

Alcohol is full of contradictions. It is a euphoriant and a depressant; it is a poison and a medicine. For these reasons, discussion of alcohol and its place in society and culture engenders much debate and disagreement. We often overlook the fact that alcohol is a cultural artifact that can tell us about society: although alcohol is ultimately consumed, it plays an important part in the construction or breaking down of social norms. Alcohol can be an identity marker that denotes status, cultural capital, or gender differences. Rituals that focus on alcohol are often associated with rites of passage and life stages. All of these aspects of the culture of alcohol consumption and production have a rich history in the United States. One of the goals of this volume is to engage the reader in reconsidering everyday perceptions and discourses about alcohol.

How has alcohol shaped American society, and vice versa?

Historically, this country has had a turbulent relationship with alcohol, and at the same time, drink played an essential role in the founding of the United States from trade to social cohesion. Excess grain produced by farmers on the western frontier was distilled, making it easier to ship, and traded to the market in the east. Alcoholic drink and public drinking places helped build civil society in this young nation. Intertwined with the past and with America's cultural diversity, this well-lubricated history is multifaceted and complex. This work is a starting point for contemplating alcohol production, commerce, and consumption from its most social and convivial forms to its most destructive and antisocial aspects, which all make up the culture of alcohol in the United States.

Approaches for Studying Cultures of Alcohol

One of the most challenging aspects of compiling and editing a cultural encyclopedia of alcohol has been balancing voices and approaches to studying the complex subject of alcohol and culture. Scholars have mainly taken two approaches to looking at the cultural aspects of alcohol: one camp focusing on alcohol as an individual pathology or social problem, and another looking at "normal drinking" and alcohol as an integrated social element, something that has cultural value (Dietler 2006). This dichotomy is not meant to preclude approaches that lie outside of this spectrum. There are many positions between these two poles.

Most alcohol studies in North America tend to take the "alcohol as a social problem" approach, and this is largely due to the well-developed field of alcohol studies, which is usually part of health sciences research in epidemiology, addiction, and psychology (Hunt and Barker 2001). The United States has high rates of alcoholism: half the population is considered regular drinkers (conservatively defined by the Centers for Disease Control and Prevention [CDC] as those who consume at least 12 drinks in the past year). There are many serious social and health issues related to this situation, from domestic violence to driving under the influence, but these must be understood within a larger cultural context. It is important to understand how Americans came to be so preoccupied with their often-troubled relationship with alcohol. This is where the true complexity begins, and where the anthropologist and historian's work can come into play. It is also necessary to take a critical look at the way in which this research has been shaped by cultural beliefs and dominant moral values. This book tries in no way to deny the problems related to excessive alcohol consumption; however, we have tried to be aware of the way in which much of the alcohol research in the United States has been couched in anti-alcohol and temperance rhetoric. Alcohol is a political, economic, and moral subject. Studies that help understand the problems related to alcohol abuse can be biased by political views, strong economic interests, and religious beliefs. It could be said that culture has shaped both research agendas and public opinion about drinking. In this work, we have attempted to be critical of our sources while encompassing a wide range of perspectives.

The flip side of the coin is the "normal drinking" approach to studying alcohol. Looking at the most recent literature in alcohol studies, this type of research is rarer. It is true that histories and ethnographies of drinking in the United States focus on the cultural and anecdotal risk glossing over the negative impacts of drinking; yet, it must be possible to find a balanced picture of alcohol consumption that looks at both sides of the coin. There certainly is some "normal" drinking going on in the United States, but it is not the central focus of alcohol research in this country. The term "normal drinking" is even contentious, subjective, and nearly impossible to define in a concrete manner. There is even a large population of Americans who abstain, and this group is not often considered when studying drinking habits. Still, only a limited amount of research focuses on moderate, social drinking in the United States (Heath 2000). It is difficult to find a balanced account of alcohol use and its place in American culture (Barrows and Room 1991). This is indicative of a larger cultural issue in America: alcohol is largely seen as a problem. In turn, this stance is reinforced by popular politics and culture. Many Americans have argued that alcohol is one of the few legalized drugs that is normalized through a culture of consumption. It is this uneasy relationship with alcohol that teeters between control and out of control that makes it such a difficult subject to study from a cultural perspective. What is certain is that any work that attempts to address alcohol as a positive or negative is entering into the fray of a hot debate.

This cultural encyclopedia of alcohol tries to understand the positive cultural aspects of alcohol consumption in America (for example, community creation, social cohesion, and culinary culture) while also looking at the cultural roots of some of the most dangerous and damaging aspects of alcohol consumption and production in this country. We have also tried to include topics that deal with alcohol as a cultural artifact by including entries such as "drinking vessels" and "beer bongs" and, in contrast, others that look at the social aspects of popular American drinking culture such as the "barfly" and "temperance."

Colonists, Natives, and Drink

It would be impossible to create a cultural encyclopedia of alcohol in America without considering the historical relationship between this land, its native people, the first colonists, and the streams of immigrants who populated the country from east to west. Most native populations of America did not originally have a culture of drink, but tribes such as the Zuni and Huron were fermenting grains as part of food preparation. The native people of the area that we now refer to as the United States used other state-altering substances, such as peyote (*Lophophora williamsii*) and jimsonweed (*Datura stramoium*), as part of religious ceremonies and usually in highly ritualized contexts. In contrast, Central and South American native people had both fermented beverages and food.

Alcohol quickly entered into relationships between Native Americans and European settlers. It was traded for commodities and goods (furs, corn, and tobacco, for example) and quickly altered the social structures of many native bands. The "firewater myth," which suggests that Native Americans have a predisposition to drink a lot of alcohol and are prone to uncontrollable behavior while intoxicated, was born out of this focus on heavy or binge drinking that was initially due to a foreign intoxicant being introduced to a culture that had no social norms to control its use. However, as Caetano et al. argue (1998), different tribes responded differently to the introduction of alcohol into their societies. These responses ranged from Navajo acceptance of social drinking to the Hopi view that drinking is irresponsible (Mail and Johnson 1993). Many native tribes have dealt with problematic relationships by turning to abstinence as the answer (Duran and Duran 1995). Other groups have not escaped the predominance of binge drinking that has shaped popular stereotypes, and alcohol abuse remains a major social and health issue for many American tribes.

European colonists were the first immigrants to come to America and bring their culture of drink. Europeans brought the plants that would provide their alcohol and went through some difficult agricultural shifts as they adapted to the new climate and soil. When settling in New World, ensuring a supply of alcohol was given a high priority. Even before British colonization, Spaniards had attempted to plant grape vines brought from the Old World. In most cases, these vines, *vitis vinifera*, failed to take root because of the inhospitable climate, soil type, pests, and disease. Early vineyards planted with Native American grapes, such as *vitis labrusca*, did not produce palatable wines. Wines like Madeira were shipped from the Old World to satisfy the colonial elite, but the "masses" were left to produce their own alcoholic beverages from what they could grow and what was available. This was serious business because alcohol was an important social, nutritional, and religious element in most European cultures. Michael Pollan eloquently outlines this symbiotic relationship between plants and humans in his book *Botany of Desire* (2001), explaining that early colonists brought apple seedlings and cuttings with them to ensure a supply of alcohol from hard cider. The pioneer nursery man Johnny Appleseed was busily planting orchards in what is now Ohio, Indiana, and Illinois to make sure early American settlers had their tipple. Barley, malted and used for making both beer and whiskey, and hops were planted by early Dutch and English settlers, and beer brewing and distilling were soon booming business in the new colonies. Alcohol was also a major source of revenue for colonial governments—taxation often was the central cause of tension between thirsty colonists and European governments, who tried to control the consumption of alcohol and profit from its sale. Much of alcohol production was on a very small scale and produced in the home. Where barley and wheat were difficult to cultivate, the central crop was usually corn. Early settlers began producing corn-based whiskey. Distilled alcohol of this type, such as bourbon, came to be America's most popular drink. Bourbon shows how immigrants bring with them their own culture, whiskey distilling in this case, and adapt it to a new environment, eventually creating something novel and distinctive. America is full of Old/New World cultural hybrids.

Colonial American history is dotted with lore and accounts of excessive drinking and associated violence. Early colonists came to America in many cases to escape the oppressive politics in Europe, and part of the newfound liberty for some was expressed through drinking culture. Alcohol also had other practical functions in the colonies. Adding alcohol to water was a common way of purifying otherwise unpotable water. Besides being used to sterilize wounds, alcohol was also an ingredient in many medicines and common remedies. It certainly helped dull pain before modern painkillers were invented. The medicinal uses of alcohol in early America are an often-overlooked area of alcohol culture and common use of alcohol.

After the American Revolution ended with the symbolic signing of the Declaration of Independence in 1776, alcohol continued to be heavily taxed and was an important source of revenue for the new republic's coffers. Alcohol was a constant bone of political contention, which culminated in Prohibition from 1920 to 1933. During this period, the sale, production, and transportation of alcohol was, for all intents and purposes, banned in the United States.

American Diversity: Drinking Cultures

Besides Native Americans, all the inhabitants of the United States are immigrants. Consequently, a country made up largely of immigrants is a country with immense cultural diversity. The original immigrants to the United States—mainly British, Scottish, French, Irish, German, African, and Dutch—brought with them their own cultural and social norms concerning alcohol. At the same time, climatic and social differences in this new land played a big part in creating a unique American drinking culture. New beverages were developed, particularly corn-based alcohol, and new social spaces, such as saloons, for consuming alcohol abounded. Due to the heterogeneity of the American population, drink and drinking cultures have often been a cause for conflict. Social norms surrounding the consumption of alcoholic beverages are still evolving in this country.

Each wave of immigration to the United States has brought with it new forms of drinking culture. New cultures were often greeted with suspicion, and the subject of alcohol was usually where cultural difference and xenophobia showed its uglier side. For example, Italian immigrants to America in the early twentieth century were seen as lazy and immoral because of the inclusion of wine in their daily diet (Cinotto 2001). Conversely, the Chinese who came to build the railroads in America were viewed with distain and distrust because they did not drink (Barnett 1952). The social space of the bar or the saloon was frequently a place where racial and ethnic boundaries were transgressed. This was not always a peaceable affair, and these drinking establishments became associated with social disorder and interethnic conflict—to the point where official and unofficial segregation took place (Powers 1988).

The same sort of segregation is largely true of the gendered differences of American drinking culture. American women's relationship with alcohol changed greatly throughout American history. Women were initially seen as keepers of the domestic hearth, and drinking was an unacceptable activity for respectable women. This is not to say that women did not drink; however, where they drank and what people thought of them when they imbibed changed over time. Again, class, ethnicity, and race played an important part in the social norms surrounding women's drinking. Drinking eventually became a way for American women to cross social barriers and challenge gender identity. This was a long and difficult struggle that often ended in social ostracism and dangerous alcohol abuse. By the end of the mid-twentieth century, American women had made their way to the bar and exercised their right to partake in all areas of social life in this country.

Bars and saloons offer social spaces for people who may not be welcome in other public spheres. In addition, the consumption of alcohol can help break down inhibitions and create social openness. This has certainly been the case for gay, lesbian, and transgendered Americans. Alcohol and bar culture has played an important part in their communities' social lives. Bars have also been important sites of protest and transgression for these groups, such as seen in the Stonewall riots in New York in 1969. This police raid on the Stonewall Inn, a bar in Greenwich Village, is often cited as the moment in American history when the homosexual community started to fight back against government persecution. It is significant that this symbolic conflict took place at a bar.

Alcohol in the United States is not a free-for-all; some overlying cultural norms relating to the consumption of alcohol have been established. For instance, it is considered socially unacceptable (and unlawful) to let minors drink. Meanwhile, other norms remain exclusive to specific ethnic or racial groups; for example, Chinese Americans have a higher rate of abstinence from alcohol compared with most other ethnic groups. That said, it is difficult to identify overarching behavioral patterns. As Caetano et al. (1998) noted, although ethnic minorities are underrepresented in American alcohol research, the utility of looking at racial or ethnic stereotypes is limited because of the variations with in each group. Variability is one of the defining factors of alcohol consumption in the United States.

Role of Culture in Alcohol Consumption in the United States

Alcohol is both a product of human culture and a substance that shapes this same culture. Human skill, tradition, and scientific knowledge have developed over time to produce a range of different intoxicating alcoholic substances. Both the agriculture and the technique involved in fermenting or distilling alcohol make it a complex cultural product. Europeans brought their agricultural know-how to America and planted crops that were familiar to them while adapting new crops, such as corn, for the purpose of making alcohol. Adaptation and innovation are part of nearly all cultural processes. Hybrids in the consumption and production of alcohol that came out of the meeting of diverse cultures began to form new and distinctly American forms of alcohol culture. The saloon was the American answer to the British pub, while bourbon was the New World adaptation of whiskey.

American literature, theater, art, and film reveal a great deal about this country's relationship with alcohol. But culture, at a more pedestrian level, is also shaped by alcohol. The ways in which social spaces for drinking are organized, and in which the laws and legislation regulating alcohol are constructed, reveal another way in which alcohol shapes American culture. Someone younger than 21 years of age cannot walk into a bar and order a pint of beer, but a 21-year-old can go to a drive-through and purchase a daiquiri in Louisiana. These laws are culturally constructed barriers that shape society through limiting or attempting to limit who can consume alcohol and who cannot. Alcohol both breaks down barriers and sets up limitations.

This encyclopedia has attempted to capture some of the cultural complexity created by Americans' relationship with alcohol. From Prohibition to college binge drinking, Americans are still struggling and defining social and cultural norms concerning alcohol. By trying to understand the cultural and historical place of alcohol in the United State, we can see where the troubles arise in various forms of alcohol abuse and where the positive points can lead to a socially integrated, responsible drinking culture.

References

Barnett, Milton Leonard. *Alcohol and Culture: A Study of Drinking in a Chinese-American Community*. Ithaca, NY: Cornell University Press, 1952.

Barrows, S., and R. Room, eds. *Drinking Behavior and Belief in Modern History*. Berkeley: University of California Press, 1991.

Caetano, Raul, Catherine L. Clark, and Tammy Tam. "Alcohol Consumption among Racial/Ethnic Minorities: Theory and Research." *Alcohol Health and Research World* 22, no. 4 (1988): 233–41.

Centers for Disease Control and Prevention. "Alcohol Use." May 15, 2009. http://www.cdc.gov/nchs/fastats/alcohol.htm.

Cinotto, Simone. *Una famiglia che mangia insieme: Cibo ed etnicità nella communità italoamericana di New York, 1920–1940*. Torino: Otto Editore, 2001.

Dietler, Michael. "Alcohol: Anthropological/Archeological Perspectives." *Annual Review of Anthropology* 35 (2006): 229–49.

Duran, E., and B. Duran. *Native American Postcolonial Psychology*. Albany: State University of New York Press, 1995.

Heath, Dwight. *Drinking Occasions: Comparative Perspectives on Alcohol and Culture*. Ann Arbor, MI: Sheridan Books, 2000.

Hunt, Geoffrey, and Judith C. Barker. "Socio-cultural Anthropology and Alcohol and Drug Research: Towards a Unified Theory." *Social Science and Medicine* 53 (2001): 165–88.

Mails, P. D., and S. Johnson. "Boozing, Sniffing, and Toking: An Overview of the Past, Present, and Future of Substance Use by American Indians." *American Indian and Alaska Native Mental Health Research* 5 (1993): 1–33.

Pollan, Michael. *Botany of Desire: A Plant's Eye-View of the World.* New York: Random House, 2001.

Powers, Madelon. *Faces along the Bar: Lore and Order in the Workingman's Saloon 1870–1920.* Chicago: University of Chicago Press, 1998.

Timeline

1500s	The Spanish begin to set up colonies in North America in the areas that are now Georgia and Florida. The first African slaves are brought to America.
1600s	The Spanish continue to colonize in the south and west, but their defeat in Europe places the British in a dominant role in North America. The Dutch, Swedes, Russians, French, and British set up colonies on the eastern seaboard. The brewing and distilling of alcohol becomes an important trade in these colonies.
1600s–1800s	Triangular trade between the American colonies, West Africa, the Caribbean, and Europe thrives. In particular, molasses from the Caribbean was sold to New England or to Europe, where it was distilled into rum and traded in Africa for slaves and gold.
1654	Massachusetts creates laws against home-brewing in attempt to gain greater control over the production and consumption of alcohol.
1673	Puritan Increase Mather writes *Wo to Drunkards*.
1770s	The first grape vines for winemaking are planted in what would become California and one of the country's finest wine regions.
1781	Reverend Samuel Peters first mentions "Blue Laws" with relation to the laws in Puritan colonies that prohibited certain business activities during the Sabbath.
1784	Prominent citizen, physician, and politician Benjamin Rush publishes *An Inquiry into the Effects of Spirituous Liquors on the*

1784 (*cont.*)	*Human Body and Mind*, one of the first temperance texts written in America.
1791	U.S. Congress imposes an excise tax on domestic whiskey distilleries.
1794	The Whiskey Rebellion takes place in western Pennsylvania as farmers revolt against the distilling tax. This is the first time the federal government imposes order by sending in federal troops.
1802	Congress passes laws that prohibit the sale of alcohol to Native Americans.
	The Whiskey Tax is repealed by President Thomas Jefferson.
1810	First Oktoberfest, to celebrate a royal marriage in Munich, Germany.
1814–17	A temporary alcohol tax is levied to help finance the War of 1812.
1826	The American Society for the Promotion of Temperance is founded.
1833	The Congressional Temperance Society is founded.
1837	The Temperance Union is founded.
1838	Massachusetts is the first state to place severe restrictions on the sale of alcohol.
1842	The Sons of Temperance organization is formed in New York and spreads across the nation, laying the groundwork for the prohibition movement.
1844	The temperance play *The Drunkard* is presented in Boston.
1860	Nearly 1,140 distilleries produce 88 million gallons of liquor in the United States.
1862	Congress develops a modern alcohol taxation system as a means to fund the Civil War. It remains in place even after the war. Through the Act of July 1, an Office of Internal Revenue is created within the Department of the Treasury to collect taxes on distilled spirits and tobacco products.
	The United States Brewers' Association is formed in response to the new federal excise and license taxes on alcohol.
1869	The Prohibition Party is launched in Chicago.
1873	The Women's Temperance Crusade starts in Fredonia, New York.
	The Woman's Christian Temperance Union is formed
1875	The "Whiskey Ring" is broken up by the federal government. Made up of an association of grain dealers, politicians, and revenue agents, this group defrauds the government of millions of dollars in distilled spirits taxes.

1886	The National Union of United Brewery Workmen becomes one of the first industrial unions.
1893	The federal government investigates the "Whiskey Trust," which bribed distributors to not carry competing brands.
1895	The Anti-Saloon League is founded.
1900	Carry Nation begins to lead attacks on illegal saloons in Kansas.
1906	The Pure Food and Drug Act regulates the labeling of products containing alcohol.
1912	The importing of absinthe into the United States is banned.
1917	The Lever Act is passed by Congress, limiting the production of beer and banning distilling as a wartime measure.
1918	The Association against the Prohibition Amendment (AAPA) is founded.
1919	The Eighteenth Amendment of the U.S. Constitution is adopted, ushering in the Prohibition period.
	The Volstead Act (the National Prohibition Act) passes despite President Woodrow Wilson's veto.
1920–33	Despite Prohibition, the illicit alcohol trade flourishes.
1931	The Wickersham Commission acknowledges that Prohibition laws are not being upheld.
1933	Repeal of Prohibition. The Twenty-first Amendment is ratified, officially ending Prohibition.
	Despite the Twenty-first Amendment, many local governments do not repeal Prohibition. Dry counties result.
1935	Alcoholics Anonymous is founded.
1936	The Federal Alcohol Administration Act lays the post-Prohibition framework for regulation of alcohol. Excise taxes on alcohol began to climb again.
1938	Professor Rolla Harger invents the Drunkometer—a breath-testing device to measure alcohol levels. It is the predecessor of the breathalyzer.
1939	The Alcoholics Anonymous *Big Book* is published.
1944	The National Council on Alcoholism (NCA) is founded to promote the disease concept of alcohol.
	The U.S. Public Health Service reports that alcoholism is the fourth-biggest health problem.
1946–96	Liquor companies ban television advertising.

1969	Riots break out after a police raid against homosexuals at the Stonewall Inn, a bar in the Greenwich Village neighborhood of New York City.
1973	Physicians Kenneth Lyons Jones and David Weyhe Smith identify and name Fetal Alcohol Syndrome.
1976	One of America's first microbreweries, the New Albion Brewing Company, opens in Sonoma, California.
1978	The home-brewing of beer is made legal for the first time since Prohibition.
1980s	The microbrewery trend spreads from the United Kingdom to the United States. A microbrewery produces fewer than 15,000 barrels of beer a year.
1980	Candy Lightner, whose daughter is killed by a drunk driver, founds Mothers Against Drunk Driving (MADD).
1982	The Betty Ford Center, a drug and alcohol rehabilitation center that becomes renowned, is cofounded by former First Lady Betty Ford and Leonard Firestone in Rancho Mirage, California.
1984	The federal government passes the National Minimum Drinking Age Act, essentially requiring all states to raise the legal drinking age to 21.
1988	The Harvard Alcohol Project is launched to reduce incidents of driving under the influence.
1990s	"Designated driver" becomes a household term.
	The manufacture and sale of absinthe is reauthorized in some European countries.
2000	Congress creates a standard for defining drunk driving (a blood-alcohol concentration [BAC] of 0.08).
2003	The Alcohol and Tobacco Tax and Trade Bureau (TTB) is established by order of the Homeland Security Act of 2002.
2006	The United States and the European Union sign an agreement that restricts the use of regional names on wine labels (for example, Champagne and Burgundy).
2007	St. George Spirits of Alameda, California, sells the first bottle of absinthe in the United States since the drink was banned in 1912.

List of Entries

Absinthe
Advertising
African Americans
Alcoholics Anonymous (AA)
Alcoholism
Alcopops
Anti-Saloon League
Applejack
Arts
Bar Bets
Bar Games
Barfly
Bars
Bartending
Beer
Beer Belly
Beer Bongs
Beer Goggles
Beer Pong
Beer Runs
Binge drinking
Blackouts
Blood Alcohol Content (BAC)
Blue Laws
Bootleg Alcohol
Bourbon
Breathalyzer Test
Breweriana

Brewing
Burping
Carding
Champagne
Cider
Class
Cocktail Parties
Cocktails
College Drinking Culture
Designated Driver
Distilling
Distribution
Drinking Age Legislation
Drinking Games
Drinking Glasses and Vessels
Drinking Rituals
Drinking Songs
Driving under the Influence (DUI)
Dry Counties
Economics
Elderly
Fermentation
Fetal Alcohol Syndrome
Films
Food and Drink Culture
Free Drinks
Gin
Hair of the Dog

Hangovers
Happy Hour
Health Effects of Alcohol
Home-Brew
Hooch
Internet
Interventions
Keggers
Kosher Wine
Last Call
Liquor Boards
Liquor Licenses
Liquor Stores
Literature
Madeira
Mardi Gras
Martinis
Medical Uses of Alcohol
Men and Boys Drinking
Microbreweries
Mothers Against Drunk Driving
   (MADD)
Music
National Identity
Native Americans
Oktoberfest
Peer Pressure
Perry
Politics
Prohibition
Pub Crawls

Pubs
Punch
Race and Ethnicity
Rehab
Religion
Rum
Sake
Shooters
Skid Row and the Bowery
Sommeliers
Speakeasies
Sports
St. Patrick's Day
Television
Temperance
Tequila
Terroir
Toasting
Underage Drinking
Violence, Alcohol-related
Vodka
Whiskey
Wine
Wine Coolers
Wine Tasting
Wine Tourism
Winemaking, Home
Winos
Woman's Christian Temperance Union
Women and Girls Drinking
Workplace Drinking

Guide to Related Topics

Alcoholism
Alcoholics Anonymous (AA)
Alcoholism
Barfly
Binge Drinking
Blackouts
Blood Alcohol Content (BAC)
Fetal Alcohol Syndrome
Health Effects of Alcohol
Interventions
Rehab
Skid Row and the Bowery
Violence, Alcohol-related
Winos
Workplace Drinking

Bar Culture
Bar Bets
Barfly
Bar Games
Bars
Bartending
Carding
Cocktails
Drinking Games
Drinking Glasses and Vessels

Drinking Rituals
Drinking Songs
Food and Drink Culture
Free Drinks
Hair of the Dog
Happy Hour
Last Call
Pub Crawls
Pubs
Shooters
St. Patrick's Day
Tequila
Toasting
Violence, Alcohol-related

Celebrations
Drinking Rituals
Mardi Gras
Oktoberfest
St. Patrick's Day
Toasting

College Drinking
Alcopops
Bar Games
Beer Bongs

Beer Pong
Beer Runs
Binge Drinking
Burping
Carding
College Drinking Culture
Drinking Games
Hair of the Dog
Keggers
Peer Pressure
Pub Crawls
Shooters
Underage Drinking

Drinks
Absinthe
Alcopops
Applejack
Beer
Bourbon
Champagne
Cider
Cocktails
Gin
Hair of the Dog
Hooch
Martinis
Perry
Punch
Rum
Sake
Shooters
Tequila
Vodka
Whiskey
Wine
Wine Coolers

Entertainment
Arts
Bar Bets
Bar Games
Bartending
Cocktail Parties
Drinking Games
Drinking Songs

Films
Oktoberfest
Pub Crawls
Sports
Television

Fermented Drinks
Applejack
Beer
Beer Belly
Beer Bongs
Beer Goggles
Beer Pong
Beer Runs
Brewing
Champagne
Cider
Drinking Glasses and
    Vessels
Fermentation
Home-Brew
Kosher Wine
Madeira
Microbreweries
Perry
Sake
Sommeliers
Terroir
Wine
Wine Coolers
Wine Tasting
Wine Tourism

Gender
Barfly
Bars
Class
Cocktails
Drinking Rituals
Fetal Alcohol Syndrome
Men and Boys Drinking
Pubs
Sports
Woman's Christian Temperance
    Union (WCTU)
Women and Girls Drinking

Health and Medicine
Alcoholics Anonymous (AA)
Alcoholism
Beer Belly
Binge Drinking
Blackouts
Blood Alcohol Content (BAC)
Burping
Fetal Alcohol Syndrome
Hair of the Dog
Hangovers
Health Effects of Alcohol
Internet
Interventions
Medical Uses of Alcohol
Rehab

Law and Politics
Blood Alcohol Content (BAC)
Blue Laws
Bootleg Alcohol
Breathalyzer Test
Carding
Designated Driver
Distribution
Drinking Age Limit
Dry Counties
Driving under the Influence
    (DUI)
Economics
Liquor Boards
Liquor Licenses
Liquor Stores
Mothers Against Drunk Driving
    (MADD)
Politics
Prohibition
Punch
Temperance
Underage Drinking

Material Culture
Advertising
Arts
Breweriana
Drinking Glasses and Vessels

Drinking Songs
Films
Food and Drink Culture
Literature
Music
Television

Production
Brewing
Distilling
Fermentation
Home-Brew
Winemaking, Home

Prohibition and Temperance
Alcoholics Anonymous (AA)
Anti-Saloon League
Blue Laws
Bootleg Alcohol
Cocktails
Designated Driver
Dry Counties
Economics
Home-Brew
Hooch
Prohibition
Speakeasies
Temperance
Woman's Christian Temperance
    Union (WCTU)

Social, Ethnic, and Racial Groups
African Americans
Class
College Drinking Culture
Elderly
Men and Boys Drinking
National Identity
Native Americans
Race and Ethnicity
Religion
St. Patrick's Day
Underage Drinking
Woman's Christian Temperance
    Union (WCTU)
Women and Girls Drinking

Spirits
Absinthe
Bootleg Alcohol
Bourbon
Cocktails
Distilling
Gin
Hooch
Martinis
Punch
Rum
Tequila
Vodka
Whiskey

A

ABSINTHE

Absinthe is a potent spirit ranging from 45 to 75 percent alcohol, based on worm-wood (*Artemisia absinthium*) and other aromatic herbs including hyssop and anise. It is normally consumed by placing a shot in a large absinthe glass and then slowly dribbling in cold water through a sugar cube positioned on a perforated spoon. This creates a *louche*, or swirling green clouds. The chemical thujone in absinthe makes the mind alert, creative, and expansive, and some claim it can cause hallucinations. Absinthe's great mystique is due to its association with Impressionist-era painters such as Vincent van Gogh, poets such as the symbolist Arthur Rimbaud, as well as Oscar Wilde and Charles Baudelaire. Only after a notorious absinthe-induced murder case in Switzerland in 1905 was absinthe made illegal in most of Europe and the United States. Various forms of pastis, without wormwood, took absinthe's place.

Until 2007 absinthe was not manufactured or legally sold in the United States, and aficionados were forced to smuggle the drink from abroad, normally from one of the countries where it was still produced, such as Switzerland, Spain, or the Czech Republic. The Val du Travers in Switzerland is reputed to be the birthplace of absinthe, though older forms had been distilled centuries before as a medicinal, and even the ancient Romans flavored **wine** with wormwood. Since legalization, a number of absinthes are produced in the United States to wide acclaim, although some insist that it is no longer as special because it is legal. Nonetheless, brands such as Lucid and Kübler were the first to appear, followed by St. George made in California and Mansinthe by heavy metal singer Marilyn Manson. Other manufacturers quickly followed suit and the renaissance of absinthe continues unabated.

Further Reading

Cargill, Kima. "Distilling the Scientific Truth about Absinthe." *Food, Culture and Society: An International Journal of Multidisciplinary Research* 11, no. 1 (March 2008): 87–99.

Conrad, Barnaby. *Absinthe: History in a Bottle.* San Francisco: Chronicle Books, 1998.

Ken Albala

ADVERTISING

Before the late 1800s alcohol advertisements by major producers in the United States were primarily targeted to the upper class, taking the form of artistic depictions of the product or people enjoying their drink. Other advertising was local and simpler in the form of signs and occasional newspaper advertisements from area brewers and distilleries or local drinking establishments.

Beer advertisements in the 1940s and 1950s attempted to normalize women's consumptions of beer, at the time a beverage associated with masculinity and male drinking in America. At the same time, images of women were used to sell beer to men. (Bettmann/Corbis)

Advertising escalated with the advent of mass literacy and mass production. Innovations in production and refrigeration combined with larger concentrations of literate citizens in America's cities made the business of alcohol more lucrative and easier to advertise. As lithography prints slowly gave way to simpler mass-produced posters, old styles intersected with new trends. An 1889 poster for Burke Ale featured Cap Anson and Buck Ewing, two prominent baseball players, raising tall glasses while sitting next to a large tent. The combination of alcohol advertising and sports had arrived.

The twentieth century witnessed massive growth in the advertising business. Early twentieth-century advertisements provided traditional depictions of drinking as a pleasant experience, but alcohol was also advertised as possessing health benefits. Exotic liquors claimed to ease digestions, throat pain, headaches, and even the ills of pregnancy. **Prohibition** paused developments from 1919 to 1933, and the Great Depression dampened spending and advertising in the 1930s as well. However, a rush of alcohol-related advertisements appeared following the repeal of Prohibition—liquor and **beer** advertisements appeared throughout the pages of the *New York Times* as new companies sought to corner the reopened market. One of the longest-lasting advertising symbols from an American company, the Budweiser Clydesdales team pulling a delivery wagon, became prominent in the 1930s. Since delivering a case of beer to President Franklin D. Roosevelt in the White House during a promotional tour of the eastern United States, these horses have been nationwide symbols of the Budweiser brand. Advertisements from the nineteenth and early twentieth centuries are popular collector's items and commonly reproduced art prints today. In this enthusiasm for the consumer culture of yesteryear **beer, wine,** and liquor posters from the United States and abroad figure prominently.

When alcohol advertising returned to prominence, historical events and new forms of media changed its methods. Poster ads during World War II associated alcohol, particularly beer, with the military. Companies fought to have their beer, as well as cigarettes and other "necessities" of the time, available to off-duty soldiers at military bases throughout the world in order to promote their connection with the troops. Budweiser was among the companies linking their brand to patriotism along with many others, including Schlitz, which featured a poster boasting that "every fourth bottle of Schlitz goes overseas."

New media dramatically shaped alcohol advertising. Radio and **television** meant that sound substituted for or combined with image to sell products. Although sponsorships were not unheard of before, the ability of celebrities to lend their actual voice or presence to an advertisement greatly expanded the practice. Like much of early television, early televised alcohol ads often appeared unprofessional and awkward, particularly because the celebrities endorsing the product were unlikely to have acting experience.

A new golden age of advertising began as companies experimented with new styles to match the cultural tumult of the 1960s and 1970s. From abstract art to minimalist simplicity, alcohol was depicted in a wide array of colors, shapes, and sizes. American pop art, epitomized by Roy Lichtenstein and Andy Warhol, often depicted commercial images artistically and in turn impacted advertising. Contemporary alcohol advertising contains the promise of popularity and high living toned down with exclusivity, or a hearkening back to tradition. Imported liquor embraces the former. Tanqueray **gin** and Captain Morgan **rum** advertisements associate their drinks with wild yet exclusive parties and attractive women, though men have appeared more often, for example as handsome bartenders. American-made **whiskey** and beer are advertised in a similar style but with an old-fashioned image, and appeal to tradition. Coors, Miller, Budweiser, and Jack Daniel's advertisements often describe the historical origin of their product. These advertisements often feature a strong, quiet male character or voice-over, either a Western cowboy or an Average Joe figure.

However, not all this advertising was in favor of alcohol consumption. After the Civil War, the **Temperance Movement** produced advertisements calling attention to the abuse of alcohol and advocating prohibition. From the 1990s to the present, a new wave of ads appeared reminding viewers of drinking's dangers. Numerous lawsuits were filed in the 1990s seeking to limit alcohol advertising, and controversy has led to the regulation of alcohol advertising, particularly liquor, at sporting events, in print publications, and on billboards in areas where children may be present. Alcohol ads have begun to include reminders to "drink responsibly" and avoid driving while intoxicated. As alcohol advertising continues to evolve, brewers and distillers try to sell not only their drink but their image and dedication to public safety. (*See also* **Politics**.)

Further Reading

Balko, Radley. "The Government Should Not Censor Alcohol Advertising." In *Alcohol: The History of Drugs and Alcohol*, ed. Ann Manheimer. New York: Thomson Gale, 2007.

Dade, Penny. *Drink Talking: 100 Years of Alcohol Advertising*. London: Middlesex University Press, 2008.

Jernigan, David H. "Alcohol Advertising to Young People Should Be Limited." In *Alcohol: The History of Drugs and Alcohol*, ed. Ann Manheimer. New York: Thomson Gale, 2007.

Manheimer, Ann, ed. *Alcohol: The History of Drugs and Alcohol*. New York: Thomson Gale, 2007.

Michael Lejman

AFRICAN AMERICANS

African Americans have had a distinctive relationship with alcohol throughout history due largely to laws and policies that the white majority aimed at the black population. Alcohol was familiar to early African Americans—**beer** was common in Africa before the transatlantic slave trade ensued, and, on the plantations of the West Indies, many slaves received **rum**.

In continental North America, alcohol restrictions grew with the institution of slavery in the seventeenth century. Fear of slave uprisings and a desire to maximize labor production convinced owners to forbid alcohol to slaves, except at Christmas when work was light. Recognizing that intoxication reduced African American deference to the white population, authorities also restricted free blacks' access to alcohol.

The free black population formed **temperance** societies during the early nineteenth century, and these church-based groups grew in size and number after slavery ended. Black drinking habits changed—consumption moved from public to domestic places, and beer replaced hard liquor as the preferred beverage, reducing drunkenness. Despite this, white concern over black intoxication grew. Fears of drunken black men assaulting white women and committing other crimes led to numerous state and local alcohol laws.

In this way, issues of gender, race, and drink were intertwined at the start of the twentieth century. **Prohibition** supporters in Georgia, Alabama, and elsewhere asserted that a liquor ban would improve white control of African Americans. They accused black voters of blocking past prohibition measures. Additionally, they voiced concern about racial mixing in saloons while Jim Crow laws segregated the races in respectable venues.

Presenting prohibition as a racial issue increased white support for a liquor ban, particularly after the 1906 Atlanta race riot. White observers, spurred by false news reports, accused black drunks of sexually assaulting white women, and white Atlantans consequently attacked their black neighbors. Following this, white Georgians supported prohibition as the surest way to prevent another riot.

Black views on prohibition varied. Clergymen supported it, believing the actions of drunken black laborers confirmed white assertions of black inferiority. Many black laborers, however, viewed prohibition as a means to tighten white control of the black population. Drinking was a form of defiance. In Oklahoma, Georgia, Alabama, and elsewhere, these black voters opposed prohibition and supported the alcohol industry.

Under state and subsequently national Prohibition, some African Americans sold alcohol illegally. Racial prejudices excluded them from lucrative jobs, and the illicit liquor industry offered high rewards, though at high risk. Some prospered in these positions and gained greater social influence. Many, however, were at the mercy of white authorities who singled out black violators for arrest.

Following Prohibition, black alcohol consumption mirrored that of American society generally, particularly if economic factors are considered. Certain brands of alcohol, particularly malt liquors, have been marketed to African Americans, though this is tied as much to their low economic status as to ethnicity. Black participation in self-help groups such as **Alcoholics Anonymous** also paralleled that of American society at large, and black clergymen maintained their opposition to alcohol.

Further Reading

Martin, Jack K., Steven A. Tuch, and Paul M. Roman. "Problem Drinking Patterns among African Americans: The Impacts of Reports of Discrimination, Perceptions of Prejudice and Risky Coping Strategies." *Journal of Health and Social Behavior* 44, no. 3 (2003): 408–25.

James Klein

ALCOHOLICS ANONYMOUS (AA)

Founded in 1935 by Bill Wilson and Ebby Thacher, Alcoholics Anonymous (AA) is a mutual aid society that offers support for those who want to stop drinking alcohol.

Wilson and his wife joined the Oxford Group, a nondenominational movement based on "Four Absolutes"—honesty, purity, unselfishness, and love. Wilson tried to reach out to a group of alcoholics who wanted to stop drinking. Initially, he was unsuccessful in helping this group stay sober. Wilson sought the help of physician William Silkworth, who suggested that Wilson begin by addressing **alcoholism** as an illness. During a business trip to Akron, Ohio, Wilson met Bob Smith, a fellow recovering alcoholic, who would later help Wilson work out the best way to approach alcoholics. Wilson and Smith developed a strategy that dealt with one day at a time, "the twenty-four hour concept." By 1936, Wilson began to outline a 12-step program for recovering alcoholics based on American philosopher William James's *The Variety of Religious Experience* and the Oxford Group's six steps. Wilson went on to write a book called *Alcoholics Anonymous* (also known as the "Big Book").

The idea behind AA is to change the alcoholic's way of thinking, not just drinking habits. AA does not purport to be a religious movement, but its philosophy is certainly spiritual; the group openly states that they are "not allied with any sect, denomination, **politics**, organization or institution." The first step in the AA program is to admit that the alcoholic is powerless over alcohol and that drinking makes life unmanageable. Through the 12 steps, recovering alcoholics are asked to take stock of their actions and shortcomings and be "ready to have God remove all these defects of character." The last step is to come to a spiritual awakening, continue to practice the principles of the program, and carry the AA message to other alcoholics.

To help maintain sobriety, AA members are encouraged to volunteer in the organization and attend regular meetings. Each member seeks out a sponsor, who has preferably maintained sobriety for at least a year and who is the same gender as the person being sponsored. This relationship is beneficial to both parties and provides support to stay sober. There are no governing officers, no rules, and no regulations or fees. At the local level, there is little formal structure, and responsibilities within the group are rotated on a regular basis. Although founded in the United States, AA has become popular throughout the world.

Further Reading

Alcoholics Anonymous Web site. http://www.aa.org.

Cheever, Susan. *My Name Is Bill: Bill Wilson—His Life and the Creation of Alcoholics Anonymous.* New York: Simon & Schuster, 2004.

Wilson, Bill. *Alcoholics Anonymous: The Story of How Many Thousands of Men and Women Have Recovered from Alcoholism.* 4th ed. New York: Alcoholics Anonymous World Service, 2001.

Rachel Black

ALCOHOLISM

Popularized by the growth of the **Alcoholics Anonymous** movement, the term "alcoholism" is contentious, and it has changed greatly over time. The *American Heritage Dictionary* defines alcoholism as "a chronic disease associated with the excessive and habitual use of alcohol; the disease, if left unattended, worsens and can kill the sufferer." Most American dictionaries underline that alcoholism is a physical disease, while also mentioning that there are psychological factors. Rarely do these definitions address the social and cultural aspects of this disease. For instance, the use of this term outside of medical communities has had derogatory underpinnings, particularly when used in the context of **politics** and **religion**. Throughout the twentieth century, the use of the term alcoholism has become increasingly clinical. In the 1960s Elvin Jellinek coined the term "the disease concept of alcoholism," and his research was quintessential in bring about the medicalization of alcoholism. The acknowledgment of alcoholism as a physical disease has helped change the way alcoholics are treated, and this medical approach has moved alcoholism away from the moral discourses that have condemned individuals suffering from this disease.

Not all individuals who consume alcohol are alcoholics. Medical and psychiatric practitioners use qualifying terms that vary from use to abuse when talking about alcohol consumption. Dipsomania is the term used to refer to the condition characterized by uncontrollable cravings for alcohol or other intoxicating substances that can occur for unknown reasons. Dipsomania is often confused for alcoholism. Most modern medical definitions of alcoholism focus on the physical damage to an individual's health that is the outcome of heavy drinking. The social effects of alcoholism are in many ways just as damaging as the physical effects. Domestic **violence**, assault, and loss of employment are just a few of the negative social outcomes that can be caused by alcoholism.

With the high social and economic costs of alcoholism in the United States, numerous government policies try to curb alcoholism and educate the public about the outcomes of alcohol abuse. These policies range from campaigns against drunk driving to educational initiatives to inform people of the hazards of drinking while pregnant. The National Institute on Alcohol Abuse and Alcoholism (NIAAA) is part of the U.S. National Institutes of Health. The NIAAA funds 90 percent of the research on alcoholism and alcohol-related problems. Consequently, political agendas play a large role in shaping what is defined as alcoholism and how this disease is treated at a clinical and social level. (*See also* **Health Effects of Alcohol.**)

Further Reading

Alcohol Policy Information System Web site. http://www.alcoholpolicy.niaaa.nih.gov.

Edwards, Griffith. *Alcohol: The World's Favorite Drug*. New York: Thomas Dunne Books, 2002.

National Institute on Alcohol Abuse and Alcoholism Web site. http://www.niaaa.nih.gov.

Page, P. B. "E. M. Jellinek and the Evolution of Alcohol Studies: A Critical Essay." *Addiction* 92, no.12 (December 1997): 1619–37.

Valliant, George E. *The Natural History of Alcohol Revisited*. Cambridge, MA: Harvard University Press, 1995.

Rachel Black

ALCOPOPS

Alcopops, a term largely used by prevention advocates, are sweetened alcoholic beverages. They are usually sold in single serving sizes and marketed to younger consumers. As the name suggests, these beverages are often fruit-flavored, bubbly, and sweet. The industry refers to these beverages as "flavored malt beverages (FMBs)." Although these drinks may begin as un-hopped **beer**, **vodka** or grain alcohol is often added along with sugar and coloring and flavoring agents. They are usually stronger than beer, with an average alcohol volume of 5 percent. **Wine coolers** can be seen as the predecessor of alcopops. Due to a federal tax on **wine**, these types of drinks all became largely malt based. Alcopops grew in popularity in the 1980s and early 1990s, and a few of the most widely consumed alcopops include Mike's Hard Lemonade, Hooper's Hooch, Zima, and Smirnoff Ice.

Many prevention advocates argue that alcopops are of great concern because they contribute to **underage drinking**. This is due to the way they are packaged and promoted, and because many consumers believe that they are lighter and easier to drink compared with beer. In California, flavored malt beverages of this type must bear a label stating that "this drink contains alcohol."

Further Reading

"About Alcopops." Marin Institute Web site. http://www.marininstitute.org/alcopops.

Mosher, James, and Dianne Johnson. "Flavored Alcoholic Beverages: An International Marketing Campaign That Targets Youth." *Journal of Public Health Policy* 26 (2005): 326–42.

Rachel Black

ANTI-SALOON LEAGUE

A political force to reckon with during **Prohibition**, the Anti-Saloon League (1893–1933) started in Ohio and quickly spread throughout the United States to become one of the strongest lobby groups in support of Prohibition. Allied with the

Anti-Saloon League's War on Alcohol

This April 1912 piece exemplifies the type of writing found in *The American Patriot*, one of the Anti-Saloon League's periodicals.

The Day the Ghost Walks
By W. E. JOHNSON

In factory parlance, pay day is the day that "the ghost walks."

Pay day is a day of reckoning for the grocer who balances his weekly accounts with Smith, Flanagan, Campbell and Harrison and Davis and Mulligan.

There are others that the grocer is not quite so certain about, for on pay day the "ghost walks" in those families.

Pay day is the day that the landlord and rental agent write out receipts for Hanrahan and Rhodes and Loomis and Mitchell and others. But there are certain ones that he looks out after, because in those families, pay day is the day the "ghost walks."

In some families in Workingtown, pay day is a day of gladness. Alice rubs her nose against the windows, waiting for "Dad," because she is sure of a new dress and a bag of candy.

In the house down the lane, pay day is the day of fear and trembling. Little Hortense crawls under the bed, and mother, with reddened eyes, looks anxiously into the glimmering shades. In that family, pay day is the day that the "ghost walks."

The father of Hortense is having his "time" at the "poor man's club" around the corner. He is beginning to reel and sway and curse and open his pocketbook upon the bar.

The ghost is "walking."

In the grey dawn of the morning, he staggers home, bruised, beaten and penniless. The shrinking, shivering shadows of the hovel hide in the closets and the garrett.

For the "ghost is walking."

In the "all night" saloon down the side street, there is a shriek. Some one is stabbed and hurry calls are sent in for the police. A pay day father is sweltering in his own blood while another pay day father is being dragged to the calaboose amid hoots and cries for a "rope."

It is the "ghost walking."

In the new psychology, the licensed saloon is the "medium" which summons the shades of darkness and causes these "ghosts to walk."

Does the "ghost walk" in your town on pay day? Or have you voted the spooks out?

If your town hasn't taken this step, don't you think that the "ghost has been walking" long enough?

If your labor union has not taken steps to drive this "ghost" out of your family circles, the opportunity is wide open to you at the spring elections.

Why not take a hand at the next local option contest and let the "ghost walk" clear out of your community?

Source: Anti-Saloon League, Westerville Public Library. http://www.wpl.lib.oh.us/AntiSaloon/pmaterial/ghost_walk (accessed June 4, 2010).

Woman's Christian Temperance Union and the Prohibition Party, the Anti-Saloon League actively promoted a national ban on the manufacture and sale of alcohol. What started as a moral crusade eventually led to a constitutional amendment.

Their motto was "the saloon must go," and this message was broadcast loudly at the local and national level. The Anti-Saloon League influenced **politics** through the printed word, protest, and lobbying. Although nondenominational, this group used local churches to spread the word against alcohol and to raise funds for their political projects. During elections, they supported "dry" politicians. They were a nonpartisan group that worked hard to elect politicians who supported Prohibition, regardless of whether they were Democrats or Republicans.

A major victory occurred in 1919 with the passage of the Eighteenth Amendment, which made obtaining alcohol legally difficult, but this was short lived when it was repealed by the Twenty-first Amendment in 1933. The Anti-Saloon League is an excellent example of the way in

Many posters for the Anti-Saloon League showed alcohol as a menace to society. (Library of Congress)

which the question of alcohol was couched in moral terms for political ends at the beginning of the twentieth century. (*See also* **Temperance**.)

Further Reading

Anti-Saloon League Museum Web site. http://www.wpl.lib.oh.us/AntiSaloon/.
Kerr, Kathel. *Organized for Prohibition: A New History of the Anti-Saloon League.* New Haven, CT: Yale University Press, 1985.
Pegram, Thomas R. "The Dry Machine: The Formation of the Anti-Saloon League of Illinois." *Illinois Historical Journal* 83, no. 3 (1990): 173–86.

Rachel Black

APPLEJACK

Applejack is truly an indigenous North American spirit distilled from apples and was once among the most popular forms of alcohol in the Colonies. This was due to the ease of planting orchards, the absence of **wine** grapes, and the use of grains for bread making rather than distillation. With poor inland transportation, it also made sense to trade in spirits high in alcohol rather than more bulky **cider** or **beer**. Although it resembles in some ways Calvados from Normandy, the flavor of applejack is distinctly sweeter because it is made from sweet apples such as Winesap and Delicious rather than dry cider apples, and there is no direct historical connection between the two spirits. A simple kind of applejack was originally made by freezing fermented cider. As water freezes before alcohol, the ice could be removed, leaving a higher concentration of alcohol. This process, called *jacking*, is said to be the origin of the term, though applejack in England usually refers to a turnover-like dessert. True distillation, or boiling the cider and then condensing the steam, is the only way to make a spirit high in alcohol, applejack being 40 percent concentration. It is usually then aged in charred oak barrels, much like brandy is.

Most applejack in the Colonial era was distilled on a small scale by orchard owners, but commercial **distilling** dates back to 1780 with the founding of Laird's Applejack company in Colt's Neck, New Jersey, as the country's first licensed distillery. George Washington is said to have received the recipe for applejack from Robert Laird, the company founder, who fought under Washington in the American Revolution. The operation moved in the nineteenth century, after a fire, to nearby Scobeyville and is still owned by the same family, which traces its origin to William Laird, who arrived in Monmouth Country from Scotland in 1698 and proceeded to distill applejack.

Applejack is also entwined in the history of westward expansion. When Johnny Appleseed spread saplings through the Ohio Valley in advance of settlement, it was not actually for apples to eat, but to make into drink. These trees were open pollinated rather than grafted, meaning that a wide variety of apple types would result—some good for eating, but most only fit for **fermentation**.

Why applejack lost dominance is partly due to the emergence of other spirits in competition and manufactured on a larger scale. **Rum** was distilled from molasses, a by-product of the sugar industry, **bourbon** or sour mash **whiskey** was distilled from corn in Kentucky and Tennessee, and increasingly whiskey was made from barley or rye grown throughout the expanding young republic.

In the twentieth century, applejack was pushed even further into obscurity by the popularity of **gin, vodka,** and **tequila,** though a number of mixed drinks kept Laird's in business producing "Jersey Lightning." The most popular of these is no doubt the Jack Rose, made with applejack, lemon juice, and a dash or two of grenadine, the proportions of each varying wildly depending on the authority. Today, Laird's Applejack is made in a factory in Virginia and is mixed with grain neutral spirits, essentially flavorless grain alcohol. But they also make a bonded 100-proof "apple brandy" made exclusively from apples, which is intensely perfumed and best sipped on its own. It probably most resembles the original applejack.

Ken Albala

ARTS

The arts and alcohol in North American culture have a multidimensional relationship. Alcoholic beverages figure prominently at arts events, providing an economic resource for arts organizations. Such sales are well integrated and expected at a variety of events. Alcohol itself can also be a subject of the arts, figuring prominently in paintings and providing a text-enhancing function in plays. Drinking alcohol is a behavioral literary device that can refer to a wide range of things: from a character's emotional baggage and mental decline, to another person's sophistication and cosmopolitanism. **Cocktails, wine,** and **beer** have flooded the movie industry, providing not only ambiance and a setting for the action, but often getting star billing for mixed drinks themselves. Alcohol has also had an impact on the decorative arts and design where the objects for serving alcohol are artistic in their own right. Finally, alcohol has had an uneasy relationship with the arts. Some painters and musicians are notorious substance abusers. Ultimately, however, the path to creativity cannot be paved with artificial stimulants. **Alcoholism** nonetheless seems to be the downfall of many in the creative professions.

Alcohol Sales at Arts Events

Alcohol sales at arts events serve an economic function for arts organizations. Sales of alcohol at intermission and exhibit openings, **wine tastings,** and beer fests provide needed revenues to symphony orchestras, museums, and cash-strapped theater companies. Wine, beer, and even cocktails are sold in the lobbies of arts centers across the United States and constitute a type of earned income for arts organizations. The brief **cocktail party** at intermission provides an atmosphere of conviviality, with alcohol acting as a stimulant for conversation. No museum opening or fund-raising event is complete without alcohol, which serves as a kind of catalyst to let loose the purse strings of invited guests. Art sales, donations, and favorable publicity hopefully follow if these guests enjoy the opening event with its tasty hors d'oeuvres and accompanying drinks. Sophisticated cocktails, microbrewed beer, and wines lend an air of sophistication and glamor to a night out at the theater, the symphony, or at an art gallery or museum exhibition opening. While it is difficult to find specific statistics that determine the direct impact of alcohol sales on the financial health of arts organizations, alcohol sales no doubt are a significant portion of the 33 percent of earned income that healthy organizations can expect in their yearly budgets from ticket sales, events, and facility rentals.

Wine Art

Today, alcoholic beverages are not only served in art galleries during openings to enhance the atmosphere, but wine itself has become the subject of artists. Thomas Arvid is one of a number of contemporary artists in North America and Europe whose subjects are wine bottles, glasses of wine, and related objects such as corks and corkscrews. These still-life paintings of wine in the bottle or the glass evoke pleasant associations and brighten the walls of middle-class American homes. Wine was chosen as his subject matter, Arvid states, because it was approachable: "Wine is a great subject because people are familiar with it; they really connect to it. My paintings are really the landscapes between people sharing wine."

The use of wine as a subject is not a new idea in still-life painting. Dutch master painter Willem Kalf (1622–1693) portrayed clear crystal wine goblets and drinking horns in his works. French painters in the eighteenth and nineteenth centuries, such as Jean Simeon Chardin (1699–1779) and Paul Cezanne (1839–1906), painted wine along with fruit, cheese, and wild game. The American painter Raphaelle Peale (1774–1825) did several paintings of cake and wine. Wine glasses and decanters, too, were favored subject matter. The painter's skill was tested regarding his technique of showing the wine through the glass and the play of light on the surfaces. Wine enhanced the abundance of produce or game on the table in the still-life. It was an everyday display, yet one that symbolized wealth and prosperity.

Poster art adds another dimension to the discussion of wine and alcoholic drinks as the subject for visual artists. Posters of beverage labels often appear as art in **bars** and restaurants. These items cannot be dismissed as simple ephemera of the alcoholic beverage industry or the detritus of **advertising**. Campari umbrellas may be simple marketing tools to sell the famous Italian aperitif, but poster art of that brand and others goes a step further. It not only promotes a brand of alcohol, but the poster or the beer clock that graces the bar uses bold, new graphic design. Eye-catching and memorable, these items constitute popular art. They are not only used by restaurant chains and bar owners to sell products, but they are acquired by collectors and brought home to middle-class American suburbia to grace kitchen and den walls. Few can forget the Absolut **vodka** ads, where the shape of an ordinary bottle became a graphic statement of not only a brand, but art. An artistic photograph of a skyscraper's windows lit in the shape of the Absolut bottle became an image of 1990s prosperity in Manhattan. Even special bottles themselves become collectibles on eBay and other auction Web sites.

Wine and art are so popular together that a number of entrepreneurs have linked them in special tours. "Art and Wine Tours" are found globally, from Key West, Florida, to Deloraine, Tasmania, to Santa Fe, New Mexico. At each venue, tourists are invited to taste the wines produced in local vineyards and encouraged to buy paintings by local, contemporary artists.

Alcohol, Design, and the Decorative Arts

The tools of the trade for preparing cocktails and serving various types of drink are themselves often art, created by America's top artists and designers. The art of serving alcohol includes crystal decanters, silver **punch** bowls, wine glasses with delicate grapes and vines etched on their bowls, metallic seltzer bottles, colored cocktail glasses, hand-painted wine glasses, silver pitchers, gold-rimmed **champagne** flutes,

Tiffany cocktail shakers, cut-glass old-fashioned glasses, and **martini** sets of all descriptions, to mention only some forms. The full range of nineteenth- and twentieth-century art styles runs from the heavily ornamented Belle Epoque to the sleek styles of Art Deco and Modernism. Today, examples of these objects grace wealthy and middle-class homes and the collections of museums nationwide.

These decorative objects associated with alcohol and drinking are symbols of wealth and social prestige. In eighteenth-century America, silver objects carried the cultural capital of a public display of a family's wealth. One could not display the coveted silver coins that were needed for proper social standing without seeming crass. However, a well-placed silver punch bowl on a sideboard in one's home indicated to guests that the homeowner had a good social standing. Owners of silver objects were the pillars of the community and important families.

In the nineteenth century, cut glass and crystal joined silver as the medium for the display of middle- and upper-class wealth. Etched wine glasses and colored cordial glasses were objects that were pleasing to the eye, a joy to hold as the drink was brought to one's lips, an enhancement for the experience of drinking in a refined, domestic sphere. They were also status objects, admired by guests in the home and displayed proudly before one's wedding among women, who visited to review a bride's trousseau.

The twentieth century saw drinking in the public sector shift from the rough domain of working-class men, cowboys, and gold prospectors in rude taverns and saloons to the exclusive clubs as the **speakeasies** of the 1920s became transformed into jazz clubs and nightclubs in the 1930s and 1940s, where alcohol played an important role. Cocktail culture beginning in these years, and coming into its own in the 1950s and 1960s, represented sophistication and success as new drinks were invented by barmen in large, urban hotels where business deals were made and trend-setters wanted to be seen. In these years, modernism and contemporary design went into the creation of Manhattan sets, martini glasses, and elaborate types of glassware for the vast variety of cocktails that were available.

Alcohol and Character Development

Alcoholic beverages and their associated material culture not only serve as subjects for paintings, photographs, and posters, but they also are essential to plays. A character's personality, motivation, psychological conflicts, and/or their social status can be encapsulated in their relationship to alcohol. Tom Wingfield, a character in Tennessee Williams's (1911–1983) play, *The Glass Menagerie* (1944), is an example of how alcohol plays a role in helping the audience to better understand a character. Tom appears in one scene of the play with ticket stubs and an empty bottle, props that convey important information. The audience knows by seeing these objects that he had gone to the movies and that he had been drinking. Tom's mother, Amanda, reacts to the empty bottle, and the audience learns of her fear of alcoholism; her husband drank to excess, and she is afraid for Tom. Eugene O'Neill (1888–1953) takes things one step further. Three of the main characters in *A Long Day's Journey into Night* (1956, produced posthumously) are alcoholics, and the play's theme is addiction. Both Williams and O'Neill were writing about subjects close to their own experience. They both suffered from depression and alcoholism.

Alcohol, Alcoholism, and Artists

Many artists of all varieties, from painters, sculptors, photographers, and film-makers to musicians and composers, have an uneasy relationship to alcohol. For many, alcohol has served as muse. Artists sometimes see reality in different ways from other people. Painters, for example, notice color, shape, perspective, and light. Musicians hear in different ways, hearing texture in tone and constructing their own worlds in sound. Sculptors see statues in blocks of stone before the first blow is struck by chisel and hammer. Photographers and filmmakers take the everyday and make it extraordinary by focusing their audience's attention in new ways. For many in these creative professions, alcohol at one time or another has served as muse: loosening inhibitions, altering reality, building a sense of community with strangers who drink together, or filling the void of loneliness. But alcohol for many creative people also has a darker side through addiction and its related maladies.

Alcoholism has been seen to characterize the New York School of twentieth-century abstract painters (Lane 1998). Wilhem de Kooning and his wife, Elaine, Robert Motherwell, and Mark Rothko were victims of this environment. In Rothko's case, his alcoholism led to his suicide. The painter Jackson Pollock also self-destructed in a high-speed, alcohol-fueled car crash.

Alcohol and creativity is a new field being studied by psychologists. A 2009 conference on Creativity and Cognition featured a pilot study of "Alcoholism and Creativity" by a team of psychologists at the Georgia Institute of Technology (Smith et al. 2009). While their findings are not conclusive, this study has delineated some interesting areas for further exploration. (*See also* **Film; Literature.**)

Further Reading

Arvid, Thomas. "Biography." 2000–2009. http://www.thomasarvid.com/thomas_arvid
    _bio.html.

Bogard, Travis, ed. *Eugene O'Neill: The Complete Plays*. Vol. 3, *1932–1943*. New York:
    Library of America, 1988.

Gussow, Mel, and Kenneth Holdich, eds. *Tennessee Williams' Plays, 1937–1955*.
    New York: Library of America, 2000.

Lane, Jim. "Art and Alcohol." *Humanities Web*. http://www.humanitiesweb.org/human
    .php?s=g&p=a&a=i&ID=362.

Smith, Jesse C., Teresa M. Smith, and Ellen Yi-Luen Do. "Alcohol and Creativity: A Pilot
    Study." In *Proceeding of the Seventh ACM Conference on Creativity and Cogni-
    tion*, 147–54. New York: ACM, 2009.

Pam Sezgin

B

BAR BETS

A bar bet is a type of mental or physical bar game wagered between two patrons or between a patron and a bartender. The usual objective of a bar bet is the positive social camaraderie between bar patrons and staff and bragging rights for winning a friendly bar game. Such bar bets are based on a symmetrically reciprocal exchange relationship between parties who have an equal chance of winning the bet. An example is a competitive game of darts or pool, wherein one patron bets the other that he or she can win the game.

Other bar bets, however, are confidence games between a bar patron who is a "con" (who knows the trick) and an unsuspecting "mark" (who does not know the trick). The usual objective of this type of bar bet is either **free drinks** or easy money. Such bar bets are based on a relationship of negative reciprocity, since the parties are unequally matched; the con knows the trick and depends upon the mark to be unaware of some condition established in the bet.

Examples of trick bar bets are catalogued in books and on the Internet. They tend to fall into one of two categories, word tricks and physical tricks, with word tricks predominating. For example, a con bets a mark that he can push a wine glass through the handle of a pint jar without breaking either. When the mark accepts the bet, the con places the wine glass next to the handle of the pint jar, threads his finger through the handle, and pushes the wine glass. In such word-based bar bets, the con exploits differences between common and literal meanings of words.

In bar bets based on confidence games between unmatched players, the con always wins. However, in bar bet competitions between two cons, players compete to see who knows the most bar bets. Since either con can win, this exchange is based on balanced or symmetrical (and not negative) reciprocity. (*See also* **Bar Games.**)

Further Reading

Cruit, Ron. *175 Ways to Win a Free Drink: The Complete Book of Bar Bets*. New York: Dodd, Mead and Company, 1985.

Lansky, Doug. *The World's Best Simple Bar Tricks*. New York: Dell Publishing, 1998.

Zenon, Paul. *100 Ways to Win a Ten-Spot: Scams, Cons, Games You Can't Lose*. Chicago: Chicago Review Press, 2007, 1–35.

Karen Eilene Saenz

BAR GAMES

Bar games are enjoyable and entertaining leisure activities played by bar patrons and either passively tolerated or directly promoted by a bar as part of its marketing strategy. Games may be simple challenges of chance or luck played informally between individuals; slightly more challenging games of skill between small groups; or highly structured games of strategy between teams. Objectives of game playing by bar patrons include relaxation, entertainment, and social bonding, while objectives of the bar include increasing attendance and maximizing profits.

Not surprisingly, the bar games of modern American show direct affinities with traditional English pub games, which themselves have even earlier antecedents in Roman tavern games. Specifically, British pub games were evident in the colonies as early as the 1600s; billiards was played in American taverns by the late 1700s; and darts was recorded as a popular pastime in U.S. saloons by the late 1800s.

Traditional bar games of luck or chance sometimes include **drinking games** involving consumption competitions. Bar games involving feats of mental skill include knowledge and trivia-based quiz games administered by a quiz master to small teams of bar patrons for token prizes, **free drinks**, or local bragging rights. These originated with the popular institution of pub quizzes in Britain and Ireland, as well as the American **television** quiz show genre.

Bar games involving manual dexterity, eye coordination, or other physical skills include indoor and/or tabletop sports derived from outdoor lawn sports. Popular traditional examples include darts (derived from archery); candlepin and tabletop bowling (derived from British bowls); billiards or pool (derived from golf and croquet); table shuffleboard (derived from deck shuffleboard); ping pong or table tennis (derived from lawn tennis); and paper or penny football with its obvious outdoor derivations. Bar games involving competitive strategy, rules, and specialized equipment include card games (poker, blackjack), board games (backgammon, chess), and dice (dominos, craps, liar's dice).

Modern American technological enhancements to these and other traditional bar games have resulted in the mass production of specialized bar game machinery for purchase by **bars**. Some examples of electronic bar game machines based on their live-version counterparts include pinball, slots, and video game and interactive quiz machines. Karaoke machines represent a related technological innovation originating in Japan.

Bar bets are a type of confidence game based on magic, tricks, or wagers, aimed at obtaining free drinks from the bar establishment or another patron.

Further Reading

Foley, Ray, and Heather Dismore. *Running a Bar for Dummies*. Hoboken, NJ: Wiley
    Publishing, 2007.
Masters, James. "Pub Games." The Online Guide to Traditional Games Web site.
http://www.tradgames.org.uk/index.html

Karen Eilene Saenz

BARFLY

A barfly is someone who spends a lot of time drinking and socializing in **bars**. The first appearances in print of the term were in the early twentieth century. Spoken usage probably did not predate that by much, because the word "bar" itself was not as commonly used in the nineteenth century as "tavern" or "saloon." Though pre-twentieth-century saloons, which often kept meat and other foods open on the counter as enticements to business, were no doubt filled with barflies both real and metaphorical, "saloonfly" simply does not have the same concision or mellifluousness.

A barfly can be male or female. Prior to 1987, when used to refer to women, it often implied a pejorative comment on the subject's sexual availability. A 1987 **film** titled *Barfly* with a screenplay written by heavy-drinking writer and poet Charles Bukowski, forever removed any gender implication from the term. Bukowski defined himself as the barfly of the title, as the screenplay was a thinly

Mickey Rourke and Faye Dunaway in the film *Barfly* (1987). The semi-autobiographical screenplay by Charles Bukowski truly defined this term and established it as part of popular American vocabulary. (Photofest)

disguised autobiographical character sketch of a hard-drinking writer. Mickey Rourke played the title role.

As the eponymous barfly, Rourke frequently is beaten up in drunken brawls that start for little or no reason. He halfheartedly pursues or is pursued by women who similarly spend most of their waking hours in bars. He bathes and washes his clothes infrequently, frequently confronts police and the world of sober people, and when he gets money, spends it, treating his fellow barflies to free rounds of drinks. His life is lived in bars.

Further Reading

Barfly. Directed by Barbet Schroeder. Performers Mickey Rourke, Faye Dunaway. Cannon Film Distributors, 1987.

W. Blake Gray

BARS

A bar is a long wooden counter where drinks are served, and the building that contains this counter. Some bars take pride in the physical attributes or longevity of their bar counter. Bars are credited with fomenting revolution and civilizing frontiers, introducing couples and spurring divorces, protecting cliques and creating communities. English speakers generally consider bars separate from **pubs**, inns, or nightclubs because bars do not specialize in food, lodging or entertainment; however, bars may provide all three. But someone looking specifically for a bar is generally looking primarily for an alcoholic drink.

The concept of alcohol-first, often with no food at all, is much more common in the United States than elsewhere. It developed in the eighteenth century because of the absence of **wine**, which had to be imported at great expense from Europe, and **beer**, which Americans did not initially brew in volume. Instead, pre-Revolutionary colonists drank water with their meals, which were eaten quickly and silently. Then the men went to a bar to drink the drinks of the Colonies—hard **cider** and **whiskey**— and smoke and talk. But bars that would be recognizable today have existed for at least 400 years. The first people noted for hard drinking in taverns, with little food involved, were the Dutch of the seventeenth century, a prosperous people who had elaborate **drinking rituals**—another feature that has continued to the present in **drinking games** such as "quarters" or rites of passage such as drinking shots of liquor on one's twenty-first birthday, when one becomes legally able to consume alcohol.

Bars have long been associated with lower-class people. Today it is fashionable for the upper middle class to go "slumming" in "dive bars." In France of the late eighteenth century, poor people drank and danced at "guinguettes" outside of Paris rather than the more fashionable cafes favored by the wealthy. In some of these filthy, vermin-infested bars, patrons shared the anger and **class** resentment that led to the French Revolution.

The first U.S. city known for its bars was New Orleans, in the mid-1700s. The first licensed taverns there were required to close on Sundays and holy days and were prohibited from serving soldiers, Indians, and slaves. Unlicensed cabarets served Indians and slaves and soon became known for having a livelier atmosphere.

Forced segregation of bars by class and race may sound anachronistic today, but a visit to bars in most major cities in the world will show that laws have

---

Stonewall Riots

Given the central place of bars in gay, lesbian, and transgendered culture, it is not surprising that the violent incident that symbolically marks the beginning of the gay fight against government-endorsed discrimination and the start of the gay liberation movement was in a bar.

The Stonewall Inn, a bar in Greenwich Village, New York City, was raided by police in the wee hours of June 28, 1969. The Stonewall was well known as a popular gay bar, and police raids were frequent. On this particular evening, the bar patrons and the crowd that gathered to watch the police arrest the bartender, patrons, and the doorman decided they had enough. They fought back.

The following week, protesters returned to the site to march and speak out against police violence and discrimination.

---

changed, but culture has not. A striking feature of bars is the communities that form among their clientele. The less privileged the community, the more likely it is to be fiercely loyal to its local bar.

An important example of this is what many consider as the first event of the gay rights movement. In 1969, police raided a New York gay bar called the Stonewall Inn. A typical bar on the fringe of society, reportedly owned by the Mafia, the Stonewall Inn had no food and no running water behind the bar, meaning glasses were not always cleaned between customers. But gay New Yorkers knew that it was a place for their community, and it was always crowded.

Though raids of gay bars had been going on for years, resulting in the closure of bars and the arrests on specious charges of clients, at the Stonewall Inn patrons fought back, starting a riot. Rioters shouted "Gay Power!" as they fought police for nearly three hours. Word of the riot spread throughout the world, leading to the formation of gay rights groups around the world. "Remember Stonewall" is still a rallying cry 40 years later.

With being gay itself no longer a crime, gay bars have subsequently subdivided into lesbian bars, bars for men who like leather, bars for "bears" (large, hairy gay men), bars for those into sado/masochism, and too many other categories to detail. This kind of subdivision is true in the heterosexual community as well. A city with two football teams will have separate sports bars. College towns have bars for students and bars for professors. There are bars for motorcycle riders and cops, antiestablishment rebels, and upwardly mobile professionals. These segregations are by choice. Forcibly segregating bars by gender in the United States caused a 100-year cultural war.

While women were generally allowed in bars in the wild West, East Coast bars of the early 1800s began excluding women, first by custom and then often by law. This had a strong consequence, as woman became leaders of an anti-alcohol **Temperance Movement** personified by Carry Nation, who used an axe to destroy many a bar's front door and its valuable barrels of whiskey.

Groups of women invaded saloons where they were legally not welcome, but instead of ordering a drink, they would sing hymns, fall on their knees in prayer, and prevent business from being conducted. Women formed political alliances with religious groups, always a strong force in American **politics**, and eventually made the sale and transportation of alcohol illegal in the United States.

They were assisted in this effort by the bar industry itself, which suffered from rapid unlicensed expansion. In the 1700s and early 1800s, American bars were centers of society. The Declaration of Independence was written in a bar, as was "The Star Spangled Banner." But by the 1880s, there were so many bars that in order to survive, they began breaking laws and bending standards, serving to minors, encouraging patrons to drink until their wallets were empty, watering down whiskey or diluting it with dangerous chemicals, and even indulging in robbery scams. As bars got a criminal reputation, it became harder for politicians to defend their existence.

Ironically, the advent of **Prohibition** in 1920—which made all bars in the United States illegal—rescued American bars from an era of being seedy, frowned-upon places of ill repute, once most Americans realized they really did want to drink. The greatest nightclubs of New York were all illegal **speakeasies**, some still famous today: the Cotton Club, the Stork Club, and 21.

Bars flourished during and after Prohibition but faced a strong challenge worldwide in the 1950s from two technological developments: mass-produced televisions, and beer in a can. No longer was it enough for a bar to offer liquor and a stool. Ambience became a key ingredient for a bar's success, and it remains so today.

Bars are described today not by their physical features, but by their music selection or their cultural choices. There are heavy metal bars, hip-hop bars, and bars that play only **music** from a specific decade (1960s, 1970s, and 1980s). There are candlelit bars and bars that specialize in certain spirits. One bar in San Francisco was famous for ejecting patrons who ordered anything but a martini.

In Japan, karaoke (patrons singing the lyrics of popular songs to an instrumental recording) is performed in specialized "boxes" with small groups of friends. In the rest of the world, bars have adopted karaoke as a means of attracting clients willing to embarrass themselves in front of strangers.

Some bars have higher forms of entertainment. "Quiz night" is popular in Ireland and the United Kingdom, with prizes awarded for knowledge. Irish bars, either on the Emerald Isle or for expats abroad, are also known for literary celebrations, such as festive drinking bacchanalias interspersed with readings of James Joyce.

Modern bars are also places to meet people. Other functions of bars—as inn, as restaurant, as house of prostitution, as political meeting point—have gradually found other venues. But there remains in most cultures few places with such potential for meeting future sex partners as bars. Some bars, notably gay bars where men wear color-coded handkerchiefs announcing their preferences, are more open about this than others. But even, and maybe especially, quiet hotel bars brim with sexual tension among travelers who might be hiding their wedding rings. Many bars use this in promotions. "Ladies nights," intended to bring women into normally male-dominated bars by offering them **free drinks**, are commonplace.

Ultimately, though, one drawing card for bars that has remained constant for four centuries is community. The long-running **television** sitcom *Cheers* showed an idealized Boston bar community of regular drinkers who knew each others' families and problems and gave each other encouragement or commiseration as needed. The show's famous refrain, "where everyone knows your name," is for many the dream they seek whenever they enter the doors of a nearby bar.

W. Blake Gray

BARTENDING

Something of the nature of the changing American character is revealed by the shifting landscape of "must-see TV." *Cheers*, one of the most successful sitcoms of the 1980s, was set in a bar and centered around bartender Sam Malone (Ted Danson). There was a definite sense that, just as among the casts of workplace sitcoms, the regulars of Cheers had formed among themselves a surrogate family, of which Sam was the center, if not the patriarch. In 1994, a year after Cheers ended and the psychiatrist character Frasier spun off into his own series in hip Seattle, *Friends* premiered, featuring just such a makeshift family—but one that spent its time in a coffeehouse, with limited interaction with the staff. By the time a bar returned as the setting of a top-10 sitcom—CBS's *How I Met Your Mother* (2005)—the bartender himself had been dispensed with. The characters meet at a regular table, with Wendy the waitress appearing more frequently than the bartender, who has featured in several episodes, but never as a confidante, much less a friend.

In the simplest sense, a bartender is just a drink server. But in part because of the long-standing mild taboo against drinking and the idea of the bar as a refuge from home and work—which in a sense requires that taboo, since the preparation of most drinks is a simple task and would be much cheaper at home, so for the bar to thrive, there must be some force pushing drinkers from their homes—bartenders have assumed a greater role than that in the popular imagination. Bartenders are confidantes, confessors. Like cab drivers, they have soaked up wisdom by being immersed in, surrounded by, saturated with the madding crowd. The bartender is, if nothing else, someone to talk to, someone to be there, so that one is not drinking alone. It may be for that reason that the bartender's social role seems to have diminished: bit by bit, the typical American bar has changed, not in one direction, but in many. **Bars** are no longer picketed by **temperance** supporters. They are no longer a solely male domain. With the gradual welcoming of women to bars came the advent of singles bars, "fern bars," where drinking is the excuse to be there rather than the reason—which may explain why their appearance on the landscape coincided with the partial fading away of the traditional cocktail, replaced by premade mixers, "sour mix" instead of juice, and more and more drinks that were little more than **vodka** with large amounts of something sweet to conceal it.

The first bartenders were cocktail innovators and originators. The first published guide to cocktails, and a critical source in studying their history, was *The Bar-Tender's Guide*, by bartender Jerry Thomas (a.k.a. "The Professor"), first published in 1862. The guide describes a cocktail scene that had incorporated elements from the **gin** drinks of the British Empire and the **rum** drinks of its navy, the tavern drinks that had been around since America's earliest days, the punches that were popular throughout the western world, and the patent medicine craze that contributed bitters like Angostura, Peychaud's, and dozens of brands long since defunct. Brandy featured heavily; whiskey was still a star on the rise.

Jerry Thomas's The Bar-Tender's Guide

In the first bartending/drink-making guide published in 1862 in the United States, Thomas's goal was to commit to print the oral tradition of bartending.

> This is an Age of Progress; new ideas and new appliances follow each other in rapid succession. Inventive genius is taxed to the uttermost in devising new inventions, not alone for articles of utility or necessity, but to meet the ever-increasing demands for novelties which administer to creature-comfort, and afford gratification to fastidious tastes.
>
> A new beverage is the pride of the Bartender, and its appreciation and adoption his crowning glory. In this entirely new edition will be found all the latest efforts of the most prominent and successful caterers to the tastes of those who patronize the leading Bars and Wine-Rooms of America, as well as the old and standard favorite beverages, always in general demand.
>
> —"Preface," *The Bar-Tender's Guide*, 1887 edition

Thomas was a showman as well as a bartender and author, with a flair for the dramatic. That too persisted, just as his cocktail lore did. Though the term "flair bartending" was coined in the 1980s or 1990s, the era of movies such as *Cocktail* and *Coyote Ugly*, the practice of showing off while one pours drinks has been around since Thomas's time. Though it slows down drink production, it also entertains those waiting for their drinks. Flair bartending features heavily at various competitions devoted to naming the "best bartender," such as the World Bartender Championship—a practice sometimes criticized for taking the emphasis away from the quality of the drinks the bartender is producing, like rewarding a pizzeria for the way its kitchen workers spin and twirl the dough.

Since the 1990s, there has been a strong and widespread revival of interest in traditional cocktails, as well as in cocktails that are similarly labor-intensive but a far cry from anything Thomas might have served, featuring exotic ingredients and even elements of so-called molecular gastronomy. Innovators like Toby Maloney, of the Violet Hour in Chicago, and Audrey Saunders, of Pegu Club in New York, compose cocktail menus featuring drinks such as the Juliet & Romeo, which combines gin with lime juice, simple syrup, rose water, bitters, cucumber, and mint; or the Earl Grey MarTEAni, which uses Tanqueray gin infused with Earl Grey tea leaves before being sweetened and shaken with lemon juice and egg whites. Common to these bars is the hiring of bar staff who treat their drinks as seriously as chefs are expected to treat their food, and an expectation that the clientele will be interested in expanding and exploring their palates.

This has led to something of a culture war. Bartenders who prepare their own bitters through laborious processes (even illegal re-distillation, it is sometimes rumored), source ingredients from out of state and overseas, and spend hours preparing ingredients that will be used for only one cocktail on the menu naturally feel aggrieved when someone balks at the $12 cost for a drink, or asks for a vodka and tonic water. They may also think it is unfair or inaccurate to group them in with bartenders whose contribution to the field is the preparation of layered shots for college students, or who do little more than mix two ingredients plus ice as quickly as possible. Those bartenders, in turn, may resent the "gourmet" or "traditionalist" bartenders—sometimes called mixologists, though just as many of them abhor the term—for putting on airs. It is, ultimately, a conflict neither side can win. Just as it is neither practical nor desirable for every cook to aspire to a Michelin star, neither can every bartender to be expected to prepare intricate garnishes, work with fresh ingredients and expensive liqueurs, or even juice lemons and limes à la minute. The **economics** of drinking out simply do not permit it. Many of the places where drinks are served offer them as a more or less mindless accompaniment to the meal, and enhancing the role and responsibilities of the bartender would have the same financial impact as abandoning the soda fountain in favor of bottles of boutique soda, or getting rid of complimentary tap water and offering only Italian still and sparkling waters. (*See also* **Absinthe; Bar Games; Bars; Carding; Cocktails; Pubs; Speakeasies; Television.**)

Further Reading

Bolton, Ross. *The Saloon in the Home*. New York: CreateSpace, 2008.
Haigh, Ted. *Vintage Spirits and Forgotten Cocktails*. New York: Quarry Books, 2009.
McElhone, Harry. *Barflies and Cocktails*. New York: Mud Puddle Books, 2008.
Regan, Gary. *The Joy of Mixology*. New York: Clarkson Potter, 2003.
Thomas, Jerry. *The Bar-Tender's Guide: How to Mix Drinks: A Bon Vivant's Companion*. New York: Mud Puddle Books, 2008.
Wondrich, Dave. *Imbibe!* New York: Perigee Trade, 2007.

Bill Kte'pi

BEER

Beer is America's favorite alcoholic beverage. The United States is the largest producer of beer in the world (about six billion gallons annually), and approximately 85 percent of the volume of alcoholic beverages sold in the United States each year is beer. Americans, per capita, drink about 85 liters a year. The United States is ranked eighth in the world for its consumption of beer.

Beer produced in the United States constitutes a $190 billion industry, providing 1.7 million jobs and $36 billion of federal, state, and local taxes. The craft **brewing** sector of the industry occupied $5 billion of the market in 2007. That same year, American consumers spent $97 billion on beer. Only a relatively small quantity of North American beer is exported each year: 4.4 million hectoliters as opposed to the 30 million hectoliters of beer that is imported annually.

The origins of beer in this country mimic the international origins of many of its population's national heritages. British, Dutch, German, Czech, and Irish immigrants contributed to the birth of American beer, building breweries in many of the places they settled. Beer was originally brought from England to the colonies, and, in the nineteenth century, Germans brought the newly developed lager styles better suited to large-scale production. By the late nineteenth century, there were more than 4,000 breweries in the United States, but that

Many American cultural rituals are tied to beer drinking, from college parties to watching the Super Bowl. (Corel)

number shrank after the invention of refrigeration in the early years of the twentieth century.

Steam beer is claimed to be the first beer to have originated in the United States, in San Francisco during the nineteenth century. Steam beer was no longer brewed after **Prohibition**, although the Anchor Steam Brewery has attempted to recreate the style.

Prohibition (1920–1933) decimated the brewing industry, causing almost all of the 1,400 breweries to close. Only a small number of these breweries were able to reopen after the repeal of Prohibition. Prohibition gave rise to illegal home-brewing of beer.

Prohibition set the stage for the dominance of megabreweries, which continues to the present. During Prohibition, only the largest breweries could stay in business through the production of nonalcoholic beverages such as root beer, nonalcoholic beer, colas, and malt syrup. When Prohibition was repealed in part by the amendment of the Volstead Act in April 1933, beer up to 3.2 percent alcohol by volume (ABV) was labeled as not "intoxicating" and was therefore not prohibited. Although beer was again made legal in December 1933, with the repeal of Prohibition according to the Twenty-first Amendment to the U.S. Constitution, the brewing industry had suffered enormously. Only the stronger and larger breweries had survived.

By World War II, the brewing industry had not yet recovered, and breweries were forced to use lower-cost ingredients, producing lower-alcohol beer so that grain could be employed for the war effort. This may have been the catalyst for America's taste for low-alcohol, low-flavor beer. The industry came to be dominated by the brewing giants Anheuser-Busch and Coors Brewing Company, characterized by the uniformity of their pilsner-style lager and their use of low-cost ingredients such as corn, rice, and other adjuncts, which provided the starch needed for alcohol production but gave little flavor character to the beer.

In the 1950s and 1960s, the American national brands rose in popularity, which greatly minimized the variety of beer available in the country. Although in 1880, there were more than 2,200 breweries in the United States, in the early 1980s, there were fewer than 50. Some industry experts predicted that it would only be a short time until there would be only five brewing companies left in the country. The 1970s and 1980s have been called the pre-revolutionary period of American beer. Gradually during these years, imported beer became more prevalent in the American market, and consumers sought out new choices in beer. These beers were sold at higher prices, but many consumers thought they were well worth the price.

Since the 1980s, the United States has seen what has become known as the craft beer revolution, characterized by the rise of **microbreweries**, regional craft breweries and brewpubs. Microbreweries produce fewer than 15,000 barrels (1 barrel = 31 gallons) of beer per year. Although some craft breweries produce a volume that excludes them from this categorization, annual production generally is less than 2 million barrels per year, qualifying them for the Tax and Trade Bureau's small brewers excise tax differential. The number of regional craft breweries, microbreweries, and brewpubs is currently approaching 2,000. Craft breweries brew traditional styles, sometimes interpreting them in new, creative, and unprecedented ways.

Most commercial craft beer grew out of the hobby of home-brewing. Unsatisfied with the available beer in the United States, home-brewers realized that one of the only ways to drink stronger, more flavorful beers of greater diversity was to brew them themselves. These home-brewers eventually became many of the first commercial craft brewers. While the craft brewing sector of the brewing industry faced many difficulties getting off its feet in the 1980s, and although it still composes only 3.8 percent of the beer sold in the United States, it is the fastest-growing sector of the brewing industry.

Approximately 1,440 breweries currently operate in the United States, four of which constitute about 95 percent of the industry. These four breweries produce a uniform beer, and they distinguish themselves more through their image and marketing than through their product. In recent years, the industry giants have recognized the craft beer niche market and have made attempts to develop craft beers that rival the popularity of the independently made craft beers.

Beer in the United States is produced through the same process as beer in other parts of the world: sugars from malted grains (usually barley or wheat, but also rice and corn) are boiled with hops and water and then the wort, or unfermented beer, is fermented with yeast. The strength of beer is measured in terms of ABV. The average strength of beer in the United States is 4.2 percent.

American beer can be divided roughly into two categories: ales and lagers. Ales are beers that are fermented at higher temperatures (59–77 °F) using grains that have been kilned at higher temperatures, giving more color and flavor and fermented by top-fermenting yeasts. Lagers are fermented at cooler temperatures (43–50 °F) using bottom-fermenting yeasts. These beers are lagered, or stored, after **fermentation** at cooler temperatures for a period of several weeks.

Most beer produced and drunk in the United States is the pale lager, the style of Budweiser, Coors, and Miller. This style, originated in Europe, is characterized by its pale yellow color, low alcohol content, and light flavor. Other beer styles that were developed in Europe but have grown into distinctly American versions include the pale ale, India pale ale, brown ale, porter, and stout. Some markedly American versions of these beers such as the American Stout or West Coast India pale ale are now recognized beer styles of their own. Many craft breweries in the

United States also produce Belgian-style beer such as Saison, Dubbel, Tripel, Belgian Strong Golden, and Belgian Strong Dark.

Most beer in the United States is consumed in the home, but about one quarter of the beer sold in this country is consumed in **bars**, restaurants, and breweries. A slightly lower amount is purchased in gas stations (20%), supermarkets (19%), and **liquor stores** (17%). Although beer can be sold on the premises in brewpubs (establishments that sell most of their beer on the premises), most breweries do not sell beer directly to the customer. Instead, beer is sold through a three-tier system involving the supplier, the distributor, and the retailer.

Unlike in many other countries where the legal drinking age is 18, Americans must be 21 years old to legally drink beer. Many underage Americans, however, are not dissuaded from drinking beer. Beer is one of the most common beverages for **underage drinking** in the United States because, for many, beer is considered less harmful and more socially acceptable than **wine** or hard alcohol. Young adults are also more likely to be inundated with **advertising** that promotes beer more than any other alcoholic beverage.

Beer is a beverage of relaxation and celebration in many parts of the world. However, among many consumers of beer in the United States, it is not the drink of moderation as it is in other countries. A relatively small population of drinkers consumes most of the beer drunk in the United States. Beer drinkers are overrepresented by men and young adults who disproportionately represent the heaviest drinkers. Although they constitute only about one quarter of the population, they make up almost half of adult drinking. For many Americans, beer has a negative association with elements such as sex, partying, and aggression among young males. Some mainstream beer advertising also tends to play into the negative stereotypes associated with beer.

Men drink the most beer in the United States, but women represent a growing market. Beer advertising is almost exclusively targeted toward men. Although women have historically been marginalized from the beer world, and beer drinking among women is less socially accepted than among men, women currently account for one quarter of the beer consumers in the United States. Women in their 20s drink more beer than in any other age group, although beer drinking among women above the age of 50 is also on the rise. Women tend to be more discerning beer drinkers on the whole than men, preferring beer with more flavor and character than the average beer drinker. Lower-alcohol and low-carbohydrate beers, wheat beers, and light ales are popular choices among American women. The craft beer sector of the beer industry continues to be male-dominated, as does the **home-brew** hobby, but this is changing as many talented women enter the field producing high-quality beer.

Although the average beer drinker may know or appreciate little about the process that goes into the beer, through the educational undertakings of select breweries and beer enthusiasts, beer is slowly shedding some of these negative associations and is becoming an alcoholic beverage of more integrity.

Further Reading

Bamforth, Charles. *Beer: Tap into the Art and Science of Brewing*. 3rd ed. New York: Oxford University Press, 2009.

Greenfield, T. K., and J. D. Rogers. "Who Drinks Most of the Alcohol in the U.S.? The Policy Implications." *Journal of Studies on Alcohol* 60, no. 1 (1999):78–89.

Rogers, J. D., and T. K. Greenfield "Beer Drinking Accounts for Most of the Hazardous Alcohol Consumption Reported in the United States." *Journal of Studies on Alcohol* 60 (1999): 732–39.

Matthew Russell

BEER BELLY

A person with a large and rotund stomach, but a relatively thinner body, can be said to have a "**beer** belly." This is also referred to as a "beer gut." Excessive beer drinking has become associated with abdominal weight gain, but it seems that beer might have gotten a bad rap. It is true that drinking large quantities of beer will increase the circumference of one's waistline, but so will drinking any highly caloric beverage in excess. Where a person gains weight, on the other hand, is purely genetic. Studies show men are predisposed to fat storage in the abdominal area, whereas women gain more of their weight in the thighs and buttocks. The fact that in America, more men than women regularly drink beer perhaps contributes to the reason that a large gut and beer have become synonymous.

Experts suggest that moderation is key in the fight against the bulge, as is how many drinks are consumed at any given time. **Binge drinking** is apparently worse for the waistline than drinking a beer or two a day, even if the total amount of drinks consumed in the week is the same. Essentially, beer has calories, and calories create fat. If the calories ingested are not expended, weight will be gained.

Further Reading

Bamforth, C. W. "Beer, Carbohydrates and Diet." *Journal of the Institute of Brewing* 111 (2005): 259–64.

Vaccariello, Liz, and Cynthia Sass. *Flat Belly Diet*. New York: Rodale, 2008.

Whitney Adams

BEER BONGS

Popular on college campuses, a **beer** bong is a simple device designed to allow one to consume a large amount of beer in a very short time period. The word bong is a slang term for a type of water pipe, also popular on some college campuses, that is normally used to smoke tobacco or marijuana. Resembling a large funnel, the beer bong operates on the simple principle of gravity. The smaller end of the beer bong is temporarily plugged while beer is poured into the larger end, which, in turn, is held as high as possible above one's head. Once a sufficient amount of beer is poured into the funnel, the smaller end, or "drinking end," is released, and it is quickly placed in the mouth. The user then faces the challenge of consuming the large quantity of beer that is rapidly moving through the tube.

There is no standard design for beer bongs. Some are simple, while others are elaborately decorated and include valves that can control the beer flow. Others have long tubes that can be held far above the user's head using a ladder or a staircase. Beer bongs can be designed for use by one person at a time or by several people, in which case the size of the funnel is altered and multiple tubes are attached. Popular at college parties, beer bongs are sometimes used in reckless contests that determine which partygoer can consume the most beer in the shortest period of time. These devices generally do not promote responsible alcohol consumption. (*See also* **College Drinking Culture; Drinking Games.**)

Further Reading

Ogle, Maureen. *Ambitious Brew: The Story of American Beer*. Fort Washington, PA: Harvest Book Company, 2007.

Ben Wynne

BEER GOGGLES

"**Beer** goggles" refer to the assumed change in perception of the attractiveness of others as drunkenness sets in. While it is widely accepted that drinking lowers one's inhibitions, the idea of beer goggles adds a different spin to the scenario of waking up with someone one would not ordinarily have gone to bed with: rather than acting impulsively or carelessly, the beer goggle-wearer has acted on erroneous information. Other phrases conveying the same model of drunkenness include such misogynistic expressions as "she's a 2 at 10 and a 10 at 2" and "there are no ugly women at closing time."

Over the years, there have been a number of conflicting scientific studies on the effect of alcohol on attraction. A 2005 University of Manchester study commissioned by Bausch & Lomb attempted to quantify the beer goggles effect, even taking the smokiness of the bar into account as part of the formula. Though the Manchester study does not seem to have tested whether the beer goggles effect is real, a 2002 Scottish study found that an intoxicated group of college students rated photos about 25 percent more attractive than the control group did. A 2009 study, published in the *British Journal of Psychology*, found the opposite was true—the intoxicated group in their study rated photographs as less attractive. (That most of these studies have been British may say something about differences in attitudes toward drinking, or drunken sex, in the UK and the United States.)

On the "Beer Goggles" episode of the Adult Swim cartoon *The Drinky Crow Show* (an adaptation of Tony Millionaire's *Maakies* comic), Drinky Crow buys a pair of beer goggles (made from **beer** bottles and worn after gouging out one's own eyes) from a men's room vending machine. Not only are women made more attractive, but the world itself is transformed in his perceptions, becoming a sunny landscape filled with candy and unshaking optimism.

A 2009 ad campaign for Coopers Premium Light, a beer produced in Singapore but propagated as an Internet meme, depicted conventionally unattractive women Photoshopped to emulate an "incomplete" beer goggles effect (highlighting the beer's low alcohol content), pasting an attractive leg, face, or breasts onto an otherwise unattractive body. (*See also* **Barfly; Last Call; Social Drinking.**)

Further Reading

Burns, Eric. *The Spirits of America: A Social History of Alcohol*. Philadelphia: Temple University Press, 2004.

Curtis, Wayne. *And a Bottle of Rum: A History of the New World in Ten Cocktails.* New York: Three Rivers Press, 2007.

Bill Kte'pi

BEER PONG

Beer pong is a popular team drinking game in which players throw ping-pong balls across a table into beer-filled cups. While common on college campuses, the game has crossed into the mainstream in recent years.

The basic game play involves two two-player teams, one team on each side of a table, and a number of cups set up on each side. Starting from the back of a table, 10 plastic cups are arranged in a pyramid-shaped "rack" at each end of the table. These cups are filled with a mutually agreed-upon volume of a mutually agreed-upon beverage, most often lager.

The two teams stand on opposite sides of the table and attempt to throw, bounce, or otherwise propel a regulation ball into the opponent's cups on the opposite side of the table. After the cup is "sunk," it is removed from play and the contents are consumed by the defending player. The first team to sink all their opponent's cups wins.

The game was created on the campus of Dartmouth College in the 1950s when a cup of beer was left on a ping-pong table. The leisurely and lighthearted version gave way in the 1980s to a more intense game played by throwing balls into clusters of multiple cups.

This new version, also known as Beirut, spread quickly as colleges around the country picked up the game—and began putting their own touch on the rules. With the proliferation of the Internet, these local traditions became visible and a slightly more codified version emerged. (*See also* **College Drinking Culture; Drinking Games.**)

Further Reading

Applebaum, Ben, and Dan Disorbo. *The Book of Beer Pong.* San Francisco: Chronicle Books, 2009.

Berner, Laura. "On Language, Princeton Style: The History of 'Beirut.' " *Daily Princetonian* (2004). http://www.dailyprincetonian.com/2004/11/19/11525/.

Ben Applebaum

BEER RUNS

A **beer** run entails going to a store to purchase beer and/or other alcoholic beverages. Beer runs normally occur before a social event to gather supplies or during an event to replenish low stock. The drinks purchased are usually bottled and packaged.

Most beer runs are made to a nearby supermarket, **liquor store**, or other shop selling alcohol, though some trips may involve driving across state lines or international borders in pursuit of cheaper alcohol due to different taxation laws. The drinks purchased are used primarily for consumption in a home or other private setting. A beer run can be made alone or with a group of people. Beer runs are not usually made to a pub or bar because the drinks sold in those venues are for immediate consumption unless they have take-away sales, which is illegal in many states.

Beer runs are frequently featured in popular culture. They are the plot source of countless **television** shows, movies, commercials, comedy routines, and songs.

Their portrayal in popular culture often shows the event as the grounds for an often-comedic adventure.

An alternate meaning refers to the act of stealing beer or other alcoholic beverages from a store. The thieves must run and flee before their activities are noticed.

Further Reading

Hancock, Elise. "Zoos, Tunes, and Gweeps—A Dictionary of Campus Slang." *Journal of Higher Education* 61, no. 1 (1990): 98–106.

Willa Zhen

BINGE DRINKING

The term "binge," when referring to alcohol use, has three distinct meanings. The first is the traditional and recovery-movement meaning, which refers to a lengthy period of time of drunkenness, sometimes also referred to as a spree or an orgy. The second meaning is more recent and refers to a metric adopted by alcohol researchers that defines a binge as the ingestion of a certain number of drinks in a specific period of time and is used in research on intake patterns among population groups or as a means to identify those at risk for alcohol abuse or addiction. The final meaning is popular and refers to a style of drinking that encourages large intakes of alcohol in a relatively short period of time for the purpose of becoming intoxicated.

During the nineteenth and early twentieth centuries, the noun "binge," when used in relation to alcohol, referred to spending several days drunk. The *Oxford English Dictionary* dates the first use of "binge" in drinking to 1854, from an English Midlands dialect to mean "soak" as in hydration (to soak a wooden vessel). In print, the word was used to describe a drinking bout or spree, but without negative moral or behavioral connotations. Starting in the 1930s, the term came to mean a time of overindulgence of alcohol, food, or other behaviors, and took on negative characteristics; with the use of binge to describe eating disorders in the 1970s, the word became more medicalized. The behaviors attached to a "drinking binge" are recorded in many media; perhaps the most appropriate use of the phrase in this manner is by the Big Book of **Alcoholics Anonymous (AA)**, in which many recovering drinkers describe their binges as "lost weekend" timeouts of heavy ingestion and negative behavior outcomes, often within a cycle of avoidance of alcohol followed by complete indulgence, in which it is impossible for the drinker to stop until the alcohol is gone or the user unconscious or asleep. In the stories found in the Big Book, a drinker on a binge is unable to have just one drink and must continue until an outside force ends the possibility of intake; it is perhaps the awareness of this sober/drunk binge cycle that has led to the AA belief that a drunk can never stop at just one drink ("one is too many and one thousand is never enough").

Rorabaugh (1979) used "binge" to describe the changing drinking habits of the U.S. population during the beginning of the nineteenth century. He argued that citizens of the young country were seen to shift from an eighteenth-century drinking style of daily, steady sipping of alcohol to occasional and heavy episodic usage, alone or within a social group. Rorabaugh attributed these changes to a number of factors, including the promotion of alcohol consumption as a means to demonstrate citizenship and freedom. The most common use of "binge" in the printed press is to indicate drinking a large amount in one evening. In alcohol use research, especially that focused on young people and collegians, "binge" usually means to ingest at least five drinks (alcohol equivalents) in an evening for men, and four drinks for women. This number was popularized by Henry Wechsler and his team at Harvard and used in the campus drinking habits survey of 1993 (the College Alcohol Survey, CAS) as a means to identify problematic patterns of intake that lead to negative outcomes; the survey was repeated in 1997, 1999, and 2001 (Wechsler et al. 1999; Wechsler and Nelson 2008). The team documented that at levels above five/four drinks, there are increased negative outcomes per occasion and per person, and that students who binge frequently tend to have greater problems with schoolwork and personal relationships. Furthermore, this intake level causes impairment of judgment and motor skills; the Centers for Disease Control (CDC) and the National Institute of Alcohol Abuse and **Alcoholism** defined in 2004 a binge as "a pattern of drinking alcohol that brings blood alcohol concentration (BAC) to 0.08 gram percent or above. For the typical adult, this pattern corresponds to consuming 5 or more drinks (male), or 4 or more drinks (female), in about 2 hours" (NIAAA 2004). This is a rational amount and time frame to use as an indicator of potential problematic drinking, because quick intake of five/four causes immediate impairment, and frequent binge drinking patterns are linked to specific long-term problems in public health. Accordingly, the five/four metric, or some similar number, has been adopted by the World Health Organization (WHO) for population surveys of health-related behaviors and is used in many surveys of drinking behavior as the metric that best indicates problematic drinking.

Used to measure potentially problematic behavior and health outcomes, the five/four measurement, with time limits included, provides an accurate representation of the levels of intake likely to cause negative consequences. Whether that amount represents actual behavior patterns is contested, however, as groups of drinkers identify problematic levels differently. Furthermore, a long evening of drinking during which the drinker has one drink per hour and thus remains sober (most medical research indicates that the body can clear roughly one drink per hour) could still count as a binge (and imply drunkenness) in studies without time frame metrics. However, higher-end drinkers may ingest far more (and do so quickly) per drinking occasion than other drinkers and may consider their own levels of intake to be normal. For this reason, many colleges have implemented social norming campaigns designed to make students aware of the intake habits of medium and low-end drinkers (Perkins 2002). Given that the CAS has demonstrated that only 20 percent of students regularly drink more than five drinks per occasion (Wechsler and Nelson 2008), the social norming term "four or fewer" is a potent and real description of most college drinkers' habits. Problems with the five/four metric are related not to correlations with outcomes, but to social actions and expectations of population groups that have developed drinking patterns and styles that encourage rapid and high-end intake of alcohol.

The third meaning of the term "binge" is popular and used as a verb, indicating a high intake over a short period of time specifically to become intoxicated. According to CDC and WHO measurement indices, almost any participant of a **drinking game** or of shared rounds is probably "binging," given that under those conditions there is a high likelihood of ingesting five or more drinks. But that is not the meaning of the verb "to binge," as used among English speakers. To use the phrase "let's binge" means "let's get drunk" and indicates rapid intake of drinks. Although much of the social attention about binge drinking is focused on youth and college students (presumably due to the wealth of data available for those populations), the vast majority of binge drinkers are adults. According to the CDC, using U.S.-based data from Town et al. (2006), 72 percent of all binge drinking episodes involve drinkers older than 25 years of age. In other words, while the focus is on underage and college-age drinking, most dangerous drinking episodes involve older adults. As a result, it might be argued that the word "drunk" or the phrase "to get drunk" has been replaced by the term "to binge." Certainly media all over the world highlight the problems of "binge drinking" in various population groups; rates of binge drinking among the English-speaking and northern European countries are reported to be especially high, a pattern that may have deep cultural and behavioral roots (Engs 1995). However, measurement standards differ from country to country, so it is difficult to ascertain whether these rates are accurate or a consequence of higher screening, surveillance, and reporting of drinking habits. (*See also* **Blood Alcohol Content (BAC); College Drinking Culture; Health Effects of Alcohol; Underage Drinking.**)

Further Reading

Engs, Ruth. "Do Traditional Western European Drinking Practices Have Origins in Antiquity?" *Addiction Research* 2, no. 3 (1995): 227–39.

National Institute on Alcohol Abuse and Alcoholism. "NIAAA Council Approves Definition of Binge Drinking." *NIAAA Newsletter* 3 (Winter): 3. NIH Publication No. 04-5346. Bethesda, MD: National Institute of Alcohol Abuse and Alcoholism, 2004.

Perkins, H. Wesley. "Social Norms and the Prevention of Alcohol Misuse in Collegiate Contexts." *Journal of Studies on Alcohol* Supplement 14 (2002):164–72.

Rorabaugh, W. J. *The Alcoholic Republic: An American Tradition.* New York: Oxford University Press, 1979.

Town, M., T. S. Naimi, A. H. Mokdad, and R. D. Brewer. "Health Care Access among U.S. Adults Who Drink Alcohol Excessively: Missed Opportunities for Prevention." *Preventing Chronic Disease* 3, no. 2 (2006). http://www.cdc.gov/pcd/issues/2006/apr/05_0182.htm.

Wechsler, Henry, Andrea Davenport, George Dowdall, Barbara Moeykens, and Sonia Castillo. "Health and Behavioral Consequences of Binge Drinking in College: A National Survey of Students at 140 Campuses." *JAMA* 272, no. 21 (1994): 1672–77.

Wechsler, H., and T. F. Nelson. "What We Have Learned from the Harvard School of Public Health College Alcohol Study: Focusing Attention on College Student Alcohol Consumption and the Environmental Conditions That Promote It." *Journal of Studies on Alcohol and Drugs* 69, no. 4 (2008): 481–90. http://www.hsph.harvard.edu/cas/What-We-Learned-08.pdf.

World Health Organization. "International Guide for Monitoring Alcohol Consumption and Related Harm." WHO Document No. WHO/MSD/MSB/00.4. Geneva: WHO, 2000.

Janet Chrzan

BLACKOUTS

Alcohol-related blackouts can be complete or partial and are caused by the rapid consumption of alcohol. "Blacking out" is not to be confused with "passing out," which is the loss of consciousness. **Binge drinking** is one of the leading causes of blackouts. Researchers believe that it is not necessarily the amount but rather the rapidity of alcohol consumption, hence the rapid increase in **blood alcohol content**, that leads to memory loss. Alcohol can hinder the brain's ability to form new long-term memories. Memory loss is usually only of the period while drinking or when a certain level of intoxication is reached. The amount of alcohol it takes to reach the blackout phase will vary from individual to individual and between men and women. Despite popular social perceptions of the antisocial drunk, research has found that blackouts often occur among young social drinkers.

There are many dangers for individuals who experience alcohol-related blackouts. Unprotected sex, **driving under the influence,** and violent behavior are just a few of the high-risk activities that are sometimes related with the sort of excessive drinking that can lead to blacking out. (*See also* **College Drinking Culture.**)

Further Reading

Goodwin, Donald W. "Alcohol Amnesia." *Addiction* 90 (1995): 315–17.

Rachel Black

BLOOD ALCOHOL CONTENT (BAC)

The blood alcohol content, or alternately blood alcohol concentration, is a metric determined by the amount of alcohol in relation to the volume of blood, usually as a percentage of grams per milliliter, and can be affected by the drinker's weight, height, fat percentage, sex, and metabolism. BAC is measured either by analysis of alcohol particles in the breath using a **breathalyzer** or by urine analysis; both methods assume that the human body excretes a known and regular amount of alcohol in relation to breath or urine production and that alcoholic drinks provide a known and regular amount of alcohol to the drinker. On average, each alcohol equivalent (one-half fluid ounce of raw alcohol, which is roughly one shot of 80 proof alcohol, five ounces of **wine,** or 12 ounces of **beer**) is expected to affect BAC in a predictable manner, so the BAC can indicate the number of drinks ingested.

The primary use of BAC is as a legal metric for indicating possible levels of intoxication, especially in situations where drinkers are operating machinery. Most countries have BAC laws that determine a maximum allowable BAC for operation of automobiles, with some countries opting for zero tolerance. The assumption behind the levels is that BAC affects behavior in broadly similar ways, with levels as small as .03 percent causing euphoria and small personality changes. At .40 percent, the human body becomes unconscious, and death may occur as a result of the shutdown of the central nervous system. (*See also* **Driving under the Influence (DUI); Health Effects of Alcohol.**)

Janet Chrzan

BLUE LAWS

Blue laws, also known as Sunday closing laws, require businesses to remain closed on Sundays in recognition of the Christian Sabbath. For most of American history, people had one day off from work—Sunday—and this day was considered the day of rest or the Lord's Day. No commerce, financial transactions, or even travel was to take place that day. Christians encouraged people to attend church and spend time with their families instead.

Blue laws have been in America since nearly the beginning of the colonies. The origin of the term "blue law" is somewhat murky. It may have referred to the laws printed on blue paper for the New Haven colony in 1665. Or it may refer to "true blue" principles of Puritans—that is, unyielding and dogmatic. In earlier times, punishment for violating the Sabbath could range from fines to whipping, or sometimes death. Even slaves were given a day of rest. In New Orleans, African slaves met in Congo Square on Sundays to play music, sowing the seeds for jazz.

The **Temperance** Movement allied itself with strict Sabbatarians to keep people from drinking alcohol on Sundays. Temperance reformers sought to shut down the saloons. This was especially targeted at German immigrants, who arrived in waves starting in the late 1840s, and who spent their Sunday afternoons and evenings at their local *Biergarten*, socializing with their family and friends. This behavior, known as the Continental Sunday, violated the Temperance Movement's belief in what it meant to be a good American. The blue law was designed to force all to respect Sunday as a dry day, as well as a day of rest.

Temperance finally got its wish to make every day dry—not just Sunday—with **Prohibition** (1920–1933). Likewise, Sabbatarians put a stop to the U.S. Postal Service delivering mail on Sundays in 1912.

Blue laws in the United States gradually disappeared beginning in the 1960s, largely in response to consumerism and the decline of trade unions. The two-day weekend emerged after World War II, which dissipated the cultural relevance of a single day of rest. In addition, most American families are now two-income, and the weekends are the only time when people can shop. Consumers demand that stores be open on Sundays, and legislatures responded by opening commerce. In some states like California, blue laws were uprooted.

Alcohol remains one of the few areas where retailers must close shop on Sunday, though this is largely confined to the South and Midwest. This is at odds with the fact that restaurants and **bars** (on-premise establishments) can serve drinks on Sunday, but off-premise venues like **liquor stores** cannot sell retail alcohol. Many states have repealed their Sunday closing laws, or allow only **beer** and **wine** retail sales, but not distilled spirits. Alcohol is treated arbitrarily compared with just about every other consumer product that can be sold on Sunday.

Small businesses, including some liquor stores, are often in favor of blue laws, not for religious but rather for competitive reasons. Large businesses have greater efficiencies and can offer lower prices. Requiring everyone to close means a small business does not have to lose sales to a rival because they are closed on Sundays. Economists note that this is essentially a small business subsidy, as it restrains competition and drives up prices.

Some states maintain a rational basis for blue laws, partly from the church lobby, but also out of a secular desire for a day of rest. However, consumers have increasingly showed that they do not have time to rest in an on-the-go culture. Church support for blue laws fell away as congregations demanded the convenience of shopping on Sundays. Repealing blue laws has shown to have no effect on church attendance: people still go to church, and then shop afterward.

Sunday is no longer the day of rest in American society, but the day of recreation. It is the second-busiest day for shopping, and many sports events are held on Sundays.

Further Reading

Laband, David N., and Deborah Hendry Heinbuch. *Blue Laws: The History, Economics, and Politics of Sunday Closing Laws*. Lexington, MA: Lexington Books, 1987.

Garrett Peck

BOOTLEG ALCOHOL

In the United States, "bootleg alcohol" refers in general to alcohol produced and distributed illegally in an effort to make profits while avoiding government duties or other legal restrictions. The term apparently originated in the Midwest after the Civil War in reference to traders who concealed flasks of illegal liquor in their boots for sale to the Native American population. During the **Prohibition** era, "bootlegging" became a catch-all term to describe any type of activity that involved the sale of illegal liquor.

The illegal transportation and sale of alcohol in the United States dates from the colonial period, when the British government first began placing taxes on distilled spirits, but bootlegging is most closely associated with the 1920s and early 1930s, when the sale and **distribution** of alcohol was made illegal throughout the United States. The first major **temperance** organizations in the United States formed soon after the American Revolution, and by the 1830s, the American Temperance Society, one of the largest of these groups, claimed more than 1.5 million members in 8,000 local chapters. Some industrial leaders took up the cause of prohibition under the rationale that sober workers were more productive workers and progressive politicians began to view prohibition as an important form of social reform. In rural areas, particularly in the South and Midwest, the prohibition movement picked up steam as a moral crusade. The **Woman's Christian Temperance Union (WCTU)** became the largest women's organization of the period in the United States and with the **Anti-Saloon League** pressed for the legal abolition of saloons and eventually the complete prohibition of the manufacture and sale of alcoholic beverages. The prohibition movement peaked in 1919 with the ratification of the Eighteenth Amendment to the U.S. Constitution, which banned the "manufacture, sale or transportation" of alcohol in the United States. This opened the door for bootleggers around the country.

National Prohibition, which would be called a "noble experiment" by some, did not cure all of America's problems. While the amendment did curb drinking in many parts of the nation, the violation of prohibition laws skyrocketed. Because legitimate businessmen were now barred from the lucrative alcohol trade, criminals moved in to make sure that the American public was able to purchase bootleg liquor, which was in high demand. Eventually it became almost as easy to acquire illegal alcohol in many parts of the country as it had been to purchase legal alcohol before prohibition. Criminal networks developed that brought in bootleg **whiskey** from Canada and Mexico on ships nicknamed "rum-runners." On the East and West coasts, as well as in the Gulf of Mexico, large ships with cargo holds filled with cases of bootleg liquor dropped anchor several miles off the coast, outside the so-called rum line of U.S. jurisdiction. Their cargo was then loaded onto smaller, faster boats for transportation to the mainland. While the U.S. Coast Guard tried to stop this type of activity, they did not have the manpower or resources to curb the high volume of illegal traffic. Contraband also came in overland through Mexico and Canada and by boat across the Great Lakes.

During the Prohibition era, bootleg liquor made its way to illegal nightclubs, or "**speakeasies**," located in many American cities. Speakeasies increased in popularity and number as the Prohibition era progressed, and as criminal networks distributing bootleg liquor became better defined. Although law enforcement agents would sometimes raid the clubs and arrest the owners and patrons, the business itself was so lucrative that speakeasies flourished regardless of the risks involved. In major cities, speakeasies were often sophisticated, with food, live **music**, and other forms of entertainment in addition to bootleg alcohol. Many illegal clubs stayed in operation by bribing public or police officials who were willing to turn a blind eye to illegal activity for a cut of the profits. The system fueled the coffers of organized crime and made crime bosses such as Al Capone in Chicago very wealthy. In rural areas, the criminal activity that revolved around the sale of bootleg alcohol was less sophisticated, but generally very profitable for country entrepreneurs willing to violate the law. Rural stills in the South and Appalachia produced bootleg alcohol called "moonshine" for individual consumption or to stock local nightclubs. Just as in the cities, these moonshiners—named for the assumption that they had to operate by moonlight to avoid detection—were sometimes harassed by law enforcement but many times they were, in effect, in partnership with local police officials who took a cut of their profits.

Within a few years after the ratification of the Eighteenth Amendment, many of the supporters of Prohibition began to see that the noble experiment was failing. Because of the prevalence of bootleg liquor, alcohol consumption in the United States was still high, and the only group profiting from Prohibition seemed to be organized crime and corrupt politicians and police officials. Finally in 1933, the Eighteenth Amendment was repealed by the Twenty-first Amendment to the Constitution. The end of national Prohibition was a blow to organized crime, but bootlegging did not disappear completely. Individual states could still enforce their own prohibition laws, and for years many did, particularly those states with large populations of evangelical Christians. As a result, bootlegging flourished for decades in the South and Appalachian regions. (*See also* **Politics**.)

Further Reading

Behr, Edward. *Prohibition: Thirteen Years That Changed America*. New York: Arcade Publishing, 1997.

Butts, Edward. *Outlaws of the Lakes: Bootlegging and Smuggling from Colonial Times to Prohibition*. New York: Thunder Bay Press, 2004.

Kobler, John. *Ardent Spirits: The Rise and Fall of Prohibition*. New York: De Capo Press, 1993.

Ben Wynne

BOURBON

Bourbon is a distilled spirit, an American aged **whiskey** made from corn and other grains. It gets its brown color from aging in a charred oak barrel. Unaged corn whiskey is clear and known as moonshine.

In this Kentucky distillery, bourbon is kept inside wooden barrels for aging. Regulations stipulate that bourbon must be aged in new charred oak barrels. (Shutterstock)

Whiskey making came from Scottish and Irish immigrants, who brought the know-how to make rye whiskey to the mid-Atlantic. When their descendants crossed the Appalachian Mountains into what is now Kentucky, they found that native Indian corn grew so plentiful that they soon replaced rye with corn, and corn whiskey, also known as corn juice, was born.

Kentucky was named Bourbon County in honor of the French royal family when France declared war on England during the American Revolution. The frontier farmers had no way to ship their crops to market—a national transportation network did not exist yet—so they distilled their excess corn into whiskey and poured it into oak barrels. They then floated the barrels downriver on flatboats to New Orleans. Traders noted that the whiskey came from Bourbon County, and the name bourbon stuck.

Bourbon inadvertently launched the **Temperance** Movement in the early American republic. Congress repealed the excise taxes on whiskey after the Whiskey Rebellion of 1794. The Ohio River Valley was soon settled and began producing a glut of cheap corn whiskey. It quickly replaced **rum** as the country's favorite distilled spirit. By the 1820s, the nation was on a whiskey-drinking binge, the likes of which have not been seen before or since. The Temperance Movement was a church-based response to stop people, mostly men, from drinking so heavily.

Bourbon retained its popularity until after the Civil War, when German brewers like Anheuser-Busch began shipping lager nationally. **Beer** replaced whiskey as the country's favorite alcoholic beverage. After **Prohibition** was repealed in 1933, whiskey regained its popularity, only to be eclipsed by **vodka** in the 1970s.

Bourbon: A Whiskey by Another Name

According to title 27 of the U.S. Alcohol, tobacco and firearms Code of Federal Regulations definition, the label "Bourbon" cannot be used to describe whiskey that is produced outside the United States. To be labeled as Bourbon, it must conform to the following regulations:

- Produced from a fermented mash with no less than 51 percent and no more than 79 percent corn
- It cannot be distilled at less than 80 percent alcohol/volume (160 proof)
- Stored in a new, charred, oak barrel at a maximum of 62.5 percent alcohol/volume (125 proof) for at least two years (at two years or more, it can be labeled "straight")
- The original color and flavor of the whiskey must remain the same and cannot be filtered
- Must be produced and aged for at least one year in Kentucky in order to be called Kentucky bourbon

Congress declared bourbon the national spirit in 1964. Federal law defines bourbon. It must be made from at least 51 percent corn and also includes other grains, such as barley, rye, and wheat. It must be aged in a new oak container—meaning that they cannot be reused for another batch of bourbon. Used bourbon barrels are resold for Scotch, Caribbean **rum**, and garden barrels.

Although bourbon can be made anywhere, most of it is made in Kentucky. There is an urban legend that Bourbon County, northeast of Lexington, is a dry county. It is, in fact, wet.

Bourbon saw a resurgence in the early twenty-first century, and it has become a premium product, with new brands entering the market like Buffalo Trace and Woodford Reserve. Jim Beam is the biggest bourbon brand. The Kentucky Bourbon Festival is held annually in September, centered on Bardstown, the self-proclaimed "Bourbon Capital of the World." There is also a Kentucky Bourbon Trail, modeled after the **wine** trails in Napa Valley, geared toward visitors and tourists of the various distilleries along the Blue Ridge Parkway. (*See also* **Distilling; Dry Counties.**)

Further Reading

Peck, Garrett. *The Prohibition Hangover: Alcohol in America from Demon Rum to Cult Cabernet*. New Brunswick, NJ: Rutgers University Press, 2009.

Regan, Gary, and Mardee Haigin Regan. *The Book of Bourbon: And Other Fine American Whiskies*. New York: Houghton Mifflin, 1998.

Rorabaugh, William. *The Alcoholic Republic: An American Tradition*. New York: Oxford University Press, 1979.

Garrett Peck

BREATHALYZER TEST

A blending of the words "breath" and "analyze," breathalyzer refers to a machine used to measure the alcohol level in a person's system, usually to determine whether the person is fit to operate a motor vehicle or has violated laws dealing with drinking and driving. At one time, the term described a particular brand of the machine used by law enforcement, though now it is considered a generic term to describe all such devices.

The technology behind the breathalyzer dates to the 1930s and the work of Professor Rolla N. Harger of Indiana University. A biochemist and toxicologist, Harger in 1938 developed the "Drunkometer," a device that estimated the alcohol level in a person's system by measuring the alcohol content in the person's breath. With the Drunkometer a driver's breath sample went directly into a balloon and was pumped through a chemical solution that changed color if traces of alcohol were present. Building on this technology, Professor Robert F. Borkenstein, also of Indiana University, invented in the 1950s what most consider the first modern breathalyzer. Whereas the Drunkometer was cumbersome and required significant recalibration when it was moved from one place to another, Borkenstein's machine was highly portable.

Like previous models, modern breathalyzers do not measure **blood alcohol content** or concentration, which can be accomplished only through blood sample analysis. Rather, they estimate the concentration by measuring the alcohol content in someone's breath. Different types of machines are used, including relatively large evidentiary machines housed at police stations or in specially equipped police vans, and less accurate handheld devices used by police officers in the field for preliminary alcohol screening. Because the larger machines yield better estimates than the handheld models, some states will not allow data from handheld machines to be introduced as evidence in court. Handheld devices are commonly used at sobriety checkpoints, or "roadblocks," to establish the basis for taking motorists to a police station where they would then be tested using the larger, more accurate machine. Laws vary from state to state, but it is usually illegal for adults to operate an automobile if their blood alcohol content is .08 percent or higher. In an effort to curb habitual drunk driving, scientists and engineers have in recent years developed breath-testing devices that connect to the starter or the ignition of a vehicle or to the vehicle's onboard computer system. To start the vehicle, the driver must provide a breath sample with an alcohol concentration below a preset limit and periodically provide breath samples while the vehicle is in use to ensure that the driver remains sober.

Studies show that the use of breathalyzers has reduced the number of drunk-driving fatalities in the United States, but breathalyzer technology is not yet completely foolproof. A number of factors can affect data collection, including the presence of other chemical compounds in the testing area, climate, calibration of the device, and the manner in which the breath test is conducted. (*See also* **Driving under the Influence (DUI)**.)

Further Reading

Jacobs, James B. *Drunk Driving: An American Dilemma*. Chicago: University of Chicago Press, 1992.

Taylor, Lawrence E., and Steven Oberman. *Drunk Driving Defense*. New York: Aspen Press, 2005.

Ben Wynne

Breathalyzer Statistics

Across the United States, it is illegal to operate a vehicle with a blood alcohol rate of .08 percent or higher. For drivers 18 to 21 years of age, the legal limit in most states in .02 percent.

Approximately one in four motorists in the United States detained on suspicion of driving under the influence of alcohol refuses to take a breathalyzer test in hopes that the lack of a breathalyzer score will help in court. Penalties for refusing to take the test vary from state to state.

More than one-third of all fatal traffic accidents in the United States involve at least one person with a blood alcohol content over 0.08 percent.

Nearly a third of Americans will be involved in an alcohol-related crash at one point in their life.

BREWERIANA

Nostalgia fuels a hobby-industry known as breweriana. Particularly in English-speaking countries, collectors buy and trade physical artifacts of the **beer** industry, such as beer mugs, bottles, and cans. Sometimes breweriana enthusiasts meet face to face, and at other times they use the Internet to determine prices and make deals. Some collectors join organizations that publish magazines, sponsor websites, and organize conferences. The Eastern Coast Breweriana Association claims to be the oldest such organization in the United States. The national organizations are the Breweriana Association, the National Association [of] Breweriana Advertising, and the Brewery Collectibles Club of America (founded as the Beer Can Collectors of America). Milwaukee and St. Louis have breweriana museums. Many specialized organizations also exist, as for instance, the Canadian Corkscrew Collectors Club. In Britain, the major organization is the Brewery History Society. Its journal is more scholarly than its American counterparts. In another national difference, the British pay as much attention to public houses as to breweries. British organizations include the Association for British Brewery Collectibles, the Pub History Society, the Inn Sign Society, the Labologists Society (for bottle labels), the British Beermat Collectors Society, and the British Brewery Playing Card Society. In some respects, the Campaign for Real Ale can be counted as a breweriana organization, although it focuses on traditional beers, their **brewing** and retailing, and not on collecting. Breweriana is not confined to Anglophone countries. Most beer-drinking countries have at least one breweriana society.

Further Reading

Fahey, David M. "Old-Time Breweries: Academic and Breweriana Historians." *Ohio History* 116 (2009): 101–21.

David M. Fahey

BREWING

Brewing in its broadest sense is a combination and sequence of chemical mixing processes for preparing raw cereal grains so that their starchy carbohydrates can undergo **fermentation** by yeast, thus producing ethanol or alcohol for human consumption. The modern meaning of brewing is restricted to the production of **beer**, although technically, tea, **sake**, soy sauce, and certain biofuels are also produced by brewing processes.

Process

Raw cereal grains are difficult to consume when first harvested. To extract their nutrients, brewing is required to convert the tough grain starches into a sugary liquid, which in turn is converted into alcohol by the process of fermentation via the addition of yeast.

More specifically, brewing is a lengthy process requiring the following sequence of steps: (1) "malting," or the conversion of raw grain to a malted starch, via steeping in water, germinating and subsequent heating in a dry kiln; (2) "milling," or cracking the malted grains to further soften them; (3) "mashing," or adding hot water to the cracked grain, then extracting the larger solids to leave a sugary solution called the "wort"; (4) "brewing," or boiling the wort, then mixing in selected additives (e.g., hops for flavoring), then extracting the smaller solids to produce a refined wort; (5) "cooling" the refined wort quickly in a separate cooling tank so that yeasts can be added; (6) "fermenting" the cooled wort in a separate fermentation tank by adding selected yeasts so that the sugars in the wort can be converted into alcohol; (7) "racking" in a separate conditioning tank so that the flavors of the alcohol can be improved by aging; (8) "finishing" the recipe by filtering (if required), stabilizing the flavors, polishing, fixing the final color, and so on; (9) carbonating the finished product; (10) moving the finished product to a holding tank; and (11) packaging, finally, in bottles, cans, kegs, or tanks.

Copper kettles used for brewing beer. (Kai Koehler/ Dreamstime)

Product

The end result of this lengthy brewing process is beer, a fermented alcoholic beverage based on recipes of the four basic ingredients of water, malted grains, brewer's yeast, and preservative flavoring components (e.g., fruit, herbs, hops).

Almost any substance containing sugar or starch can be substituted for the malted grains. Malted barley is traditionally used, though mixtures of starches can be used in a brewing recipe, depending on what is locally available in the natural environment and/or commercially available in regional, national, and international markets. For example, other common grain sources include rye and wheat from Europe, maize (corn) from the Americas, rice from Asia, and sugar from the Caribbean. Less widely used starches for certain locally produced beers include millet, sorghum, and cassava root in Africa, potato in Brazil and Peru, and agave in Mexico.

Culture

Though brewing involves many decisions about source ingredients and the corresponding manipulation of the physical properties of the final product, the basic brewing process itself crosses national and cultural boundaries. At the simplest level, beer style is a function of locally available yeast strains and yearly climate patterns, for these two environmental variables minimally determine whether lagers (bottom-fermenting yeasts), ales (top-fermenting yeasts), lambics (wild yeasts) or hybrids are brewed.

Beyond obvious choices of ingredients and style, culture also specifies who can brew (householders, religious specialists, craft specialists, guilds, corporations), where brewing can take place (households, taverns, monasteries, restaurants, breweries, factories, microbreweries), in what social contexts brewing can occur (domestic, religious, scientific, commercial, national, international), and how brewing can be celebrated (literary arts, performing arts, visual arts, festivals).

Origins and History

Beer is one of the oldest human-made beverages. On present ceramic and documentary evidence, brewing of fermented rice occurred in China some 7,000 to 9,000 years ago, and at that same time, brewing was frequently mentioned in the literature of ancient Mesopotamia. Specifically, in the Code of Hammurabi, laws regulate Babylonian beer production and consumption from 4,000 years ago; in the Hymn to Ninkasi, a prayer to the Sumerian goddess of beer offers a poetic brewing recipe from 3,800 years ago; and in the Epic of Gilgamesh, ancient Iraqi brewing traditions are described from 3,200 years ago.

In ancient Egypt, brewing was especially important: over 5,000 years ago, beer fed the political elites, and in later periods, it was a sacrament, a sacrificial offering, and a medical treatment. Recent research also suggests that the political elites provided beer as compensation to the laborers who built some of the monumental architectural structures in the Giza Plateau.

Diffusion of brewing practices then spread from Egypt to Greece 3,000 years ago; from Greece to Rome 2,000 years ago; and from Rome to the early Anglo-Saxon tribes in Britain 1,500 years ago. During the subsequent rise of Christianity in Western Europe, brewing professionalized in monasteries. Monks produced beer as part of their religious duties and organized themselves into early trade guilds. Monastic breweries also supported church efforts by providing shelter, food, and refreshment to travelers and pilgrims during medieval times, and some of this religious preoccupation is evidenced by numerous Christian saints who are also patrons of brewing (e.g., St. Nicholas).

Brewing practices also spread through Western Europe by Germanic and Celtic tribes some 5,000 years ago, although these brewing practices were domestic and secular. As in the early origins of beer production in Mesopotamia, women were the primary brewers—in domestic households and also in the commercial taverns of medieval Europe. Interestingly, one of the first historical mentions of the use of hops was in 1067 AD by a literate Church woman, the Abbess Hildegard of Bingen.

Industrialization and Modernity

In Western Europe, brewing remained primarily a domestic activity of the household through the medieval period. By the fifteenth century, though, domestic brewing had been replaced by a combination of brewing in monasteries, **pubs**, and early commercial brewing companies. In this early modern period, brewing practices were codified and regulated by villages, cities, and, in some cases, nations.

During the Industrial Revolution, improvements and inventions in brewing technology made mass-produced European beer a reality. In quick succession, the following inventions were introduced and adopted by brewers: thermometers in 1760, steam engines in 1765, hydrometers in 1770, and drum roasters in 1817. Finally, the discovery of the role of yeast in fermentation by Louis Pasteur in 1857 further aided brewer knowledge by describing those chemical processes that sour beer.

In North America, a similar pattern evolved with some uniquely American twists: In the colonial period, brewing occurred in a variety of social contexts, including the household, the tavern, and in both craft and commercial breweries. **Prohibition**, however, devastated the thousands of brewery businesses in existence in the early twentieth century. Some of these businesses survived by converting their operations to the production of soft drinks (a modern American contribution to global beverage production), or by running their businesses illegally, which had some impact on developing a mainstream American beer palate that preferred lighter (watered-down) beers.

After repeal, surviving commercial breweries consolidated and grew into giant beer companies with industrialized quality control, mass production and mass marketing through the new medium of **advertising**. Consolidation also happened by merger and acquisition aimed at shutting down the operations of smaller rivals. It was not until the late twentieth century that small craft brewers and **microbreweries** reemerged, and by the early twenty-first century, the number of North American microbreweries and brewpubs finally eclipsed the number of breweries during the pre-Prohibition era.

Today, modern American craft breweries exhibit an inventiveness that defies culture-bound tradition, producing traditional styles from other countries, modern re-creations of ancient styles (e.g., Belgium lambics), and even styles that have never existed before, such as chili beer and cream ales. At the same time,

---

Coors Brewing Company

The Coors brand is perhaps one of the most emblematic in American beer. In a typical American-dream fashion, this company was founded in Colorado by Adolph Coors, a German immigrant, who left the Old World in hopes of one day owning his own brewery. Coors survived Prohibition by diversifying into other products—they made malted milk, "near beer," and ceramics during this period. It was one of the few brewing companies to survive Prohibition.

Initially a regional beer company that was limited by legal restrictions that kept it from **distribution** beyond the West, it was not until the early 1990s that Coors attained nationwide distribution. Responsible for many innovations in American beer, in 1959, Coors became the first American brewery to use a two-piece aluminum can. Coors, along with Miller, was among the first major brands that promoted light beer in the United States. Light can refer to either calorie-reduced or lower-alcohol content. Brands such as Coors "Silver Bullet" light beer have been criticized for their lack of taste and for being "watered down," but they represent one uniquely American approach to beer.

Coors is a major sports sponsor and has become a household name through its multimillion-dollar advertising campaigns. The company has run into major labor disputes and been accused of racial discrimination. Nonetheless, in 2003, Coors was rated the third-largest producer of beer in the United States.

---

a handful of multinational corporations use technological advances in refrigerated transport and international shipping to market mass-produced and nondescript grain-based liquids all over the globe. Brewing, in fact, is now big business, with total global revenues exceeding $300 billion in 2007. As well, home brewing has returned to the scene, providing additional economies of scale for this ancient cultural behavior. (*See also* **Home-Brew.**)

Further Reading

Arnold, John P. *Origin and History of Beer and Brewing: From Prehistoric Times to the Beginning of Brewing Science and Technology.* Reprint, Cleveland, OH: BeerBooks.com, 2005 (1911).

Civil, Miguel, trans. "The Hymn to Ninkasi—Making Beer" (literature of Sumeria, nineteenth century BC). http://www.piney.com/BabNinkasi.html.

Nelson, Max. *The Barbarian's Beverage: A History of Beer in Ancient Europe.* London: Routledge, 2008.

Ogle, Maureen. *Ambitious Brew: The Story of American Beer.* Orlando, FL: Harcourt, 2007.

Palmer, John J. *How to Brew: Everything You Need to Know to Brew Beer Right the First Time.* Boulder, CO: Brewers Publications, 2006.

Percival, Sean. "History Lesson: The Story of Beer." *Manolith.* http://www.manolith.com/2009/04/15/history-lesson-the-story-of-beer/

Smith, Gregg. *Beer in America: The Early Years—1587–1840: Beer's Role in the Settling of America and the Birth of a Nation.* Boulder, CO: Siris Books, Brewers Publications, 1998.

Karen Eilene Saenz

BURPING

Burping or belching, more formally known as eructation, is the body's way of getting rid of too much swallowed air in the stomach. The average person can consume up to 10 cups of air and other gases per day while eating, drinking, and even just talking. That air goes on a journey down the esophagus toward the stomach, where it hides in the just-swallowed food or beverage. A great-tasting milkshake and fries receive a warm welcome into the stomach. Air, however, does not. Therefore, the body sends it on a return trip back up the passageway it just traveled. If burping does not occur, that trapped air will build up in the stomach, causing discomfort, stomach pain, and bloating. The actual sound of a burp is created from the epiglottis (the cartilage that covers the windpipe) flapping open as the air is expelled from the throat. To avoid excessive burping, one reduces the intake of the following main culprits: carbonated beverages such as **beer**, sparkling **wine**, and soda. It also helps to avoid drinking through straws or eating and drinking too quickly.

However, burping is not always a concern for everyone. Some people proudly display their belching prowess, with sound and length being crowning achievements. Burping in public, which is not considered polite by most, tends to be more accepted among men. Movies and **television** shows have glorified the communal burping bonding sessions of college-aged boys and sports game–watching men for decades. The *Guinness Book of World Records* even has a "world's loudest burp" category.

Further Reading

Hoffman, Matthew, and Eric Metcalf. "Belching," In *1,801 Home Remedies: Trustworthy Treatment for Everyday Health Problems*, 70–72. Pleasantville, NY: Readers Digest, 2004.

Masoff, Joy. "Burping." In *Oh Yuck! The Encyclopedia of Everything Nasty*, 24–25. New York: Workman Publishing, 2000.

Mayo Clinic staff. "Bloating, Belching and Intestinal Gas: How to Avoid Them." http://www.mayoclinic.com/health/gas-and-gas-pains/DG00014.

Whitney Adams

C

CARDING

Carding is the act of requesting an identification card in order to check the age of people before selling them alcohol in a bar or retail shop. Usually the only cards allowable are official state or federal documents such as driver's licenses or passports. In some cases, the clerk or bartender is instructed to visually scan the customer and make sure that the photo on the card is accurate and the birth date indicates the customer is over the age of 21. Because the purchase of alcohol by those under the age of 21 is illegal in all U.S. states, many underage youth seek to obtain a fake ID in order to purchase alcohol at stores and to enter **bars**. Because of this, increasing numbers of retail establishments and communities are requiring that sellers establish the veracity of the ID by using Automatic Identification and Data Capture (AIDC) technologies to read the card's magnetic strip. In some areas, laws have been passed to require that all buyers present a suitable card for scanning prior to being able to purchase alcohol. This is an attempt to prevent the use of fake IDs by scanning and recording the embedded data strip to ensure the card's face is the same as the data on file with the state. While this protects the establishment from charges of selling to minors, it is often perceived by buyers as inconvenient and a possible breach of privacy because it allows the stores to collect and analyze data on individual purchasing habits.

Janet Chrzan

CHAMPAGNE

Strictly speaking, champagne is a sparkling **wine** produced entirely from grapes grown in France's Champagne region, and essentially—but not exclusively—from the varieties Chardonnay, Pinot Noir, and Pinot Meunier. However, the name champagne is often used as a synonym for any sparkling wine, a confusion that France has been fighting actively on international markets by ensuring that only wines from the region Champagne can actually use the name "champagne" on their labels. France and the European Union have mounted regular legal challenges to the use of the term outside of the appellation zone around the cities of Reims and Epernay.

In the United States, the use of the term champagne by winemakers is allowed within certain limits, following a 2006 trade agreement between the United States and the European Union. Although the agreement forbids the use of European geographic indications by American winemakers, it also includes a "grandfather clause" allowing producers who had been legally using the term champagne prior to the agreement (as well as 16 other "semi-generic" terms like Chablis or sherry) to continue putting it on their labels. This explains why, for example, Korbel "California champagne," produced under that name since the 1880s, can still be served at presidential inaugurations without causing a diplomatic incident.

The conflict over the appellation is not fully resolved. The Office of Champagne USA, which represents the Comité Interprofessionnel du Vin de Champagne (CIVC), the champagne producers' trade association, has been mounting public relations campaigns in favor of its exclusive appellation, even producing a petition to Congress trying to end the use of the word "champagne" by U.S. producers.

Historically, whether regionally correct or not, champagne (and pretty much all sparkling wine on the market today) finds its origins in the nineteenth century, when winemakers in the Champagne region learned to master the **fermentation** process and the carbon dioxide it releases to generate a reliably bubbly wine. Although production of sparkling wine had been taking place before that, it was deemed until then as inferior to the region's still wines. It was also unpredictable, leading to regular explosions as the gas pressure from fermentation taking place inside the bottle grew too great for the bottles.

In the nineteenth century, Champagne houses perfected a production method that consists in provoking a controlled, in-bottle secondary fermentation through the addition of a mixture of sugar and yeast to still wine. Finding the right dose of sugar to add was key to turning this sparkling wine into a product that could be exported far and wide. This allowed Champagne producers to export to the royal courts of Europe, and innovators like Charles "Champagne Charlie" Heidseick to come to America and develop the market for their wines, starting in the 1850s.

Today, this *champenoise* method (or traditional method) is used to make the best sparkling wines of any origin, including the best Californian and American sparkling wines. "Bubbly" is the drink of choice for celebrations and special occasions, as demonstrated by the importance of sparkling sales for the holidays and, especially, for New Year's Eve. The arrival of the year 2000, for instance, saw record sales of champagne and sparkling wines around the world.

Although it represents less than 10 percent of sparkling wine sales in the United States (and around the world), Champagne has been more successful than any other region in associating its sparkling wine with luxury and class. Luxury products conglomerates like LVMH have made champagne a central part of their strategy, and French champagne has retained an image of distinction that has persisted over the last two centuries. In the 1990s and 2000s, the love affair between rappers and Roederer's Cristal brand of champagne was central to the "bling" subculture of very conspicuous consumption (at least until remarks by Roederer managing director Frédéric Rouzaud, in 2006, led to a boycott of the brand by prominent rappers such as Jay-Z).

The downside to this association of champagne with luxury is that sales of the wines of Champagne are more closely associated with the upper end of business cycles and suffer more from economic downturns as well. In 2008 and 2009, champagne sales and exports went down while sales of American, Italian, or Spanish sparkling wine kept increasing. So while people's desire to celebrate may remain intact in downturns, a more modest bubbly appears more appropriate in less luxurious times. (*See also* **Terroir.**)

Further Reading

Champagne's official U.S. site. http://www.champagne.us.

Robertson, Carol. "The Sparkling Wine War." http://www.abanet.org/buslaw/blt/2009 -05-06/Robertson.shtml.

"Sparkling Wine/Champagne." The Wine Institute. December 2009. http://www .wineinstitute.org/resources/winefactsheets/article92.

Rémy Charest

CIDER

Cider is an alcoholic beverage made by fermenting the juice of apples (*Malus pumila* Mill.). More specifically, cider is preferentially made from special apple varieties known as cider apples. These apples are high in tannins and acid, providing the complex flavors associated with cider in addition to serving as a preservative. Once the desired apple varieties have been collected, the apples are crushed into a pulp and juiced. This juice contains naturally occurring wild yeast that will ferment the juice into the cider. However, industrial methods of cider production often call for pasteurization of the juice to kill any wild yeast. Later on in the process, a known yeast variety is added to produce a more consistent taste from year to year. This juice is then blended with other fermented apple juice to meet desired tastes, before becoming the finished cider. Ciders can be still, but they are more commonly sparkling. Distilled cider is apple brandy, of which the French Calvados and American **applejack** are variants.

Occasionally, cider is made from other fruits. Although "pear cider" is traditionally called **perry**, it may be found on the shelf alongside peach cider, cherry cider, and others. In the United States, cider can be either alcoholic or nonalcoholic. Unfiltered, unfermented apple juice, which is opaque, even cloudy with sediment that has not yet settled to the bottom of the jug, and is traditionally made from the same sort of cider apples as alcoholic cider, has been called "cider" in much of the United States since at least **Prohibition,** to differentiate it from filtered clear apple juice, which is markedly different in flavor. This form of cider has become harder to find, as the number of small apple orchards producing it has diminished. In many states, unpasteurized or unfiltered ciders can be sold only at the orchard that produced them. The ciders on the shelves of supermarkets, particularly in regions where large numbers and wide varieties of apples are not produced, are blander juice products.

Alcoholic cider is typically made from cider apples such as Golden Russet and Kingston Black, cultivars grown for traits that lend themselves well to cider production (high sugar to encourage **fermentation**, perceptible tannin levels, and acidity). Often a blend of apples, which may include more familiar eating apples, is used. The apples are ground and pressed, and the resulting liquid is allowed to ferment, usually with an inoculation of yeasts so that the cider need not be exposed to air (and thus to airborne acetic acid bacteria, the bacteria that convert alcohol to vinegar).

The earliest mention of cider comes from the Assyrian version of the Epic of Gilgamesh. In this version, some 5,000 years old, Sidra was the goddess of fermented fruits. The name moved around Europe, where it became solely associated with fermented apples. Eventually the term *sidra*, under the Latinized spelling *cidre*, came into the British Isles, where cider (under local names) had long been made, and following the Great Vowel Shift of the fifteenth century, cidre became pronounced cider (sometimes spelled cyder). It is under this name that the concept of fermented apple juice came to the New World via England.

British colonists were largely responsible for the movement of apples and orchards to the New England region, where cider making was seen as a necessity for the production of clean potable liquids, as was the case elsewhere. As water supplies become contaminated, fermented beverages such as cider were seen as ways to provide a clean source of liquid, so much so that much early history in the New England colonies details daily consumption of cider by all members of a household. The advantage over **beer** was the ease of production and prevalence of ingredients. Particularly in New England, English grains did not grow well, and the rocky ground was not well suited to wheat or barley farming. Though cider sold for nearly the same price as **rum**, it could be made in the home by anyone who grew apples, a fairly low-maintenance crop by the standards of the time.

France, Portugal, and Spain were responsible for bringing their cider varieties and technologies to other parts of the New World. Spain imported cider apple trees via cuttings to South and Central America, and also to the Southwest of what became the United States. Areas of New Mexico, Arizona, and Colorado are among the highest centers of cider apple diversity in North America. French settlers brought their prized cider apple varieties to parts of Canada, where cider making is still practiced, though largely through production of ice cider (cider made from frozen apples). Settlers to the southeastern United States brought both cuttings and seeds, which gave them thousands of new varieties of apples with which to make cider. Later, cider spread to the frontiers of the American West.

Cider was extremely popular in colonial American and early U.S. history. Before George Washington became the first president of the United States, he was offering cider to his supporters while running for public office in Virginia in 1758. President John Adams is noted for drinking cider each day at breakfast to alleviate his gas and bloating. President Thomas Jefferson's estate Monticello is also an example of cider's popularity. Most of the trees in his orchards there were designated for the making of cider. William Henry Harrison is famous for having offered free cider to his supporters during his campaign for the presidency in 1840.

The solids left over after pressing the cider for fermentation, the pomace, were used to make a weak low-alcohol beverage called "ciderkin," served to children. So prevalent was cider drinking before **Prohibition** that **temperance** agitators in the early twentieth century cut down orchards as a sign of protest and impelled families to chop down any apple trees on their property, claiming there was little other use for the fruit. The typical association in the English-speaking world of the apple with the forbidden fruit of Eden was not lost on these protesters.

Cider fell into decline for a multitude of reasons, among them industrialization and availability of clean water, urbanization and decline of farming, immigration of beer- and **wine**-drinking cultures, and the various temperance movements that ended in Prohibition in the United States. Interestingly, the illegalization of alcohol in the United States created an increase in cider production in Canada as the market for brandy made from cider exploded in the bordering states.

During the time of Prohibition, many American farms were still producing apple juice intended for cider. Apple juices were mixed to the desired taste and made ready for fermentation. Despite the illegality of fermenting this juice, it was often sold to people who would take it home to make their own alcohol. During this time, it was common to continue to call the unfermented apple juice "cider." After Prohibition, this term remained, causing confusion in terms in the American dialect. This reference to unfermented apple juice as cider is largely restricted to the United States, though a few regions in Canada also have this misleading term. Historically in the United States, cider was legally defined as fermented apple juice, though this has been regionally altered with terms such as "sweet cider" referring to the unfermented juice of apples and "hard cider" referring to the fermented product. Globally, cider is understood strictly as the fermented juice of apples.

Today, cider has been recovering from years of neglect, with cultural revitalization movements often centering on cider as a cultural and economic touchstone. This has led many to seek out older varieties of cider apples, long since forgotten in old abandoned orchards. Although cider currently makes up only 1 percent of U.S. alcoholic beverages, the market has been expanding in the United States and elsewhere as consumers desire to taste a bit of history and discover this uniquely natural drink. Although there are a few national brands in the United States, cider is most often obtained from local producers either from farm shops or nearby outlets, providing much regionalism in its making and consumption.

Since Prohibition, which altered American drinking habits, hard cider has been more popular in Europe than in the United States. In some parts of the country, imported British ciders were easier to find than domestic products. Since the 1990s, cider has become more popular. New producers have offered ciders in 750 ml bottles to compete with wine as a "special occasion" beverage, and such ciders are often classed as dry or semidry rather than the more familiar sweet cider. They may also be still instead of sparkling. Cider as a "session drinking" beverage rose in popularity as a variety of drinks comparable to beer in alcohol content entered the marketplace: a plethora of **wine coolers** and malt beverages, most of them sweeter than the sweetest low-alcohol beers. Harpoon Brewery, a Boston-based brewery founded in 1986 and well positioned to take advantage of the craft **brewing** movement of the 1990s, added a cider to their line in 2000, with the opening of their second brewery in Windsor, Vermont. In the winter, Harpoon Cider is often drunk half-and-half with their seasonal spiced beer, Winter Warmer.

Cider is often associated thusly with winter, largely because of when it is produced; many apple varieties are suited for long storage even without refrigeration, and cider production can continue through much of the winter. A Quebecois technique for "ice cider" allows the apples to remain on the tree so late into the season that they partially freeze, developing the sugars to lead to a sweeter, higher-alcohol cider. Hot cider mulled with spices (typically the same kind of fruit used for apple pie) has been served around fireplaces from America's earliest days, and not until Prohibition did unfermented cider replace the hard version in the mulled drink. Indeed, while the hot hard cider would be given to children, adults often added a shot of rum for a drink called a Stonewall, after the boundaries between New England fields. (*See also* **Applejack; Beer; Perry.**)

Further Reading

Calhoun, Creighton Lee, Jr. *Old Southern Apples*. Blacksburg, VA: McDonald and Woodward, 1995.

Lea, Andrew. *Craft Cider Making*. Preston, England: The Good Life Press, 2008.

Orton, Vrest. *The American Cider Book: The Story of America's Natural Beverage*. New York: Farrar, Straus and Giroux, 1973.

Watson, Ben. *Cider Hard and Sweet: History, Traditions & Making Your Own*. Woodstock, VT: The Countryman Press, 2009.

Dave Reedy and Bill Kte'pi

CLASS

Social class is a potentially complex idea, embedding socioeconomic differences, social inequality, the division of labor, and culture. Social classes embedded into an inferred structure of social stratification raise further implications about power, control, and social influences.

In contrast to many other cultural items associated with pleasure and leisure, alcohol use over history has not been restricted to the rich and powerful. Beverage alcohol is a natural product of decay and fermentation of both carbohydrates and proteins, and is thus potentially ubiquitous. In its most basic forms, production of consumable alcohol requires no technology and thus can be accessible to all who want it. Thus drinking from the top to the bottom of the social class structure has been a captivating topic for social scientists since the first quarter of the twentieth century.

The earliest drinks may have been discovered by the less privileged members of a social group, namely those exposed to garbage and foodstuffs that may have been tossed aside by others. If this is true, the diffusion of drinking up the social class scale would be fascinating. In terms of ancient records, alcohol production and use in the form of vineyards, **wine**, celebrations and contradictory alcohol-related admonitions are documented throughout the Old Testament. In an unusual manner, alcohol production at a wedding reception for people of unknown social class membership is central to Jesus's first "miracle" in the New Testament. There is also an impressive archaeological record, particularly of material objects associated with alcohol and fermentation.

Thus, in contrast to many other cultural artifacts, alcohol has very likely had a social class–wide availability since its discovery. When efforts to prohibit alcohol access to either the totality or segments of any human population have been attempted, the failure of these efforts has often been marked by the ease of production of beverage alcohol under multiple natural conditions.

Considerations of drinking among the rich and the poor probably have an early documentation during the **Gin** Epidemic in England. Apparently this form of distilled liquor was made available at extremely low prices, and the poor were attracted to drunkenness as a short-term remedy for their miserable lives, a scenario to be later paralleled in the nineteenth century by impoverished Chinese opiate smokers in both China and the West Coast of America, and in the twentieth century by **African Americans** in urban ghettos with ready access to crack cocaine.

Despite his London base, Karl Marx never took the opportunity to use illustrator William Hogarth's visions of genial "Beer Alley" and chaotic "Gin Lane" to underline his sometimes florid characterizations of class relations and conflict. Yet there still remain empirical questions as to what really happened when technology allowed the introduction of cheap distilled spirits to the bottom classes of society with few barriers to availability.

For some, Hogarth's Gin Lane baby dropped to its apparent death or at least severe injury by its drunken mum is foundational for a projected future of first, a **temperance** movement, followed by a prohibition movement, and then in a far more complex mode, a muddled complex of temperance concepts and medicalized ideas for those whose drinking apparently exceeds their capacity for control.

The Temperance Movement in the United States and Western Europe began in earnest in the early nineteenth century. It may be seen as especially successful in the United States, since it led to over a decade of national **Prohibition** in the twentieth century. Social class elements were intense throughout this movement, with a strong emphasis on working-class and poor Americans.

The evolution of American Prohibition was seemingly centered on the elimination of alcohol in American life, but in actuality, the agenda of the drivers of the establishing legislation were a group of moral entrepreneurs who had two foci. The first was the survival of the lower-class American family, the absolutely essential fulcrum for the capitalist capture of the combined rural and immigrant workforce to sustain its initially promising opportunity for productivity. The second was for the restriction of potentially uncontrolled drinking by some of these workers in light of the uncontrolled alcohol production and **distribution** system of the second half of the nineteenth century.

Gusfield (1963) and Rumbarger (1987) point to this synthesis, with Gusfield adding valuable ideas about the intersection of "old-line" Americanism, upper-middle-class membership, Protestantism, rural and small-town residence, and female gender to greatly energize attempted control over immigrant, working-class, Catholic, urban males. Another view is that the low-key but potent involvement of male industrialists in their support of temperance was a vehicle for enhanced workplace control.

Specifically, alarming numbers of immigrant workers in urban factory settings were drawn into saloons that had no limits in their economic exploitation of these stressed, frustrated, and confused men (Clark 1976). These men were, for the industrialists, initially a miraculously cheap addition to the workforce ("wage slavery"), but this extremely profitable boon might be turned upside down into a demand for public support of families abandoned by alcohol-addicted breadwinners.

Within the larger social context extending beyond urban America that was home to most of these immigrants, American society became caught up in a "moral panic" that offered the political foundation for the eventual enactment of the national Prohibition of alcohol production and distribution.

Prohibition was to be repealed after 13 years due to its cost, perceived ineffectiveness, and the Depression-era need for both the tax revenue and employment opportunities promised by repeal. A social class aspect of Prohibition is found in the publicity given the upper classes who were apparent beneficiaries of opportunities to defy the law with illegal importation of liquor, and glamorous drinking linked with sexual freedoms and nascent trends toward female equality.

In the post-Prohibition period, a new vision evolved that initially suggested that there was no social class linkage with problematic alcohol consumption. This was the ambiguous disease concept of **alcoholism,** and its real-world partner, **Alcoholics Anonymous (AA),** both of which slowly came to center stage in Western thinking about alcohol problems over much of the next 70 years. The continuity of this approach with the Temperance Movement can be seen in its action plan for attempting to end drinking, but only among a select small group whose alcohol consumption had proven to be outside their personal control. Those without this "allergy" to alcohol could drink safely but should practice prudence as the substance remained potent according to a vague cultural overlay of alcohol education.

Overtly, AA accepted that alcoholism could affect anyone regardless of social class, but in practice, AA's membership was initially circumscribed as downwardly mobile white males who could recapture or even advance beyond their pre-alcoholic social status through conforming to AA's comprehensive program of "sobriety," a combination of abstinence and a well-outlined set of prescriptions for personal and social growth.

AA eventually gained a much broader-based membership including women and minorities, but because of its prescriptive program, there is little or no platform for those at the bottom of the class structure, including many who desire no entry or reentry into "responsible respectability." This population of "Skid Row bums" was highly visible in many urban areas and is a subgroup among today's homeless population.

Those recovering from alcoholism through AA desire to convince the public that Skid Row public inebriates do not represent the American alcoholic. Today, this effort has recently been reincarnated as a much broader, but not necessarily larger, "recovery movement." Fighting this supposed stereotype has been a theme of public relations efforts to assert that "alcoholism is a disease like any other," and that its victims deserve equal treatment.

A class-related dimension of this effort occurred in the 1960s and 1970s with a targeted attack on the Skid Row image through the diffusion of a new image, the "hidden alcoholic" (Roman and Blum 1987; Roman 1991). This individual was the middle- or upper-class man or woman whose position and resources allowed him or her to "hide" within the social structure, usually protected by "enablers" who benefited from the hidden alcoholic's sustained respectability. A campaign called "Project 95," sponsored by the Federal National Institute on Alcohol Abuse and Alcoholism (NIAAA), proclaimed in 1971 that 95 percent of American alcoholics were either employed or in the families of the employed, thus underlining the earlier suggestion by AA of no correlation between social class and alcoholism.

A public ceremony at the Grand Ballroom of the Shoreham Hotel in Washington, D.C., in 1976 was essentially centered on social class claims featured the "coming out" of 60 "celebrities" who were in recovery from alcoholism. On stage in a darkened hotel ballroom, they stepped forward one by one in a spotlighted introduction and represented entertainment stars, business and military leaders, authors, politicians, and professionals. This event presumably would add momentum to the belief that alcoholism could strike anyone, but also that recovery accompanied by continued fame was possible.

A study in the late 1940s (Straus and Bacon 1951) confirmed that alcoholics in treatment were distributed across the social class structure, although the data were geographically limited to Connecticut. A different orientation was generated initially by national epidemiological research based in California and supported by NIAAA (Cahalan and Room 1972). Sampling from the general population rather than people seeking treatment, these researchers undertook what was then a novel approach and measured not only reported alcohol consumption, but also the reported difficulties that the respondents had in association with their drinking.

These data produced evidence that ironically shadowed the targets of the Temperance Movement. Cahalan and Room's research showed that the heaviest and most problem drinking was found among young white working males in urban settings. Using this problem-definition approach, the data definitely did not show equal distribution of alcohol-related problems across the social class spectrum and in fact found lower rates of problems in the upper social classes.

This research was the foundation for what was to emerge in the 1980s as a two-pronged focus in social scientists' study of alcohol issues, those focused on alcoholics and those focused on alcohol problems. The overlap between these two categories offers strong evidence that the diagnosis of alcoholism frequently has multiple social elements, such as visibility, social protection, and perceived social value of ongoing role performances. Psychiatric diagnoses of alcohol dependence are heavily based on the perceptions of others in regard to the focal individual's performance across a spectrum of role expectations.

The new "problem drinker" definition fueled emergent attention to drinking drivers as persons whose actions should not be dismissed as those of "sick" individuals who may automatically avoid punishment. Likewise, more recent attention and resource allocation to study of drinking among college and university students has relatively little emphasis on alcoholism or alcohol dependence but is concerned with disruptive behaviors and loss of opportunities due to drinking.

A further development since the mid-1980s has been the increasing merger of the treatment of alcohol dependence and dependence on illegal drugs, and a combining of policy activities to cover both target populations. The constituency of socially powerful people who sharply distinguished alcohol issues from illegal drug issues has almost completely vanished. The consequence is a massive "downward mobility of a social problem," namely the merging of social imagery of alcohol and drug dependence such that alcohol-dependent persons now may share the stigma of those with drug abuse and dependence.

Many more challenging analytic issues are to be found at the interface between social class and alcohol. These include many emerging and unexplored patterns of cross-national social class linkages as Western-style drinking diffuses throughout the world. (*See also* **Alcoholism; Men and Boys Drinking; Women and Girls Drinking.**)

Further Reading

Cahalan, D., and R. Room. "Problem Drinking among American Men Aged 21–59." *American Journal of Public Health* 62 (1972):1473–82.

Clark, Norman. S. *Deliver Us from Evil*. New York: Norton, 1976.

Gusfield, Joseph. *Symbolic Crusade: An Interpretation of the Woman's Christian Temperance Union*. Champaign-Urbana: University of Illinois Press, 1963.

Roman P. M., and T. C. Blum. "Notes on the New Epidemiology of Alcoholism in the U.S.A." *Journal of Drug Issues* 17 (1987): 321–32.

Roman, Paul. *Alcohol: A Sociological Perspective*. New Brunswick, NJ: Publications Division of Rutgers Center of Alcohol Studies, 1991.

Rumbarger, John J. *Profits, Politics and Prohibition*. Albany: State University of New York Press, 1987.

Straus, R., and S. Bacon. "Alcoholism and Social Stability." *Quarterly Journal of Studies on Alcohol* 12 (1951): 231–60.

Paul M. Roman

COCKTAIL PARTIES

A cocktail party is an intimate social get-together that features mixed drinks and light snacks or hors d'oeuvres and typically occurs in the afternoon to early evening hours. Less formal and less time-consuming than a dinner party, the cocktail party is also called a "social mixer" because it enables its guests to mingle in a more relaxed environment for only a couple of hours.

Both Britain and the United States claim rights to the cocktail party's origin. As a widely popular party type, however, the cocktail party is a twentieth-century American invention, resulting in large part from **Prohibition** and the passage of the Eighteenth Amendment to the U.S. Constitution. Before 1920, most American drinkers publicly consumed their libations in taverns, saloons, and restaurants. Private, home entertaining was viewed as a fairly formal endeavor, with teas, balls, or dinner parties being the norm. After it was no longer legal to acquire or consume alcohol in public, liquor consumption was driven underground into **speakeasies** or as private at-home gatherings. At these house parties, "bathtub gin" was a popular homemade concoction containing the hosts' own personal combination of industrial alcohol, glycerin, and herbs. For the most part, this was a terrible-tasting and smelling DIY liquor that had to be mixed with something else to ensure drinkability. Depending on what the host had on hand, vermouth, simple syrups, juices, or other alcohols were mixed with the home-brew, and garnishes of fruit and vegetables adorned glasses as "chasers." To go along with these new drinking parties, specialized cocktail glasses and barware became the rage, so much so that one New York City department store boasted that it sold 35 different types of cocktail glasses in 1928.

As America moved into the mid-twentieth century, Prohibition and the Great Depression were in its past, and a new economic boon allowed the cocktail party to become a fixture of social interaction and middle-class entertainment. During the 1940s and 1950s, the cocktail party became a site for consumptive style and displays of socioeconomic status, with party hosts serving their drinks from personalized barware like monogrammed martini shakers and decanters, or crystal ice buckets and matching tumblers. Fashion, too, represented this era with a new type of "cocktail clothing" and "cocktail-length" dresses to be worn during these events. During the less formal 1960s and 1970s, the cocktail party waned in popularity, but it was certainly back in style in 2010. Many home entertaining magazines and Web sites attribute the contemporary resurgence of the cocktail party to the economic recession of the late 2000s. As an economical alternative to public drinking in **bars** and restaurants, cocktail parties have again become en vogue. Interestingly, many cocktail party hosts have brought back the Prohibition-era home-brew aspect to their events. An **Internet** search for "home distilling" brings up over eight million hits, with the World Wide Web providing would-be cocktail party hosts and hostesses instructions and recipes for making what is jokingly referred to as "white collar moonshine" to serve at their next cocktail party. (*See also* **Class; Cocktails; Drinking Glasses and Vessels.**)

Further Reading

Felten, Eric. *How's Your Drink? Cocktails, Culture and the Art of Drinking Well.* Chicago: Surrey Books, 2007.
Lendler, Ian. *Alcoholica Esoterica.* New York: Penguin Books, 2005.

Cristin Rollins

COCKTAILS

A cocktail can be defined as a mixture of liquids. This term is associated with mixed drinks that might consist of a simple sugar syrup, one or several distilled spirits, and perhaps fruit juices or cream. This mixture is shaken or stirred into a delightful drink to be savored at a party, reception, or before a special meal. Classic cocktails were meant to whet the appetite, served as an aperitif, and should be served "short," where the alcohol content does not overpower the drink. They were not supposed to be sweet. Sugar was used only in moderation, until very recently, to balance any tartness from lemons or other fruit. Cocktails were supposed to be served cold and "dry" (Collins 1963).

Commandments for a Perfect Cocktail

Oscar Haimo, barman extraordinaire and author of the *Cocktail and Wine Digest* (1946), presented the Drink Mixer's Commandments for success in concocting cocktails. His rules included the importance of measuring with a jigger and using the best liquor one could afford, as well as clean ice, an essential ingredient. In cocktails that use juices and sweeteners, the spirits should be poured last, and only freshly squeezed juices, never canned, should be used. He cautioned the mixologist to be aware of the distinctions between shaking a cocktail, which produces a cloudy drink, and stirring, which produces a clear one. Chilled glasses add to the finesse of a fine cocktail. Cocktails must be drunk as soon as they are made. They cannot stand, and prepared mixes should not be used.

History

Cocktails made their appearance in the early nineteenth century following a variety of drinks like the "fizzes" (liquor, lemon, sugar, and soda), the "julep" (**bourbon,** sugar, and mint), and "toddies" (hot drinks with **rum** or brandy, milk, honey or sugar, and spices). Initially, cocktails were drinks that men imbibed in the morning, at breakfast, to get their circulation going (for more, see Murdock 1998). Later in the nineteenth century, cocktails became more festive and were served as a peritifs, before-dinner drinks. In the twentieth century, cocktails appeared in the guise of the cocktail party.

In nineteenth-century magazines like *The Farmer's Cabinet* (1803) and the *Balance and Columbian Repository* (1806) cocktail recipes consisted of spirits, sugar, water, and bitters. The "Sazerac" was one of the earliest cocktails, made of two dashes of **absinthe**, a lump of sugar that has been soaked in Peychaud bitters, ice, one twist each of lemon and orange peel, and an ounce and a half of bourbon (Haimo 1946). Or it can be made with two dashes of Pernod, sugar, Angostura bitters, and bourbon (Collins 1963).

Martinis also made an early appearance, circa 1862. At San Francisco's Occidental Hotel, they

Cocktails are made to be alluring. They often reflect and express the character of the drinker. (PhotoDisc, Inc.)

were made of four parts of sweet, red vermouth to one part **gin**, with a cherry garnish. Later, olives or pearl onions were used as a garnish. Today, martinis seem to be any cocktail made with **vodka** or gin and served in a chilled, cone-shaped martini glass.

A number of cocktails were invented in the 1920s and early 1930s, during **Prohibition**, when mixers were needed to cover the taste of homemade **hooch**, illegal spirits. In the late 1930s through the 1960s, these cocktails were popularized at large, elegant hotel **bars** in major cities, as well as in the movie industry. Some of these cocktails, popular in **films**, were named after famous characters in the films. For example, James Bond's adage for a martini was "Shaken, not stirred" in the movie *Goldfinger* (1964). Another Bond film, *Casino Royale* (2006), featured not only the "Americano," the signature drink of the original novel, but also five others named for the film's characters and events: "Christmas Jones," "Kissy Suzuki," "May Day," "Vesper Martini," and "What Does James Bond Drink?" (Graham 2008).

Hollywood legends have inspired cocktails. Some of these drinks are nonalcoholic, like the Roy Rogers, named for the famous cowboy actor, made of cola and grenadine syrup; or the Shirley Temple, named for the early-twentieth-century child star, made of lemon-lime soda, ginger ale, and finished with grenadine and a maraschino cherry. These nonalcoholic examples are made with mixers, the cola and lemon-lime sodas, ordinarily used with alcohol in classic cocktails, as well as key ingredients like grenadine, which provide both color and taste, and the usual garnish for a fancy drink, maraschino cherries. Nonalcoholic cocktails are most appropriate for a hero-cowboy and pixie star.

Most Hollywood legends, though, inspired alcohol-based drinks. The brilliant Marlene Dietrich, foreign seductress of 1930s and 1940s classic films, inspired her namesake cocktail of rye **whiskey**, Angostura bitters, and Curaçao, garnished with orange and lemon peels. Greta Garbo, another leading lady of mystery in the 1930s, inspired a cocktail that adds crème de menthe to brandy, vermouth, orange juice, and grenadine. Mae West, the 1930s blonde bombshell, an epitome of feminine flamboyance with her feather boas and spicy personality, inspired a cocktail made of brandy, egg yolk, and powdered sugar, garnished with cayenne pepper. Ginger Rogers, another 1930s and 1940s screen icon, inspired a sweet martini made of gin, vermouth, and apricot brandy with a dash of lemon juice. Another cocktail using apricot brandy, with sloe gin, and lime juice, was a tribute to the phenomenal comedian Charlie Chaplin. A gin-and-vermouth concoction garnished with orange and lemon peels was named for Douglas Fairbanks, an early leading man of the silver screen. It is unlikely that any of these drinks were developed or even favored by the screen legends that they immortalized. Bars in major hotels like the Waldorf Astoria in New York created these drinks to attract their customers as a clever marketing strategy in the early and mid-twentieth century.

Hundreds of types of cocktails are known today. For example, margaritas are popular today. A margarita is a cocktail that mixes **tequila** with lime or another fruit flavoring, an orange liqueur like Triple Sec, served either over ice or as a frappe where the cocktail is blended with the ice to create a frozen drink. Both versions are served in a salt-rimmed cocktail or martini glass. Margaritas became popular in the United States in the 1960s through the 1980s as Mexican-American restaurants proliferated. Each type of cocktail has a definitive list of ingredients, a distinctive garnish, and corresponding glassware to complete its allure. Special equipment is required, too, to produce these drinks, such as an electric mixer, cocktail shakers, mixing and measuring glasses like two-way jiggers and shot glasses, stirring spoons, lemon peel zesters, wire strainers, lime and lemon squeezers, swizzle sticks, miniature paper umbrellas, ice scoop, muddler, fruit knives, snow ice shavers, and funnels.

Gender

In the United States, cocktails have both **class** and gender associations. In the late nineteenth century, cocktails represented domesticated drinking, served in the home and on festive occasions. This type of alcohol use among the upper class contrasted with the public drinking opposed by the **Temperance** Movement (1870s–1920s) that was a male-dominated activity in taverns and saloons. The **Woman's Christian Temperance League**'s platform was that these venues were dangerous for the family: working-class men were spending money on drink that could better be used to feed and clothe their families.

In the 1920s and 1930s, things changed. During **Prohibition** and the Great Depression, some middle-class and immigrant women manufactured bathtub gin and homemade **wine**, selling it from their front porches for income. Women in the 1920s bobbed their hair, shortened their skirts, and went out with their boyfriends or husbands to **speakeasies** and nightclubs where they smoked cigarettes and drank spirits. By the 1930s with the repeal of Prohibition, cocktails were depicted in films. Public drinking venues were for men, but sometimes also for couples, who were welcome at the refined bars of the best hotels and in restaurants. In the 1930s, cocktails became urban and urbane. They were the drinks of the "smart set": upper-class New York or New England aristocrats or aristocratic "wanna-bes" were knowledgeable about fashion and were trendsetters.

The 1940s and 1950s might be called the golden age of the cocktail. Movie stars, world leaders, and businessmen in gray flannel suits with their trophy wives were photographed in glossy magazines and newspapers at **cocktail parties** as endless new drinks were invented. **Advertising** also played a role, promoting certain brands of spirits by linking cocktails such as the martini and the Manhattan with representations of social sophistication and economic success.

In the 1960s and 1970s, cocktail hour was instituted at home for upper middle-class bureaucrats and businessmen in many areas of the United States. The good 1950s housewife met her husband at the door with his glass of scotch on the rocks, or other straight spirits, when he arrived home after work. She, however, probably saved her cocktail drinking for when they went out to dinner at a fancy restaurant, where imaginative drinks combining flavored liqueurs or fruit juices and spirits. Such drinks were featured as a prelude to dinner on a special cocktail menu.

Cocktails in the mid-twentieth century were gendered. Women's cocktails were frothy, colorful, exotic, and sweet, whereas men stuck to martinis, brown drinks, and straight spirits. The martini was a man's drink in its pure form, dry and bracing, sporting an olive or a pearl onion as a garnish (Edmunds 1998). Women's drinks might contain a plastic sword full of fruit slices, a tiny, paper umbrella, or elaborate glass swizzle sticks and cocktail stirrers, adding to their charm. Women often collected these objects, bringing them home to happy middle-class children in the 1950s and 1960s.

Glassware had something to do with the gender divide, too. According to O'Neil (2007), the hurricane glass, also called a Poco, had curves and was likely strictly for women. Men, if they wanted a cosmopolitan, for example, could do so most appropriately if they requested it in a tall, straight Collins glass. Martini glasses were gender-neutral, but only appropriate for men if the drink was clear like a classic martini, or brown like a Manhattan. Pastel drinks in martini glasses up through the 1970s were only appropriate for women. Starting in the 1980s, some of these rules were relaxed. For example, piña coladas were always served in a Poco glass, and men and women both drank them. Today, the gender divide regarding cocktails is not as wide as it was in the mid-twentieth century. Many men, however, might still avoid the martini glass if it contains colorful and sweet libations.

Cocktails Forever

Some examples of enduring cocktails include aperitifs, cobblers, Collins, flips, and highballs. These drinks consist of liqueurs that are served straight, like Dubonet, a sweet French wine served on the rocks with a twist of lemon, or Campari, an Italian drink served mixed with soda. "Collins" cocktails take the basic "Tom Collins" and vary the spirit used. In a tall glass with cracked ice, the "Tom Collins" is a mix of lemon juice, sugar, and gin, and finally, sparkling Canada Dry water is added.

Have You Seen Tom Collins?

> If you haven't, perhaps you had better do so, and as quick as you can, for he is talking about you in a very rough manner—calling you hard names, and altogether saying things about you that are rather calculated to induce people to believe there is nothing you wouldn't steal short of a red-hot stove. Other little things of that nature he is openly speaking in public places, and as a friend—although of course we don't wish to make you feel uncomfortable—we think you ought to take some notice of them and of Mr. Tom Collins. This is about the cheerful substance of a very successful practical joke which has been going the rounds of the city in the past week. It is not to this manor born, but belongs to New York, where it was played with immense success to crowded houses until it played out. (*Gettysburg Compiler*, 1874)

As this blurb explains, Tom Collins was not a real person, but rather part of a popular proven hoax of exposure in 1874. It is likely that the drink that was given the same name was developed around the same time as part of this practical joke.

The first recipe for a "Tom Collins" cocktail appeared in Jerry Thomas's *The Bar-Tender's Guide* in the 1876 edition:

> Use a large bar glass
> Take 5 or 6 dashes of gum syrup.
> Juice of a small lemon
> 1 large wine-glass of gin
> 2 or 3 lumps of ice.
> Shake up well and strain into a large bar-glass. Fill up the glass with plain soda water and drink while it is lively.

The other "Collins" include "Apple Jack Collins," where applejack substitutes for the gin. For Bourbon, Brandy, and Irish Collins, each respectively uses the title spirit in place of the gin. "Cobblers" mix wine with spirits and are garnished with fruit and served on ice. For example, a burgundy or claret cobbler consists of a goblet filled with fine ice over which three ounces of claret or burgundy are poured as well as four dashes each of curacao and brandy. This drink is gently stirred and garnished with mint and fruit slices. "Flips" use wine or a spirit, sugar and a whole, raw egg. A number of wines and spirits can be used, each as the primary ingredient: brandy, claret, port wine, sherry, rum, or Southern Comfort. For each of these, the ingredients are shaken, then poured into a wine glass and topped with a sprinkle of ground nutmeg. Highballs use a special glass, also called a highball, that is a short, wide beaker. Served over ice, this drink consists of liquor, ginger ale, soda, or water. The list is endless and cocktail guide help one to really explore the variety. (*See also* **Drinking Glasses and Vessels.**)

Further Reading

Collins, Dennis. *Mixing and Serving Drinks: A Complete Guide.* New York: Dell, 1963.

Edmunds, Lowell. *Martini Straight Up: The Classic American Cocktail.* Rev. ed. Baltimore: Johns Hopkins University Press, 1998.

Haimo, Oscar. *Cocktail and Wine Digest: Encyclopedia and Guide for Home and Bar.* New York: The International Bar Managers' Association, 1946.

Murdock, Catherine Gilbert. *Domesticating Drink: Women, Men and Alcohol in America, 1870–1940.* Baltimore: Johns Hopkins University Press, 1998.

O'Neil, Darcy. "Is Glassware a Barrier to Cocktail Acceptance?" February 3, 2007. http://www.artofdrink.com/2007/02/is-glassware-a-barrier-to-cocktail-accep.php.

Tranberg, Charles. *The Thin Man: Murder over Cocktails.* Duncan, OK: Bear Manor Media, 2008.

Pam Sezgin

COLLEGE DRINKING CULTURE

The culture of students attending college is commonly associated with freedom. Freshmen entering the college scene are faced with, in most cases, unprecedented liberty not only academically, but also socially. Parties become a common expression of this freedom, which often leads to a culture of drinking. Much like the freedom to go out and party without the interference of parents, drinking becomes another expression of freedom to the average student. A 2001 study

Students on spring break drink on the beach. Festivities during spring vacation have become notorious for revolving around binge drinking. (iStockPhoto)

conducted by Henry Wechsler and his colleagues at Harvard University on the drinking habits of underage and overage college students showed that 63 percent of underage students drank in the past 30 days, compared with 74 percent of overage students. The underage students drank more per occasion than their older counterparts. The media and society push, enable, and justify consumption of alcohol by college students as part of the "college experience."

The media often contains commercial advertisements for alcoholic beverages that tend to equate certain social situations or moods to consuming alcohol. Alcoholic beverages appear on **television** and in **films**, suggesting that consuming alcohol can enhance many different situations. However, the media rarely show any of the detrimental consequences of alcohol use that results in further indoctrination by portraying alcohol consumption as devoid of any negative effects. Furthermore, society constantly portrays **underage drinking** as inevitable and shifts to mitigation rather than prevention. Most notable is the various alcohol awareness groups and organizations that lecture at high schools, warning students not to drink and drive and to have a **designated driver**. Students may get the message that drinking is acceptable, if they do not drive. The focus of alcohol awareness explains to students as they are entering college that it is acceptable to drink, despite the illegality of underage drinking. Coming onto the college scene, where students experience freedom to act for themselves like adults, drinking is not only encouraged but expected in college culture.

Among college students, **binge drinking** has become an issue. Binge drinking is commonly measured as five or more drinks in a row for men and four or more drinks in a row for women (Wechsler and Nelson 2001). What is considered excessive drinking becomes a relative term and is almost never recognized as an issue because of the perceived culture among college students who view that kind of behavior as the norm. While binge drinking is a serious issue, it is not representative of every college student at every social gathering. It is only perceived as representative of the college culture because of extreme circumstances. Because the focus tends to be on the most extreme minority, the perception becomes the belief that this kind of behavior is the norm. Thus, human experiences create the image that that college culture revolves around not only the act of drinking, but the amount of alcohol that is consumed as well.

Drinking has become another strong component of the perceived college culture of freedom. College has come not only to promote underage drinking, but to reward it. As it stands, society itself has come to view underage drinking as inevitable, so students coming onto the college scene are already conditioned to believe that drinking is acceptable and are more likely to drink because of it. This further perpetuates the image of college life that is filled with partying and alcohol without any negative repercussions or responsibility. While not every student in college is an alcoholic, the perception of college life that includes excessive drinking is a result of the personal experiences of students who see the vocal minority and view the loud, excessive drinkers as indicative of the college culture as a whole. (*See also* **Keggers; Men and Boys Drinking; Women and Girls Drinking.**)

Further Reading

Perkins, H. Wesley. *The Social Norms Approach to Preventing School and College Age Substance Abuse*. San Francisco: Jossey-Bass, 2003.

Peterson, J. Vincent, Bernard Nisenholz, and Gary Robinson. *A Nation under the Influence: America's Addiction to Alcohol*. Upper Saddle River, NJ: Pearson Education, 2003.

Wechsler, Henry, and Toben F. Nelson. "Binge Drinking and American College Student: What's Five Drinks?" *Psychology of Addictive Behaviors* (2001): 287–91.

Zailckas, Koren. *Smashed: A Story of a Drunken Girlhood*. New York: Penguin Press, 2005.

DeMond Miller and Joel Yelin

D

DESIGNATED DRIVER

A designated driver is an individual who volunteers to provide a safe ride to another person or a group of people who plan to drink. The designated driver is chosen in advance and abstains from drinking. The concept of designating a driver was first used in the 1920s in Scandinavia. It was imported to the United States in the late 1980s. In 1988, the Harvard Alcohol Project was launched with the goal of not only reducing incidents of **driving under the influence (DUI)**, but to see how quickly a new social concept could be diffused throughout American society using mass communication. The goal was to cause a shift in social norms that would change the way Americans thought about drinking after driving. The U.S. Department of Transportation and the Ad Council launched the "Friends Don't Let Friends Drive Drunk" campaign, which was hugely successful and helped make Americans aware of an alternative to driving after drinking. Many celebrities and politicians, including Bill Clinton, championed the designated driver concept. "Designated driver" had become a household term by the early 1990s.

Research has shown that designated driver programs have been successful in reducing the number of fatalities caused by drunk driving. It is estimated that between 1988 and 1998, over 50,000 lives were saved thanks to increased awareness about drunk driving (Harvard School of Public Health). However, designated driver programs have also been criticized for promoting excessive drinking, particularly among underage and college drinkers. This criticism is largely outweighed by the positive effects of designated driver initiatives. (*See also* **Mothers Against Drunk Driving (MADD)**.)

Further Reading

Harvard Alcohol Project. Center for Health Communication, Harvard School of Public Health. http://www.hsph.harvard.edu/research/chc/harvard-alcohol-project/.

Rachel Black

DISTILLING

Distillation is the method of turning fermented solutions into strong spirits. Undistilled alcoholic beverages include **beer, wine, cider**, and malt beverages; distilled alcohol, or spirits, includes **whiskey, rum**, brandy, and the neutral spirits used to make **vodka, absinthe**, and **gin**. Distillation results in a higher alcohol content (the yeasts that produce alcohol will eventually die when a solution becomes too alcoholic; special strains and methods are used to produce high-alcohol beers like barleywine, and even they stop well short of the alcohol content of spirits), and a longer shelf life, so long as nothing is added after distillation. Pure spirits like whiskey and rum will last essentially forever, so long as evaporation is prevented; this is also true for professionally made gin, which is redistilled after flavoring. Flavored alcohols like liqueurs have lower alcohol contents and higher sugar contents and may have botanical ingredients that continue to age in the bottle. St. Germain Elderflower Liqueur, for instance, a newly released liqueur so popular that it has been called "bartender's ketchup" because it is used in so many house specials, ages significantly in the bottle, as its botanicals age and oxidize.

Distillation operates on a simple principle: ethanol (alcohol) evaporates at 172 degrees Fahrenheit at sea level, a lower temperature than water. By heating a fermented solution to that temperature, capturing and redirecting the steam, the steam can be condensed (cooled down) separately. Not only does this result in a product that is higher in alcohol content (much higher than what is purchased in stores; most spirits are diluted before sale), but it leaves many impurities behind, while dampening much of the flavor. Dampening the flavor is not an undesirable thing, as such; gin is a neutral spirit heavily flavored with a variety of botanicals (including juniper, citrus, and spices), a spicy and overwhelming mix that becomes "smoother," crisp, and well blended through the process of distillation.

Types of Spirits

Virtually anything with sugar or starch can be fermented and thus distilled. In the United States, the most common spirits are rum (molasses or sugar cane juice; cachaca is a variant), whiskey (various grains; includes **bourbon**), brandy (grapes), and **tequila** (agave; mezcal is a variant), as well as the neutral spirits used to make vodka (which remains flavorless, apart from "flavored vodka"), gin (which is flavored and redistilled), and various liqueurs (which are generally diluted, sweetened, and flavored). Fruit can be used to make fruit brandy such as **applejack**, *eau de vie*, schnapps, or other concoctions. Around the world, spirits are made from such things as the cashew fruit (fenny, India), coconut (arrack, India), rice (shochu, Japan; often also made from barley, sweet potato, or a blend), and sorghum (kaoliang, China).

Microdistilleries

In 2009, there were about 100 American microdistilleries, a steep increase from the half-dozen or so in business at the end of the 1980s. This trend has followed in the footsteps of the enormously successful microbrew movement, and just as **microbreweries** popularized less familiar beer styles or explored new variations on the theme, so too have microdistilleries attempted to do more than simply emulate the larger distilleries on a smaller scale. Several of these distilleries are offshoots of microbreweries, such as Rogue in Oregon and Dogfish Head in Delaware.

The barriers to entry in distilling are significant, not only because of the cost of equipment and expert labor, but also because of federal and state laws and regulations. Dogfish Head's Sam Calagione had to figuratively write the legislation himself to expand to distilling in Delaware, after his company's tremendous success in **brewing**. In many states, the laws governing distilleries were rewritten following federal **Prohibition**, sometimes as part of the process of simultaneously dismantling older state or local prohibition legislation. The few distilleries that survived Prohibition by making liquor for medicinal or industrial usage were generally very large distilleries. This limited the number of exceptions the government needed to make, and the process of producing ethyl alcohol for industrial uses naturally lends itself better to large-scale operations, so those distilleries were favored in subsequent legislation.

In some states, the laws—either directly or as a matter of pragmatic consequence—prohibit microdistilleries making whiskey. Further, there is a marketing hurdle in producing high-quality whiskey anywhere but in Kentucky. It is a widespread misconception, for instance, that bourbon must come from Kentucky; the law says only that it must be made in the United States and defines the specific processes that separate bourbon from other whiskeys. But because of Kentucky's historic association with the spirit, "Vermont bourbon" is likely to be seen the same way "California wine" was some decades ago. So microdistilleries producing whiskey tend to take another tack. Tuthilltown Spirits, for instance, in New York State's Hudson Valley, makes much of the fact that it produced the first whiskey in New York since Prohibition. It offers a number of different whiskeys, including not only a "baby bourbon" (corn whiskey aged for a few months instead of the typical two years or more) but also a single malt, two mixed-grain whiskeys, and an unaged corn whiskey. The potential microdistilling holds for whiskey is enormous. Traditionally defined by regional styles (Scotch, Irish whiskey, bourbon, and so forth), whiskey in the United States has been confined to the bourbon style, Tennessee whiskey, rye whiskey, and a handful of outliers.

Local or unique ingredients provide another niche for microdistilleries to fill. Tuthilltown uses New York apples to produce two unaged apple vodkas—Heart of the Hudson, distilled twice, and Spirit of the Hudson, distilled an additional time. Neither is "flavored apple vodka" of the sort used to make appletinis, but neither are they flavorless neutral spirits, retaining some of the flavor of the apples used to produce them, much like an *eau de vie*. Balcones Distilling, in Texas, makes what they believe is the world's first blue corn whiskey, using Hopi blue corn (an ancient ingredient with a character unlike that of the modern blue corn hybrids used to make tortilla chips). In Oregon, Clear Creek Distillery specializes in *eau de vie* using locally sourced ingredients—traditional fruits such as pears and raspberries and the tender young buds (immature pine cones) of Douglas fir trees—resulting in a pale green spirit with notes of forest floor and lemon zest, and a powerful kick.

Distinctly American styles of spirits are emerging as well. Just as the growth of the microbrew industry led to, for instance, the "West Coast IPA" (an especially hop-centric bitter beer) and chocolate stouts with actual chocolate in them (the style having been named originally for the chocolate-colored roasted malt used, not for the presence of real chocolate), microdistilling has significantly changed the world of gin. Not all of the new gins introduced in the last 15 years are American in origin, but American-produced gins have been a major part of that trend and have especially favored unusual blends of botanicals, which in many cases challenge the boundaries of what "gin" has traditionally meant.

Distilling, like other forms of producing alcoholic beverages, has a natural affinity with the "slow food" movement and other trends within artisanal food production, and the emphasis on uniquely American or regional ingredients in microdistilling parallels that of other food producers focused on, say, corncob-smoked bacon, Virginia ham, shagbark hickory syrup, kudzu jelly, paw paw beer, and huckleberry pie.

Home Distilling

The microbrew movement was able to piggyback on the **home-brew** movement, which had had the effect of increasing the brewing skills of the general populace. However, while making beer and wine for personal consumption was made legal without a license in 1978, distilling alcohol without a license remains illegal for any purpose, a law that originated to protect the tax interests of the federal government. Home distillers remain hobbyists (apart from the tiny illegal moonshine industry), gambling that they will not attract the attention of the Bureau of Alcohol, Tobacco, Firearms and Explosives or other authorities, and have not had significant impact on the microdistillery movement yet. It is becoming easier to buy stills on the Internet, and just as home-brewers will often experiment with a new or unusual beer style rather than just replicating something they can buy in the store (at a generally higher cost, given the economies of scale favoring breweries), some home distillers have begun experimenting at home and are even showing up at conferences intended for distilling professionals, to share their experiences. However, home distilling is not without its dangers: if the "head," first flush of alcohol, is not discarded, there is a risk of having a high methanol content. Large doses of methanol can cause blindness. Regardless of the physical dangers, distilling alcohol without a permit or selling it is a federal crime. (*See also* **Cocktails; Hooch.**)

Further Reading

Blue, Anthony Dias. *The Complete Book of Spirits*. New York: William Morrow, 2004.

Bryson, Lew. "Make Way Next Wave: Microdistillers New Pioneers." Ale Street Online. http://www.alestreetonline.com/content/view/193/45/.

Burns, Eric. *The Spirits of America: A Social History of Alcohol*. Philadelphia: Temple University Press, 2004.

McHarry, Samuel. *The Practical Distiller*. New York: BiblioBazaar, 2008.

Owens, Bill. *The Art of Distilling Whiskey and Other Spirits: An Enthusiast's Guide to the Artisan Distilling of Potent Potables*. Bloomington, IN: Quarry Books, 2009.

Rothbaum, Noah. *The Business of Spirits*. New York: Kaplan Publishing, 2007.

Bill Kte'pi

DISTRIBUTION

Today, most states in the United States have a three-tiered distribution system for alcoholic beverages. Producers sell to distributers, who then supply retailers. As a general rule, consumers can buy only from the retailers. An exception to this rule includes some commercial wineries, where customers may buy bottles or cases of wine directly from the manufacturer to not only enjoy onsite, but to take home. **Microbreweries** or brewpubs are another exception, where glasses and pitchers of **beer** can be enjoyed on the premises where the beer is manufactured.

The main reason for a three-tiered system is that first the federal government, and later, state governments, wanted to tax the sales of alcoholic beverages, as well as limit the influence of organized crime in this industry. Controlling distribution made taxation more uniform in the mid-twentieth century, following **Prohibition** (1920–1933) compared with early federal efforts to make money off of whiskey sales, which in the eighteenth century resulted in a "Whiskey Rebellion" in post-Revolutionary America (1791–1794). However, states now are responsible for this taxation, and rules vary across state lines.

During Prohibition, in the Roaring Twenties and at the beginning of the Great Depression of the 1930s, alcohol sales were unregulated because they were illegal. Bootleggers and organized crime groups smuggled whiskey and other distilled beverages from Canada across the frozen Great Lakes in the winter in touring cars that were stuffed to the gills. Also, clever rumrunners left the Caribbean on fast ships bound for Charleston, South Carolina. Debarking, they hid their stash in the secret compartments of hollow, neoclassical monuments that decorated South Carolina cemeteries, until sales were made. This type of Prohibition-era distribution was done in the dead of night and accompanied by men with tommy guns.

The federal government put the three-tiered system in place a few years after the ratification of the Twenty-first Amendment to the Constitution (1933), which provided states with powers and authority to regulate the sale and distribution of alcohol. Manufacturers or producers were the first tier. They were responsible for **brewing** the beer, making the **wine**, and **distilling** the hard liquors. Importers might also be included in this first category, a category of middlemen who bring specialty beverages from abroad. The second tier consisted of independent distributors. The distributors were the wholesalers, responsible for bringing particular brands to a market, bounded by geography. The purpose of this second tier is to avoid competition in the same geographic area among the producers. These distributers were also designed to insulate retailers, the third tier, from the manufacturers. Retailers were licensed to sell to consumers.

The three-tiered system was designed to avoid some of the problems when alcohol, though banned, was unregulated during Prohibition. For example, sales and marketing efforts were controlled in this system. Only licensed entities could participate. State and local governments decide when and where alcohol can be served and sold. State and federal government agencies could better supervise the taxes collected. Purity and safety standards could better be enforced, avoiding the problems of unregulated distilled beverages like moonshine, where lead poisoning was sometimes a problem. Freshness and efficiency were built into this system, too, as it was well organized and national in its scope.

Today, distribution is regulated by the Alcohol and Tobacco Tax and Trade Bureau (TTB), a unit of the Department of the Treasury. This bureau employs 600 analysts, chemists, computer experts, investigators, and auditors across the United States, in their central office in Washington, D.C., and at the National Revenue Center in Cincinnati, Ohio. The TTB collects excise taxes not only on the sales of alcoholic beverages, but also on tobacco products, firearms, and ammunition. It provides oversight and administers the laws and regulations. The states today fall into two categories: 18 "control states" and 32 "license states." In the control states, alcohol distribution and retailing are regulated directly by the state governments. In the license states, the state governments issue licenses to private sellers.

Further Reading

"About Alcohol Policy." National Institute on Alcohol Abuse and Alcoholism Web site. 2009. http://www.alcoholpolicy.niaaa.nih.gov/About_Alcohol_Policy.html.
Alcohol and Tobacco Tax and Trade Bureau Web site. http://www.ttb.gov.

Pam Sezgin

DRINKING AGE LEGISLATION

Before 1933, the concept of a "drinking age" was foreign in the United States. In Puritan and early colonial communities, childhood was undefined. Youth and young adults drank like adults—usually in moderation, and without drunkenness. In 1673, Reverend Increase Mather, a prominent Puritan minister in the early Massachusetts Bay Colony, preached that "The wine is from God, but the Drunkard is from the Devil." During the late nineteenth and early twentieth centuries, youth were seen as the victims of adult alcohol abuse, but not as abusers themselves. However, during Prohibition, it became clear that young adults, particularly those attending college, did drink, often in unsafe ways. Thus, when Prohibition was repealed in 1933, state legislatures thought it wise to establish an age at which youth could purchase and imbibe alcohol. As 21 had traditionally been the age of majority, most states established their first "minimum drinking age" at 21.

During the 1950s and 1960s, state officials, educators, and parents struggled with the inconsistencies in state law. For example, New York State had been one of the few to set a minimum drinking age lower than 21. Its drinking age of 18 lured teens from Pennsylvania, Connecticut, Massachusetts, and Vermont across its borders and into its taverns. Many of these teens died on the highways home, sparking concern and alarm. However, by the early 1970s, many state legislatures thought that perhaps New York was correct. If kids could go to risk their lives in Vietnam, they should be able to drink. Between June 1970 and October 1973, 24 states lowered their minimum legal drinking age. However, by 1975, many states questioned that decision. Although border deaths had decreased, drinking and driving fatalities had increased. In the late 1970s, most states raised their drinking age back to 21. The states recognized that although the youth of the late 1960s had shown great maturity in many ways, they still needed boundaries, set by their parents and the law.

In 1984, President Ronald Reagan relieved the states of this burden. The new National Minimum Drinking Age Act established a uniform drinking age at 21. States who failed to comply were subject to a loss of 5 percent, soon raised to 10 percent, of federal highway funds. Although the 1987 Supreme Court case, *South Dakota v. Dole*, questioned its legality, the 1984 National Minimum Drinking Age Act was upheld and is still in effect today.

Despite the Supreme Court's ruling, the act is continually questioned. College administrators and students highlight its futility, noting how many students drink illegally behind closed doors, afraid to call for medical assistance if needed. In 2006, Middlebury College President Emeritus John McCardell, founded "Choose Responsibility." Dedicated to questioning the current drinking age and exploring new options, Choose Responsibility has had much publicity but limited success. Many claim that the drinking age has saved hundreds of thousands of lives and fear the lives to be lost if the age is changed. Both sides are strong, and it is clear that the debates will continue for many years to come. (*See also* **Mothers Against Drunk Driving (MADD)**.)

Further Reading

Hingson, Ralph W. "The Legal Drinking Age and Underage Drinking in the United States." *Archives of Pediatric and Adolescent Medicine* 163, no. 7 (2009): 598–600.

Lender, Mark Edward, and James Kirby Martin. *Drinking in America: A History*. New York: The Free Press, 1982.

"24 States Drop Drinking Age in 3-Year Period." *Alcohol and Health Notes*, October 1973, 1.

Joy Newman

DRINKING GAMES

Drinking games are social activities where alcohol consumption is utilized as either a rule or the ultimate goal. They are played almost exclusively in social situations and typically involve more-than-casual levels of consumption. The most basic and common formula for a typical drinking game involves a participant being offered a challenge that tests either a physical or mental skill set, with success in the game depending on the player's ability to meet the challenge. Failing to meet the challenge results in alcohol consumption.

Drinking games have appeared through history. Various games are cited as early as ancient Greece (500–400 BC) and the Tang Dynasty in China (618–907 AD). And while drinking games have a storied past, the most common associations with these games are with college students and recent college graduates, particularly in the United States.

Drinking games are most commonly played in private or "at-home" settings, such as residences, dormitories, hotel rooms, and campgrounds. On some occasions, these games are brought out into more public settings, such as parking lots outside of sporting events and concerts. They are less prevalent in "on-premise" venues like **bars** and **pubs**—due in part to laws against promoting overconsumption of alcohol.

With very few exceptions, drinking games typically present alcohol consumption as a penalty for poor playing skills. This behavior may seem counterintuitive to game play, until one realizes that the detrimental effects of consistent alcohol consumption affects a player's skills, thus offering a strategic factor to other players. Along with using the effects of constant alcohol consumption as a strategy, a player's ability to handle consistent consumption is often used as an affirmation of social norms equating drinking ability with personal fortitude. The ability to handle extended periods of punishment via alcohol consumption often earns appreciation from fellow players, whether after a victory or not. With very few exceptions, drinking games typically present alcohol consumption as a penalty for poor playing skills. This behavior may seem counterintuitive to game play, until one realizes that the detrimental effects of consistent alcohol consumption affects a player's skills, thus offering a strategic factor to other players. Along with using the effects of constant alcohol consumption as a strategy, a player's ability to handle consistent consumption is often used as an affirmation of social norms equating drinking ability with personal fortitude. It is this willing demonstration of alcohol mastery that is the true social currency amongst many groups of young adults. The winning or losing of the game is thus rendered irrelevant, and the game is an elaborate excuse to drink a lot.

Alcohol consumption, while the core element of drinking games, is achieved in one of two different means: democratic means and hierarchical means. Drinking games that facilitate democratic means of drinking encourage similar amounts of consumption for all players, while hierarchical means usually involve a particular player being singled out for consumption.

Another common theme in drinking games is the fact that almost all of them utilize a minimal amount of equipment. This is because drinking games are often played at a moment's notice with very little planning. Also, the lack of intricate and cumbersome equipment makes drinking games more versatile and easier to transport and set up, and conversely, easier to disassemble and clean up.

Most drinking games also share a lack of codified rules. Partly due to their unstructured occasional nature, there has never been any governing entity to declare or enforce a definitive set of rules for any particular drinking game. Because of this, even the most popular drinking games can have a different set of rules and regulations depending on where the players are from.

Drinking games differentiate themselves from other games in that alcohol consumption is an essential component. Drinking games are similar to any other game in that they involve pitting players in a battle of skills; however, the skills required to play can vary greatly, ranging from games that require sharp physical precision to games that simply require listening for a key word to initiate drinking.

Many of the most popular drinking games revolve around simple hand-eye coordination. Some of these games include **beer pong**, a game in which players throw ping-pong balls into beer-filled cups to make an opponent drink; Flip-Cup, a game in which players attempt to consume a set amount of **beer** and then flip their cup over faster than their opponents; and quarters, a game in which players bounce a coin into their opponent's cups.

Other popular drinking games revolve around strategy and mental skills. For example, the game "Asshole" is a card game in which players attempt to rid themselves of all cards they were dealt while attempting to make other players drink.

Another is "Thumper," in which players pound a drum roll onto a table while a particular player tries to remember and act out a pre-specified series of body motions, which results in heavy drinking if the motions are portrayed inaccurately. A third is "Drug Dealer," another card game that declares one player a cop who has to find the player dubbed a drug dealer, with false arrests and wrong guesses leading to severe drinking penalties.

Another, simpler variety of drinking game could actually be categorized as "stunts." These games often require little strategy or skill and rely mostly on endurance against alcohol. A popular example is "Power Hour," in which players consume a shot glass full of beer once a minute for 60 consecutive minutes. Another is the untitled movie- or television-themed drinking game, in which participants watch a program select a word or event guaranteed to be seen frequently (such as a main character, occurrence or phrase) and drink when specified words or events are presented. A more recent example is "Edward 40 Hands," during which participants simply duct-tape 40-ounce bottles of malt liquor to their hands—only to remove them when the contents are consumed.

While popular, drinking games are always facing unprecedented amounts of criticism and scrutiny due to the fact that, by nature, they encourage potentially dangerous amounts of alcohol consumption, which in turn could lead to potentially loud, dangerous, and/or illegal behavior. Because of this, drinking games are rarely played in public. While some bars, night clubs, and even beer manufacturers have tried with mixed results to capitalize on the popularity of drinking games, often times many proprietors are afraid to take such risks due to the potential liabilities that come with hosting drinking games. Despite their negative status in the public eye, drinking games continue to enjoy a strong underground presence, showing ever-increasing popularity at private parties and social functions. (*See also* **College Drinking Culture**.)

Further Reading

Bash, Alex. *The Imbible: Drinking Games for Times You'll Never Remember with Friends You'll Never Forget*. New York: St. Martin's Griffin, 2008.

Griscom, Andy. *The Complete Book of Beer Drinking Games*. Rev. ed. Memphis, TN: Mustang Publishing, 1999.

Ben Applebaum and Michael P. Ferrari

DRINKING GLASSES AND VESSELS

Over the centuries, a special material culture has developed alongside the development of alcoholic beverages. Drinking vessels blended form and function, as the shape of the vessel impacted the aroma and taste of a beverage. Aesthetics played a role, too, as drinking vessels were often decorated or made from precious substances that reflected the owner's social and economic status. Tradition, convenience, and chemistry each played a part in the morphology of the glassware and other barware that are now associated with different libations. People collected the appropriate glassware for the types of beverages they preferred. Etiquette developed about the appropriateness of the type of vessel could be used for a particular beverage. For example, it would be considered socially inappropriate to serve **champagne** in plastic cups. Champagne is a festive, expensive,

Glass Shape Enhances the Wine-Drinking Experience

In the chemistry of how wine works its magic, flavonoids, a group of poly-phenols, are aromatic compounds found in plants that provide the flavor and antioxidant properties of wine. Tannins are flavonoids found in grape skins, seeds, and stems that occur in greater quantities in red wines since these portions of the plants are fermented during the winemaking process. Tannins act as preservatives so red wines can be given long period of time to "age" during which the tannins oxidize slowly and increase the flavor and complex taste of red wines. With younger wines, those that have not aged in the casks or bottle, the oxidation process occurs when one lets the wine "breathe"—mix with the air—before serving.

The shapes of modern wine glasses are specifically designed to enhance the oxygen flow to their particular type of wine, accounting for and accen-tuating the differences in wine-to-oxygen ratio to get the best taste and aroma during the wine-drinking experience. The basic models of wine glasses are (a) a large, balloon-shaped glass to allow the most air exposure and to let the oenophile swirl the liquid around in the glass so as to savor the wine's bouquet; (b) a narrow-mouthed glass to concentrate the aroma; (c) smaller glasses for white wines that preserve their temperature as they must be served chilled; and (d) champagne flutes.

effervescent white **wine** that is associated with important celebrations like wed-dings, graduations, and job promotions.

Some 200 years ago, as middle-class families began to gain political and eco-nomic power with the decline of absolutist monarchies and the rise of nation-states in Europe and the Americas, glassware began to be preferred as the vessel of choice for serving wine. Wine glasses became composed of a bowl, stem, and foot. The glassware for serving wine was diverse and decorated. As the mass mar-keting of consumer goods burst forth during the 1890s in the United States, special sets of wine glasses in different sizes and shapes began to be used for different types of wines—for example, delicate cordial sets for dessert wines and larger-bowled stemware for red wine than white. With the further development of commercial, domestic wine production in the United States, a science and art developed that matched the type of bowl in a wine glass with the type of wine it was meant to serve. The shape of the bowl was designed to enhance enjoyment via focusing the sense of smell toward specific properties of the wine with which it was matched.

In today's bar culture, special drinks require special glasses. Brandy is served in a snifter, a balloon-shaped bowl on a short stem with a wide foot. The large surface area of the bowl enables the brandy to evaporate while the narrower top catches the aroma and lets it linger in the glass. As the bowl of this stemware is so large, it has to be cupped in the hands. The hands thus provide warmth to heat the brandy, pleasurably increasing the evaporation process and intensifying the aroma.

Quite the opposite effect is engineered into the shot glass. The beverages enjoyed in these tiny, stemless, glass tumblers are intense enough on their own.

Shot glasses are used for strong liquors with high alcoholic content. A swift drink of a small amount is all that is needed for the desired effect. Drinkers, in this case, do not linger to enjoy the aroma of **whiskey**, grappa, **bourbon**, or tequila straight. Shot glasses increased in popularity in the 1940s in the United States, although they also were used before and during Prohibition. In the late nineteenth century, **advertising** began to appear on these glasses, and today, they are decorated in many ways—for example, to promote tourism with the logo of cities or **sports** teams.

Cocktail glasses come in a great variety of shapes and sizes. The martini glass is a stemmed glass with a cone-shaped bowl and a flat, round, foot. Its stem and foot look similar to the same structures on wine stemware. The cone-shaped bowl, though, is more an aesthetic feature designed to make the drink look interesting. It amplifies the colors of the liquors mixed to make the cocktail, or highlights the olives or onions at the bottom of the bowl in a clear drink, or enhances the trademark froth that tops many cocktails. Other **cocktails** use tumblers like the Collins, highball, and old-fashioned glasses. These cylindrical glasses vary in height and width depending upon the mixed drink with which they are used. They are larger than the martini glass because several types of liquors are used and/or diluted with fruit juices.

Beer, like wine and cocktails, has its own taxonomy of drinking vessels. Tankards and steins serving a pint of ale or beer were initially used in Europe. These vessels were made from metals and ceramics. In the colonial and early republic periods in the United States, similar vessels were used, and homemade beer also was kept and served in earthenware bottles.

Like wine stemware, as consumer culture grew in the nineteenth and twentieth centuries, so did specialized glassware for drinking beer. The pilsner glass was developed to serve light beers. It served a smaller amount of beer than the tankards, steins, and pint glass. The pint glass was a British innovation to serve a standard amount of beer in **pubs**. Beer glasses have distinct shapes. Tulip-shaped beer glasses are often marked with the beer company's trademark or logo and are taller than the aforementioned types.

Further Reading

Angelakis, Manos. "Flute, Tulip, or Coupe?" Oenophile Blog, 2007. http://www .oenophileblog.com/html/flute__tulip__or_coupe_.html.
DeGroff, Dale. *The Craft of the Cocktail*. New York: Clarkson Potter, 2002.
Kirsner, Gary. *The Beer Stein Book: A 400 Year History*. 3rd ed. Coral Springs, FL: Glentiques, 1999. http://www.beerstein.net/articles/bsb-1.htm.
"Types of Wine Glasses—Stemware." Pinot Noir Wines.com, 2009. http://www.pinot _noir_wines.com/winestemware.
"Wine Glasses, Oxygen and Phenolic Compounds." The Wine Doctor, 2009. http:// www.thewinedoctor.com/advisory/technicalphenolics.shtml.

Pam Sezgin

DRINKING RITUALS

Drinking rituals are behaviors associated with the consumption of alcohol by groups of people so that strong identification is formed between individuals. These rituals can be found as part of traditional religious practices as well as secular behavior that involves membership in occupational, political, ethnic, national, or social groups. In all cases, drinking rituals serve to separate and distinguish one group of people from another, and participation is either by invitation in the form of initiation or by a cultural mandate to maintain membership within the group. Drinking rituals are closely associated with the customs, ceremonies, festivities and the etiquette of group drinking and are often undifferentiated from them. The word "symbel" for instance, in Germanic culture derives from a meaning for "feast" or "banquet" and involves ritualized drinking, which was at one time solemn and serious. A celebrant would drink ale or mead from a drinking horn and then either make a speech or engage in a rote form of boasting, followed by the giving of gifts.

In Japanese culture, there are certain expectations of drinkers to conform to group customs, and this expression is often regarded as ritualistic. It is considered rude in a social group to refuse a drink unless one is medically unable to do so or to drink before everyone is served. Ritual custom also proscribes drinking from a bottle instead of a glass. These rules function in a way that establishes a social order and ranking within the group and, just as importantly, marks outsiders. Much of this behavior is also based on cultural business etiquette, but in the context of interpersonal relationships that are formed over a long period of time, the etiquette becomes ritual. The ritual ensures that over the course of an evening, every person will pour a drink for every other person in the group, thus demonstrating respect for everyone present and instilling a sense of community and companionship.

For every culture in which alcoholic beverages are created and consumed, ritual activity surrounding the act of drinking is present. **Brewing** or **distilling** of alcoholic beverages was viewed in the ancient world as an art and so demanded an attention equal to the effort. Archaeological evidence has been uncovered in Europe, Africa, Asia, the Middle East, and the Americas that sheds light on early drinking rituals. Excavations in Spain's Ambrona Valley, for example, has revealed tombs containing Middle Neolithic pottery in the Bell Beaker tradition, in which the placement of **beer** vessels contributes to an interpretation of a ritual social use because of the context with other material goods. With the development of certain religious cults in Egypt and Mesoamerica, rituals developed that determined what particular alcoholic beverages were appropriate as offerings to the priests and to the gods. In essence, by drinking alcoholic beverages in ritual celebration, humans were consuming them for the gods as well, placing them in direct communion with deities. As another example, ancient Indian texts and sculptures from the subcontinent describe drinking scenes in conjunction with deities, demonstrating that imbibing alcohol was a strong aspect of religious practice, and thus part of a theological ritual. During religious practice, according to the texts, drinking was done in a careful, calm manner in a relaxed atmosphere. Small bowls or cups filled with alcohol would be placed on the head as a show of respect and subservience, and then they were ritually poured into ornately decorated dishes. The nature of the receptacle was an integral part of the drinking ritual. Invocations calling upon the gods to visit the faithful were then chanted.

These religious drinking rituals maintain a similarity to contemporary Christian practice. In the Roman Catholic Mass, the priest raises a chalice of sacramental **wine** above his head, offering a prayer to God, and in this way, the wine is symbolically transmuted into the blood of Jesus Christ. The wine is then offered to the congregation to sip. By taking communion with the wine, the worshipers thus express their belief and acceptance of church doctrine and reinforce their membership in the Roman Catholic Church.

In secular, everyday life, communal drinking is a social activity that strengthens cultural bonds. These bonds indicate positions of power and influence, thereby establishing a social order within a community. Drinking rituals are marked by the level of consumption of alcohol during the activity, and as a whole, a particular body of rituals forms together to determine the social networks required for the maintenance and perpetuation of a culture. There are precise rules about ritual behavior that are often nonverbal or recorded, so they can only be learned either through lengthy exposure and involvement in a culture, or under the sponsorship and guidance of a member in the drinking ritual society. These rules are fluid over time, only remaining static until a particular event or change in the group requires a consequent change in the rules. Research has been done on the Xhosa tribe in South Africa, where beer drinking is highly ritualized, involving both formal and informal speeches along with set performances that focus on a political point of view, in the past marking a resistance to apartheid and more recently at the upheavals in race relations. These rituals serve as dynamic cultural adaptations as the Xhosa experience a transition from an agrarian, family-centered life to an urban one. In essence, drinking rituals demarcate cultural survivals. One such ritual is that of *umsindleko*, a beer-fueled event that celebrates the return of migrant workers to the communal fold. The Xhosa's particular beer-drinking rituals change over time, serving always to maintain the cultural unity of the tribe. In this way, drinking rituals become a social offering between members.

And in some cultures, such as the drinking of *ouzo* in Greece, selection of the particular type of alcohol is a ritual choice, suitable to specific occasions such as weddings, funerals, and anniversaries. Toasts also represent a ritual in which a respect or esteem for the company at hand is shown. A drinking ritual following a toast can involve draining a drink in a single draught, symbolizing boldness and strength of character, such as "gan-bei" in China, which means "dry glass."

There are also social drinking rituals associated with certain types of alcohol, again complementing custom and etiquette. One of the more historically romantic because of its association with France in the late nineteenth century, with artists such as Degas and van Gogh and symbolist poets such as Rimbaud, is the ritual associated with drinking **absinthe**. A shot of absinthe is poured into a glass. An ornate, perforated spoon is placed atop the glass, a sugar cube is placed on the spoon, and then chilled water is poured over it, dissolving the sugar into the absinthe.

Another area of drinking ritual involves college-age students, most particularly in the United States. Among this social group, there are many **drinking games** that are frequently paired with the ritual of drinking heavily and to excess in a very short time. A social and health problem for many colleges and universities, as well as the communities in which they are located, these rituals involve an indoctrination of freshmen, or first-year students, into college life. Numerous studies have found that engaging in these rituals results in **binge drinking** as a way of ingratiating oneself with other students, becoming part of a social group, and forming friendships. In extreme cases, of which there is more oversight now than in past years, forced drinking is part of the initiation or hazing practices of fraternities and sororities. Additionally, the fact that many of these drinkers are under legal drinking age involves legal issues and liabilities. In some regard, drinking in college can be viewed as a ritual in the transition between childhood and adulthood. This heavy, episodic drinking is predominantly American in nature where the legal drinking age is 21. In studies of **college drinking culture** in other countries, where the legal drinking age is lower, the rituals associated with binge drinking and excessive celebration are largely absent. However, in Norway, there is a similar occasion of ritualized binge drinking. "Russ" involves students wearing specific trousers for 17 days straight while engaging in binge drinking. At the end of the 17 days, the drinker may wash his trousers and proudly call himself a "student." This ritual began in the eighteenth century and traditionally took place between the time of taking final exams and learning of the results.

For culturally significant events, the sharing of drink is special. Because festivities and celebrations often form from religious practice, the drink has to be such that it alters behavior and perspective in some way. Thus, by attaching ritual to alcoholic beverages, the drinker is able not only to communicate with fellow celebrants, but to communicate with a higher manifestation of a culture as well, thereby preserving cultural traits. Due to released inhibitions in drinking, sharing in ritual activity results in increased social bonding, again emphasizing the validity of the group. In a happy social occasion with inhibitions lowered, the celebration becomes more evident.

Further Reading

Gately, Iain. *Drink: A Cultural History of Alcohol.* New York: Gotham Books, 2008.

McAlister, Patrick. *Xhosa Beer Drinking Rituals: Power, Practice and Performance in the South African Rural Periphery.* Durham, NC: Carolina Academic Press, 2006.

Pollington, Steven. *The Mead-Hall: The Feasting Tradition in Anglo-Saxon England.* Norfolk, UK: Anglo-Saxon Books, 2003.

Kevin Grace

DRINKING SONGS

While singing often takes place alongside **drinking rituals**, particularly within the context of a religious event, the genre of drinking songs owes its existence to the celebration and conviviality that is associated with the consumption of alcohol. These songs are most commonly associated with male behavior. In this regard, drinking songs undoubtedly have been part of group drinking throughout human history, but the first written accounts of specific songs date to England in the mid-sixteenth century. The tunes derived from traditional folk ballads or melodies, with the lyrics sometimes the result of specific literary efforts or evolved from impromptu group singing in taverns. Thus, Robert Herrick's seventeenth-century composition "The Cobblers' Catch" became popular with the lyrics "Come sit by the fireside, and roundly drink we here; Till that we see our cheeks ale-dyed And noses tann'd with **beer**." A folk melody from the same era has the refrain "And bring us in good ale," preceded by a long string of verses, such as, "Bryng us no bacon, for that is passing fat, But brynge us in good ale, and gyfe us i-nought of that." The most famous American drinking song is one sung by people of all ages, but especially by schoolchildren. "Ninety-nine Bottles of Beer on the Wall" is a counting-down song, used by groups traveling from one place to another as a way of passing the time: "Ninety-nine bottles of beer on the wall, 99 bottles of beer. Take one down, pass it around, 98 bottles of beer on the wall."

Drinking songs are most often marked by ribald or bawdy verses, or by political or social commentary. The underlying basis for these themes is that the songs serve to reinforce group identity and behavior to the exclusion of other groups, and that in an atmosphere where inhibitions are lowered, so are social constraints against obscene language, political points of view, or general insults. The songs reflect the pleasures of the company one keeps. Some drinking songs are specific to distinct occupations or organizations. A group of athletes, military men, college fraternities, or **sports** fans will have their own drinking songs, and the verses are often fluid in word and context. For example, the followers of a football team may always sing the same song, but with different lyrics depending on the opposition, again with the intent being to reinforce the camaraderie of the group and to insult the other team. By the early twentieth century, college fraternities published their own drinking songs as part of general college songbooks. The songs form a bond between singers, emphasizing masculinity and like experiences or backgrounds. There are also regional and ethnic varieties of songs involving the use of the same tunes. The result is a validation of cultural community membership, both at the group and at the individual level.

Drinking songs are found worldwide, but because they are often ephemeral, there has been little recording of them outside the British and American traditions. With the folk **music** revival in England and in the United States in the 1950s and 1960s, many of the less objectionable traditional drinking songs were commercially recorded and preserved. Obscene songs, with the lyrics fitted to familiar tunes, became a staple of surreptitious copying and distribution from the 1960s to the twenty-first century and are now most often circulated through social sharing sites on the Internet. Drinking songs continue to be a dynamic rather than a static cultural expression of group behavior. (*See also* **Men and Boys Drinking; College Drinking Culture**.)

Further Reading

Cray, Ed. *The Erotic Muse: American Bawdy Songs*. Urbana: University of Illinois Press, 1992.

Laing, Robin. *The Whiskey Muse: Scotch Whiskey in Poem and Song*. Edinburgh: Luath Press, 2002.

Powers, Madelon. *Faces along the Bar: Lore and Order in the Workingman's Saloon, 1870–1920*. Chicago: University of Chicago Press, 1988.

Kevin Grace

DRIVING UNDER THE INFLUENCE

Driving under the influence (DUI) has been a public health concern since cars have been driven. Police and other community officials quickly recognized how alcohol consumption negatively affected drivers' reflexes and judgment, impairing their abilities on the road. However, despite the clear recognition of DUI as a problem, regulating it proved to be extremely difficult.

During the 1950s, 1960s, and 1970s, the primary obstacle to effective regulation of DUI behavior was individual state standards for what level of **blood**

Drinking and Driving Statistics

In 2008, an estimated 11,773 people died in drunk driving–related crashes in the United States. This is a decline of 9.8 percent from 2007. However, the costs are still huge in terms of the tragic loss of lives as well as from an economic perspective: alcohol-related accidents are estimated to have cost the public $114.3 billion in 2000. In part thanks to groups such as Mothers Against Drunk Driving (MADD) and designated-driver campaigns, alcohol-related traffic fatalities have decreased by nearly 50 percent since 1980, from over 30,000 per year to under 15,500. There is obviously still progress to be made. In 2008, more than 1.46 million drivers were arrested for driving under the influence of alcohol or narcotics.

Source: MADD, http://www.madd.org/Drunk-Driving/Drunk-Driving/Statistics/AllStats.aspx #STAT_1 (accessed July 10, 2010).

alcohol content (BAC) determined "intoxication." For example, in 1962, New York State Vehicle and Traffic Law set the BAC standard for "driving while intoxicated" at 0.15 percent. This standard was not uncommon. For example, in 1962, Illinois also had a BAC standard of 0.15 percent for "drinking while intoxicated." This standard was not lowered until January 1967. These varying standards of legal intoxication hindered police ability to charge many drivers under the influence. Police routinely pulled over drivers clearly affected by alcohol, but who technically were not legally drunk. Unable to arrest or charge the intoxicated driver, police were left with no recourse for ensuring public health and safety. Today, most states have a lower standard for "driving while intoxicated." The typical standard is 0.08 percent, although some states maintain that an individual is not "intoxicated" until 0.10 percent.

During the late 1960s and 1970s, some public health officials, as well as members of state legislatures, questioned the efficacy of BAC policies in reducing drunk driving. Many specifically questioned the efficacy of these policies when regulating youth and young adult drinking and driving behavior. By the early 1970s, research clearly demonstrated that a primary cause of the high rates of young adult drinking and driving crashes and fatalities was the compounded effect of inexperienced drinking and inexperienced driving. Whereas a more experienced driver and drinker may be better able to adjust to the driving impairments caused by alcohol, young adult drivers did not have that ability.

As public concerns rose, state legislatures looked for answers. In 1962, members of New York State Governor Nelson A. Rockefeller's Joint Legislative Committee for the Study of Alcoholic Beverage Control Law advised that New York State set a separate standard for DUI for drivers younger than age 21. The Committee advised in their "Report and Recommendations on Legal Minimum Drinking Age" that this standard should be 0.05 percent, with violators subject to the possible suspension or revocation of their driving license.

Today, one of the primary obstacles to the enforcement of DUI statutes is the courts' system of sanctioning. In many communities, DUI is seen as a minor infraction. Individuals convicted of DUI, or driving while intoxicated, often serve minimal jail time. For example, the man who killed Cari Lightner, the daughter of the founder of **Mothers Against Drunk Driving (MADD)**, struck Lightner just two days after being released from jail, where he had been held for another drunk-driving crash.

Driving under the influence of alcohol continues to be a major public health concern for adults and young adults alike. A combination of education, sanctioning, and policy analysis would likely help lessen its effects. (*See also* **Drinking Age Legislation; Health Effects of Alcohol.**)

Further Reading

DeJong, William, and Ralph Hingson. "Strategies to Reduce Driving under the Influence of Alcohol" *Annual Review of Public Health* 19 (1998): 359–78.
"Minimum Legal Drinking Age." American Medical Association Web site. http://www.ama -assn.org/ama/pub/physician-resources/public-health/promoting-healthy-lifestyles/ alcohol-other-drug-abuse/facts-about-youth-alcohol/minimum-legal-drinking-age .shtml.

Joy Newman

DRY COUNTIES

Dry counties are those that forbid the sale of alcohol from within their borders. The idea originated with the **Anti-Saloon League (ASL)**, founded in 1893, as a political tool to pressure wet states to go dry. The ASL was determined to use the force of law to impose its vision of morality on the country. The idea is credited to Wayne Wheeler, the organization's general counsel.

First, the ASL pressured the states to adopt local option laws. This allowed counties and towns to declare themselves dry, thus shutting down the saloons. With dry laws in place, the state was pressured to adopt statewide prohibition. A number of states amended their constitutions to outlaw alcohol, and some states, such as Oklahoma, entered the Union as a dry state in 1907.

Once the states were dry, the congressmen and senators would have to vote dry, no matter if they consumed alcohol in private. By the time the United States entered World War I in 1917, most states had some form of prohibition on the books, so the idea of nationwide prohibition was not so far-fetched. Dry laws were thus a stepping-stone to **Prohibition**.

While dry counties and the Deep South seem inextricably linked, the reality is that the South came late to the **temperance** game. Temperance had originated as a movement in the Northeast, and Southerners had never been abstainers. After the Civil War, the Southern Baptist Convention rose to cultural dominance, and it allied with the Anti-Saloon League in the 1890s. The Southern Baptist Convention came to believe that alcohol was sinful and that people should not drink it. Yet even in the Deep South, urban areas like Atlanta and New Orleans resisted going dry. The ASL had its greatest support in rural areas dominated by Protestants, and thus one hears of dry counties, but almost never of dry cities.

In a state like Kentucky, producer of most of the country's **bourbon**, counties are classified as "wet," "dry," and "moist" (towns within a county can sell alcohol). Kentucky is home to large numbers of Southern Baptists and Catholics,

The dance band the B-52s immortalized growing up in Georgia with their song, "Dry County" (from their *Cosmic Thing* album, 1989), which recounts a hazy, hot summer and no chance of getting booze to party because the county is dry.

who are at opposing ends of the alcohol spectrum theologically. Baptists oppose drinking, while Catholics have never had a theological issue with alcohol.

After Prohibition ended in 1933, many counties and even some states like Mississippi and Oklahoma remained dry. This is a legacy of Prohibition. Mississippi went wet only in 1966, becoming the last state to legalize alcohol.

Dry counties today are concentrated in the South and Midwest, where Southern Baptist churches insist on keeping them that way. Loopholes abound in dry counties, such as for private clubs like golf courses that allow their members to drink. As Americans have become increasingly comfortable with drinking and the stigma against alcohol has diminished, the number of dry counties has been in decline.

Further Reading

Clark, Norman H. *Deliver Us from Evil: An Interpretation of American Prohibition.* New York: W. W. Norton & Company, 1976.

Gusfield, Joseph R. *Symbolic Crusade: Status Politics and the American Temperance Movement.* Urbana: University of Illinois Press, 1986.

Kerr, K. Austin. *Organized for Prohibition: A New History of the Anti-Saloon League.* New Haven, CT: Yale University Press, 1985.

Kobler, John. *Ardent Spirits: The Rise and Fall of Prohibition.* New York: Da Capo Press, 1993.

Garrett Peck

E

ECONOMICS

The alcoholic beverage industry in the United States is a significant economic driver. By 2007, alcohol was averaging $189 billion a year in revenue, according to the Beverage Information Group. The industry accounts for several million jobs, including brewers, winemakers, distillers, bartenders, restaurant workers, truck drivers, salespeople, brand managers, and corporate executives. In addition, it has launched tangential industries, such as **wine tourism**.

The Twenty-first Amendment repealed **Prohibition** in 1933 and gave states the power to regulate alcohol. At the time there was significant distrust of distilled spirits, the favored product of bootleggers because of their profitability, so states put more stringent controls on spirits than on **beer** and **wine**. States had a choice for regulation after repeal. Thirty-two states chose to become license states, adopting the three-tier system (producer, wholesaler, retailer) of the soft drink industry. The other 18 states became control states, where the state itself serves as the retailer.

American drinking habits are cyclical, and so are spending habits on alcohol. Since the end of Prohibition, Americans have shifted in and out of different alcoholic beverages, from straight **whiskey** to **cocktails**, to light lager, to high-end wine, and then to craft beer. Drinking has never been a static activity, and few drinkers stick to the same drink their entire life. They change their favorites as their needs change. Baby boomers, for example, readily took to red wine after the television program *60 Minutes* broadcast an episode in 1991 on the "French paradox" that demonstrated greater longevity from red wine. This produced a boom in spending on red wine among a more affluent generation.

American consumers can buy alcohol in one of two ways: *on premise* is for establishments that sell drinks to be consumed under the same roof, such as a bar, club, or restaurant. An *off-premise* venue is a retail location, such as **liquor stores** or supermarkets, that sells the product to a consumer, who then takes it home for consumption. "On-prem" and "off-prem" require different kinds of state licenses, and distilled spirits are generally the most difficult licenses to buy.

In economic terms, alcohol has a relatively inelastic demand, meaning that consumers buy it regardless of the price, just as they buy gasoline and food. What they buy—and where they drink it—depends on their economic fortunes. In good times, people tend to drink more often at on-premise establishments. But in times of economic hardship, people drink at home instead to save money.

During the Internet boom of the late 1990s and the housing bubble of the early 2000s, consumers felt rich and so traded up to more expensive, premium brands of alcohol—craft beer, Napa Cabernet Sauvignon, imported Scotch, and specialty **vodka**. Grey Goose, a vodka made in France, was emblematic of this trading up: at $30 or more, it cost double that of other premium vodkas. Yet to be seen drinking Grey Goose was to announce one's place in society. When the housing bubble finally burst, triggering the Great Recession, consumers began trading back down to value brands. They continued to drink—they just spent less, opting out of ultra-premium, luxury products for less expensive brands.

There are three main categories of alcoholic beverages: beer, distilled spirits, and wine. Beer has been America's favorite alcoholic beverage since after the Civil War. At $98 billion in sales in 2007, it accounts for about half the alcohol market—and half of all beer sold is light beer (Anheuser-Busch's Bud Light is the world's best-selling beer). Beer is overwhelmingly drunk by men and is the preferred beverage at sporting events. Brewers focus much of their **advertising** on **sports**. The nation's three largest brewers are Anheuser-Busch, Miller, and Coors. All were acquired by foreign companies during the first decade of the twenty-first century.

Craft brewers grew in popularity after President Jimmy Carter signed a law in 1979 legalizing **home-brewing**. Home-brewers are defined as those producing fewer than two million barrels of 31-gallon beer a year. The nation's largest craft brewer is the Boston Beer Company, producer of Samuel Adams Boston Lager. Craft brewers have proliferated across the country—by 2008, the United States had 1,406 breweries, though they accounted for only 6 percent ($5.7 billion) of the overall beer market. Most craft brewers remain small businesses.

Distilled spirits account for about a third of the alcoholic beverage market, or $62.6 billion in 2007. Within the distilled spirits category, vodka has been the king among consumers since the 1970s; its lack of flavor makes it mixable with just about anything. Young adults in particular, who account for a large part of alcohol consumption, favor vodka, tequila, and **rum**. Aged liquors, known as "brown spirits" from their color (they are aged in oak barrels, which imparts a golden color), saw a resurgence in popularity. These included **bourbon**, Scotch and Irish whiskey, and rum. The margarita, a tequila and lime–based cocktail, was the nation's favorite in the early twenty-first century, having supplanted the popular cosmopolitan from the decade before.

Most distilled spirits are made by multinational corporations, such as Diageo, Pernod Ricard, Fortune Brands, and Beam Global Spirits and Wine. But with spirits' popularity, craft distillers began popping up to produce hand-crafted spirits in limited batches. Similar to craft brewers and family wineries, these are often small companies or even mom-and-pop operations. They usually focus on **gin** or vodka, spirits that do not require aging. Many craft distillers got their start working in craft **brewing**.

Wine, the third category of alcohol sold in the United States, is by far the smallest at $28.1 billion in sales in 2007. Wine did not reach mainstream appeal in American culture until the 1960s, when California winemakers made significant improvements in quality. At the same time, Americans discovered the European penchant for pairing wine with food. The world woke up to Napa Valley in 1976, when Napa beat Bordeaux and Burgundy wines at a blind tasting, known as the Judgment of Paris. Compared with beer and spirits sales, however, the wine market is much smaller—about 15 percent of U.S. alcohol sales. Wine is more expensive, and many consider it more of an elite beverage—a drink for collectors but not for regular folks. Wine is now made in all 50 states, though 90 percent of American wine comes from California. In terms of vines planted, Chardonnay is the leading wine grape varietal, followed by Merlot, then Cabernet Sauvignon. Wine is made at all price levels: from bulk wines like the Charles Shaw Winery's "Two-Buck Chuck" to cult wines favored by collectors that could costs hundreds of dollars. The movie *Sideways* (2004) demonstrated both wine tourism and wine fanaticism—especially for Pinot Noir.

Wine tourists can visit a winery and sign up for the wine club. This club then ships wine regularly to their customers and is known as direct-to-consumer shipping or simply direct-ship. This is a very small part of the market—wine is heavy and thus expensive to ship—but an important service for collectors. Some states tried to block direct-ship from out-of-state wineries while allowing in-state wineries to ship. The U.S. Supreme Court struck down this practice in 2005 in *Granholm v. Heald*, arguing that states could not discriminate.

Because of wine's popularity, many restaurants added **sommeliers** to assist customers in pairing wine with their food. Restaurants often double or triple the price of a glass or bottle of wine above its retail cost—and since they often buy it at a wholesale discount, the markup can be even more significant. Wine is a significant part of a restaurant's profitability, thanks to the price markup.

As the generations that supported the **Temperance** Movement died off, the stigma against drinking alcohol faded from American society. According to the annual Gallup poll conducted almost every year since 1939, nearly two-thirds of American adults drink alcoholic beverages. This was affirmed again in the 2009 survey, when 64 percent admitted they drank, while 36 percent abstained. Drinkers are a supermajority, and thus alcohol is much more recognized as a fundamental part of American society today. (*See also* **Distribution; Politics.**)

Further Reading

Beverage Information Group. *Handbook Advance 2008.*
Gallup. "Drinking Habits Steady amid Recession." June 29, 2009. http://www.gallup.com.
Peck, Garrett. *The Prohibition Hangover: Alcohol in America from Demon Rum to Cult Cabernet.* New Brunswick, NJ: Rutgers University Press, 2009.

Garrett Peck

ELDERLY

The relationship of the elderly to alcohol raises definitional questions: one of the identifying features of the old-age category is its diversity. "Elderly" has been defined as anywhere from 60 upward. Some studies work with subcategories of young-old (55–64), medium-old (65–74), old-old (75–84) and oldest-old (85+). Others use levels of health and independence, or retirement/working status. For market research, the 50+ group constitutes the "mature market."

Research into older people and drinking has been primarily medical- or problem-centered in nature, exploring, for example, the relationship between alcohol consumption and mortality in old age; the effects of combining medication and drinking; the use of alcohol as a painkiller; the relationship between heavy drinking and age-related problems such as memory loss; levels of tolerance and family support for older drinkers; the balance between risk management and the rights of older people in relation to drinking, for example, in care home settings; and ethnic and gender differences relating to such issues.

Research indicates that older people are more susceptible to alcohol-related impairment, but in general, alcohol consumption tends to decline in old age. Abstinence is higher among older than younger people. There is also evidence, however, that moderate drinking has some beneficial effects for older people: a number of studies show lower mortality rates among moderate drinkers than non-drinkers. The incidence of "late-onset" drinking problems has also been studied, attributed in many cases to age-related stress, arising, for example, from physical pain or widowhood; in some U.S. studies, this changed pattern is linked more prevalently to women.

Less research has been conducted into non-problematic forms of drinking. The main areas of research are in marketing, aging studies, and the social science of consumption and leisure. There is a growing field of market research into the drinking preferences and habits of older people, who now include in their ranks the postwar generation of "baby boomers" (born approximately between 1946 and 1964). With an aging population, the U.S. alcohol industry is currently targeting the affluent 50+ market as the fastest growing consumer group, displacing a traditional focus on young consumers. In 2006, there were over 79 million people in the 50+ range in the United States (28% of adults). Market research for this group suggests, for instance, that **wine** is the preferred drink, and they also constitute the largest market for spirits. Social scientists in this field study patterns of consumption, leisure, and sociability. Older consumers are more likely to drink at home than at drinking establishments. Some U.S. studies have found that socializing with family and friends remains a key activity for older people, while drinking outside the home and dancing declines. There is ongoing academic debate over whether the "baby boom" generation of consumers initiated new forms of spending behavior; those now in their 60s are closely associated with the rise of "consumer lifestyles." There are signs that "age norms" are becoming more diverse among the current 60+ cohort. More research is needed into specific drinking choices and routines across the life course, and how and why these change over time.

In popular culture, representations of the "aging alcoholic" abound but are generally non-age-specific, often including anyone from the late 30s upward—suggesting the "washed-up" figure (e.g., Gladys George in *The Hard Way* [1943],

Walter Matthau in *The Bad News Bears* [1976], and Jeff Bridges in *Crazy Heart* [2009]). More positive images of older people drinking are also to be found; however, though they may be less prevalent. In the United Kingdom, the public house is often represented as the site of community and sociability for adults of all ages, including older people—for example, in the TV soap *Coronation Street* (since 1960) and the 2001 film *Last Orders*. The beer drinking of the father, Martin Crane (aged 61–72), in the U.S. sitcom *Frasier* (1993–2004) suggests his down-to-earth qualities in contrast to his sons' rarefied wine drinking. *The Golden Girls* (1980s) showed older women drinking as part of their normal social routine.

Further Reading

"Alcohol Use in Older People." National Institute on Aging. http://www.nia.nih.gov/HealthInformation/Publications/alcohol.htm.

Beresford, T., and E. Gomberg, eds. *Alcohol and Aging*. New York: Oxford University Press, 1995.

Breslow, R. A., and B. Smothers. "Drinking Patterns of Older Americans: National Health Interview Surveys, 1997–2001." *Journal of Studies on Alcohol and Drugs*, 65 (2004): 232–40.

Rees, I., et al. *Consumption and Generational Change: The Rise of Consumer Lifestyles*. New Brunswick, NJ: Transaction Publishers, 2009.

Vanessa Taylor

F

FERMENTATION

Fermentation (from the Latin verb "*fervere,*" meaning "to boil") is a set of naturally occurring biochemical processes relating to carbohydrate metabolism. In fermentation, the sugars that exist naturally in plant or animal sources are transformed into alcohols or acids via the use of yeasts, bacteria, or a combination thereof, under conditions of decay that lack oxygen.

The modern scientific study of fermentation is known as zymurgy and was pioneered in the 1860s and 1870s by the French chemist Louis Pasteur, who was the first to accurately describe the role of live yeast organisms in the production of alcohol by fermentation. Later, in 1897, the German chemist Eduard Buchner refined Pasteur's work by showing that the yeasts did not actually have to be alive to yield the fermentation process, as it is an enzymatic secretion of yeast that metabolizes sugar to produce alcohol. This refinement led to Buchner's receipt of the 1907 Nobel Prize in Chemistry for advancements in zymurgy.

Today, fermentation has many modern industrial uses, including the creation of certain pharmaceutical products such as antibiotics and insulin, as well as the transformation of toxic sewage waste into harmless fertilizer. However, it is the archaic domestic uses of fermentation that provide the primary benefit to human beings, particularly the transformation of certain foods into even more desirable foods. Common global examples include fruit into **wine** and **cider**; honey into mead; grain into **beer** and bread; milk into cheese and yogurt; and vegetable sugars into acids used in food preservation and storage. Common examples of fermented products with source carbohydrates from specific regions include cocoa powder, chocolate, coffee, vanilla, and Tabasco sauce.

In the United States, the main indigenous grain used for the production of ethanol is corn. Corn is used to create alcoholic beverages (e.g., **bourbon**—distinctly

What turns grape juice into the alcoholic beverage we know as wine? The process of fermentation is responsible for this transformation. Fermentation is also responsible for producing the alcohol in cider and beer. (Yurok/Dreamstime.com)

American **whiskey**) as well as biofuels. Approximately three gallons of ethanol fuel can be produced from one bushel (0.42 liter) of corn. Currently, sorghum (Plains states) and pearl millet (southeastern United States) are also being studied as possible source grains for biofuels.

Since fermentation can occur spontaneously, without human intervention, the process logically predates human history. Some anthropologists believe that the human discovery of alcohol fermentation motivated foragers and incipient horticulturists to settle and become agriculturists some 10,000 years ago. Since fruits are some of the easiest foods to ferment spontaneously, anthropologists hypothesize that a fortuitous discovery of wine likely predated the more complicated technologies necessary to produce bread and beer from fermented grains. They further hypothesize that the domestication of grains for production of bread and beer likely contributed to the development of urban centers and the rise of early civilizations some 10,000 to 12,000 years ago.

Though fermentation can occur spontaneously in nature, humans have sought to influence, manage, and control the process for at least the last 10,000 years due to its potential to yield both positive and negative effects. Some desirable outcomes of fermentation include the production of certain acids that can cook or otherwise preserve foods without the requirement of refrigeration; and the production of ethanol that is the basis for alcoholic beverages such as beer, cider, and wine. Some undesirable outcomes of fermentation include the production of fusel alcohols that can yield certain unpleasant aromas and flavors, as well as the growth of the bacterium responsible for inducing botulism, a rare but serious and potentially fatal paralysis caused by ingesting contaminated foods.

Corn and cacao were fermented into alcoholic beverages by the pre-Columbian civilizations of Central and South America. Alcoholic beverages from corn were not known among indigenous groups in North America, though early ethnographers noted that a few groups were fermenting grains as a food preparation. Some examples are fermented corn gruel (Cherokee, Huron, Zuni) and manzanita berries (California Indians at the time of contact—though this may have been an imitation of mission behavior they observed).

In general terms, knowledge of fermentation is beneficial because it permits a community to adapt to and thrive in a particular natural environment with a particular set of native plants and animals. Main adaptive advantages of this knowledge include improvements to the local diet and improvements to food-processing technologies.

Specifically, fermentation increases nutritional variety in the diet because the process can create nutritional elements like proteins, vitamins, and amino acids not found in the source carbohydrate. It also can decrease or even eliminate some toxins and inedible parts of the original carbohydrate, thereby increasing the digest-ibility of available food in the environment. And fermentation can increase the aesthetic variety in an otherwise starchy and bland diet because a small number of staple plant items can be fermented in a variety of ways to produce an increased diversity of flavors, aromas, and textures. Finally, fermentation can improve food processing by its potential for decreased cooking time and increased food safety resulting from food preservation and salvaged waste.

Further Reading

Battcock, Mike, and Sue Azam-Ali. "Fermented Fruits and Vegetables: A Global Perspective." *FAO Agricultural Services Bulletins No. 134*. Rome: Food and Agriculture Organiza-tions of the United Nations, 1998.

McGovern, Patrick E. *Uncorking the Past: The Quest for Wine, Beer, and Other Alcoholic Beverages*. Berkeley: University of California Press, 2009.

Nobel Foundation. 1907 Nobel Laureate Biography of Eduard Buchner. http://nobelprize.org/nobel_prizes/chemistry/laureates/1907/buchner-bio.html.

"Pasteur Brewing—Works of Louis Pasteur." http://www.pasteurbrewing.com/articles/works-of-louis-pasteur.html.

Steinkraus, Keith H. "Fermentations in World Food Processing." Institute of Food Technol-ogists. *Comprehensive Reviews in Food Science and Food Safety* 1 (2002): 23–32.

———, ed. *Handbook of Indigenous Fermented Foods*. New York: Marcel Dekker, 1995.

Karen Eilene Saenz

FETAL ALCOHOL SYNDROME

Fetal Alcohol Syndrome (FAS) is one particular diagnosis available under the diagnostic umbrella of Fetal Alcohol Spectrum Disorder. The Institute of Medicine defines FAS as the presentation of the following symptoms: specific facial abnormalities, growth retardation, structural brain abnormalities, and neurological impairments as well as cognitive or behavioral deficits that emerge in childhood.

Reported rates of diagnosed FAS in the United States range between 1 and 3 cases for every 1,000 live births. While alcohol consumption during pregnancy is the primary cause of FAS, there exists an inverse relationship that has been labeled the "American paradox." In a global context, the United States has the world's highest incidence rate of FAS, while scoring quite low on measures of *per capita* alcohol consumption. With equivalent alcohol consumption between Americans and the British, and the simultaneous disparities in FAS diagnoses, Americans have 3 cases for every 1,000 live births, while the British have fewer than 0.1 incidents for every 1,000 births. The unequal outcomes of similar alcohol consumption patterns point to social epidemiological factors, such as socioeconomic status or access to health care. For example, in Canadian aboriginal communities, where

Former President George Bush presents the Daily Point of Light award to Karli Schrider of Damascus, Maryland, on March 12, 1999, at a Washington ceremony. Schrider, then 26, is a Fetal Alcohol Syndrome (FAS) survivor and has dedicated her life to raising the awareness of FAS. (AP/Wide World Photos)

socioeconomic indicators show extraordinary levels of poverty and access to health care is often very limited, rates of FAS of 100 to 190 per 1,000 live births are fairly common.

Historically, concerns about alcohol consumption during pregnancy date back to antiquity. Aristotle, in his *Problemata*, warned that drunken women often gave birth to children like themselves. Ancient Jewish wisdom dictated that pregnant women should not drink **wine** or "strong drink" as codified in the Old Testament (*Judges* 13, verse 7). Concerns about excessive drinking during pregnancy continue through recorded history, but become subjects of public debate primarily around periods of moral outrage around the abuse of specific substances. In England, during the "**gin craze**" of the 1700s, the College of Physicians warned Parliament that maternal consumption of alcohol was having prenatal consequences for children. These warnings came on the heels of a moral panic about the widespread consumption of cheap gin among the lower classes, and the social and moral implications this was seen to have. Among these concerns was a form of "degeneracy" wherein consumption of alcohol created hereditary deficiencies, most often seen as the reason for the absence of social and economic capital in certain classes of people.

While the general concerns about alcohol consumption are found in the medical research literature from 1726 onward, FAS gained the status of a medical diagnosis only in 1973. The timing of the formalization of the FAS diagnosis is not coincidental. Before the late 1960s, other physician-researchers had attempted to forward a theory of complications arising from prenatal alcohol consumption, but this was received with academic rejection and strong personal criticisms of the authors. One theory suggests that the timing relates to the revelations about Thalidomide and its role in birth defects as well as the 1973 *Roe v. Wade* ruling in the U.S. Supreme Court. This view sees the development and formalization of FAS as a social counter-movement to these challenges to the socially accepted place of procreation.

A challenge from the Foucauldian notion of "surveillance" sees the emphasis on choices made by pregnant women to be another form of social control over the pregnant female body, possibly a backlash to reproductive autonomy that emerged from *Roe v. Wade*. Others note that this represented a specific form of social control over women, which depends on the perceived validity of science and technology to achieve these patriarchical goals.

From an ethics perspective, placing an obligation on pregnant women to avoid all alcohol was partly informed by the arguments that went into the abortion debates of that period. Questions of the personhood of the fetus played a central role in philosophical and judicial debates about abortion. One argument suggests that with the legalization of abortion, the sanctity of the fetus has been irreversibly diminished, and to simultaneously obligate women to sobriety is absurd.

The enforcement of sobriety used strong measures in the United States of the late 1980s and 1990s, when pregnant women with known or merely suspected alcohol abuse issues were arrested and jailed under child abuse and endangerment statutes. Warning labels appeared on alcohol containers and harsh public service announcements appeared on **television**, radio and in print **advertising**. None of these reversed the increase in FAS in the United States. (*See also* **Health Effects of Alcohol; Women and Girls Drinking.**)

Further Reading

Golden, Janet. *Message in a Bottle: The Making of Fetal Alcohol Syndrome*. Cambridge, MA: Harvard University Press, 2005.

Gray, R., R. A. S. Mukherjee, and M. Rutter. "Alcohol Consumption during Pregnancy and Its Effects on Neurodevelopment: What Is Known and What Remains Uncertain." *Addiction* 104 (2009): 1270–73.

Ken Kirkwood

FILMS

Films are an extremely powerful medium of communication that can educate, propagandize, entertain, and inspire aesthetic awe. As such, movies are very much cultural artifacts, and their study is based on the idea that movies both influence and are influenced by the cultures that originate them.

Some recent film studies research on alcohol in American culture shows that alcohol is present in virtually all genres of film, even when not central to a movie's narrative or story, which reflects its ubiquitous presence in American society. Furthermore, drinkers of alcoholic beverages are nearly always portrayed positively (except when the purpose of the story specifically is to show misuse of alcohol), and drinking is a widespread cultural activity that is treated positively or neutrally more often than it is treated negatively. Also, though a small subset of movies specifically portrays deleterious effects of alcohol use, by far the greater percentage of movies trivialize, glamorize, or even celebrate alcohol.

Ultimately, the study of American movies reveals a culture that has been and still is deeply conflicted about alcohol and its place in American life.

Cultural History

To understand the deep ambivalence about alcohol that one can see in American movies, it is helpful to understand the source of this ambivalence in American history. Specifically, this history is a struggle between two opposite cultural forces

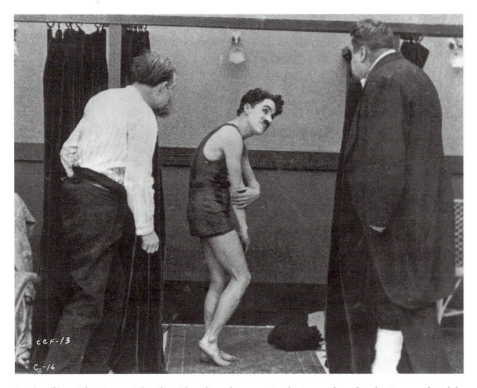

In the film *The Cure*, Charlie Chaplin plays an inebriate who checks in to a health spa to try to stop drinking. He proceeds to wreak havoc. (Photofest)

that have coexisted since the early era of formation of the new republic and that are still evidently in opposition today: a well-established tradition of heavy drinking and the cultural backlash to this tradition that promotes not moderate consumption of alcohol, but complete abstinence from drinking altogether.

Alcohol use has been featured in American life since the colonial era, and by the early nineteenth century, a very hearty and uniquely American drinking tradition was well established, especially on the frontier. The symbol of the "frontier" (defined as a political and geographical region near and beyond a settled region) is particularly salient in American culture and film because westward expansion by explorers and settlers did not have a contemporary equivalent in Europe and so is uniquely American.

Nineteenth-century Americans drank a lot and in distinctive ways. On the frontier, Americans either drank small amounts of cheap corn-based alcohol regularly and throughout the day, usually at home or alone; or they drank publicly and to the point of intoxication in group binges during elections, militia musters, holidays, neighborly get-togethers and other public events. These two characteristic styles of American drinking are well established in contemporary American culture.

In response to the development of this American drinking culture, a seminal sequence of events ensued—the **Temperance** Movement and **Prohibition** (1919), repeal (1933), and the foundation of **Alcoholics Anonymous** (AA, 1935)—all of which defined a characteristically American ambivalence toward alcohol that can be witnessed in American films.

Film History

The U.S. census of 1890 declared the death of the frontier, but the impact of its symbolism endured and became mythologized in popular culture, particularly in the new medium of silent movies and the culturally specific genre of the American Western.

By 1910, the motion picture industry had permanently relocated to southern California from the East Coast; in 1911, the first movie studio was founded; and in 1915, on the eve of Prohibition, the American motion picture industry (Hollywood) produced its first full-length American feature film. Not long thereafter, Charlie Chaplin began his creative projects, many of which featured inebriated behavior for comedic effect (e.g., *The Cure* [1917]).

Movies produced during the early silent era reflect the "dry" values of the national Temperance Movement. Alcohol was portrayed as evil, drinkers and drinking were seen as sinful, and abstinence was equated with happiness. Abuse of alcohol occurred, and either it was not commented upon (because it was not central to the story) or it was central to the story and explained as a moral failure. Examples include D. W. Griffith's *A Drunkard's Reformation* (1909) and *What Drink Did* (1909), both dramas, and Chaplin's *The Cure*, a comedy.

The early sound era of film corresponded with national Prohibition (1919 to 1933). However, an aesthetic change from highly stylized silent movies to more realistic depictions resulted in the production of movies showing "wet" values, contrary to the law of the land. Movies capture and reflect the hypocrisy of social reality, showing drinking by major and minor characters of both genders and all ages and socioeconomic classes—for example, *The Mad Whirl* (1925). If Prohibition was not central to the story, alcohol still appeared in the background of the lives of the characters, as in *The Front Page* (1931). If Prohibition is central to the story, then **speakeasies** are often featured as settings, as in *After Midnight* (1927) and *Our Dancing Daughters* (1928). During this period, the crime genre and film noir emerged, with commentary on the morals of the nation as a result of Prohibition (*Big News* [1929], *Doorway to Hell* [1930], Little Caesar [1931], *The Public Enemy* [1931], *Scarface* [1932]). Alcohol is seen as the source of a lucrative underground business, a form of subversive recreational entertainment, and/or the cause of the downfall of a character. Alcohol abuse was shown, but in a much more gritty and realistic manner than the stylized dramas and light-hearted comedies of the earlier silent era (*The Struggle* [1931] and *What Price Hollywood?* [1932]).

Repeal and the development of Alcoholics Anonymous (AA) coincided, but in this period, Hollywood became newly shackled by the moral guidelines of the 1934 Motion Picture Production Code, which limits its abilities to tell stories directly about the negative effects of alcohol. By way around this restrictive code, Hollywood created a loophole film genre that exploited cultural notions of creative artists as tortured souls who are vulnerable to **alcoholism**. In this period, excessive drunkenness was for the first time taken as the central subject of film, with the possibility for treatment. The AA conception of alcoholism as a "disease" had not yet entered the pictures, nor had the term "alcoholism"; but there was the recognition of an alcohol-related "problem," and its source was the Hollywood studio star system, the industry's own institution for selecting, creating, promoting, and exploiting movie star personas, which had its heyday in the period just after Repeal of Prohibition. Classic movies from this period include *What Price Hollywood?* as well as *A Star Is Born* (1937). Significantly, the characters in these two movies fail to solve their career and alcohol problems, and both fading stars end up committing suicide.

In the classic period of Hollywood, from 1945 to 1962, the classic alcoholism story was born and developed. For the first time in film, excessive drinking was described as "alcoholism," the condition was presented as a "disease" with a corresponding medical vocabulary, and AA was specifically referenced as a viable treatment option. The social locus of the alcoholism problem was no longer restricted to Hollywood stars, and movies began to explore the disease in main characters of both genders; indeed, the narratives were usually presented as heroic struggles toward health. During this period, no fewer than 30 films were made in this vein, many in consultation with AA, commencing with *The Lost Weekend* (1962) and culminating with the iconic *Days of Wine and Roses* (1962). By the end of this period, the problem of the disease of alcoholism plus its attendant AA treatments had become fixed in the popular cultural imagination.

The 1960s and 1970s reorganized and reassessed the cultural narratives of alcohol, drinkers, and drinking in American film. Where the preceding period had developed a singularly consistent portrait of a disease and its cure, this period of reassessment explored other options. This is due in part to the popular rise of **television** and its movie-of-the-week treatment of social problems on the small screen, such as *Sarah T—Portrait of a Teenage Alcoholic* (1975). As well, the feature film began creative explorations of old themes in new genres and new remakes of older movies. For example, in a format that is neither pure comedy nor pure drama, *The Graduate* (1967) shows an alcoholic main character whose problems are not connected directly to alcoholism. In another creative blend of light and dark moods, *M*A*S*H* (1970) shows excessive alcohol use by main characters as unproblematic and merely recreational. In the 1976 remake of *A Star Is Born*, the classic story was re-visioned for a new era. This period also witnessed the new genre of the biography, and in some of these "biopics," the life of a famous alcoholic is portrayed, including *Lady Sings the Blues* (1972) and *W. C. Fields and Me* (1976).

Since the 1980s, Hollywood has continued to explore, refine, and even challenge the main disease and cure story, although the disease became firmly located in a male or female hero who is defined not only as being an alcoholic, but who also has a career and/or is part of a couple or family who share the effects of the disease, as in *Under the Volcano* (1984) and *The Morning After* (1987).

Other developments in the current period include the packaging of drug addiction with alcoholism (*Round Midnight* [1986], *Bright Lights, Big City* [1988], *Vital Signs* [1990]); the continued mention or presence of AA (*Arthur 2: On the Rocks* [1988], *Clean and Sober* [1988], *Hannah and Her Sisters* [1986]); and the development of movies outside the studio system in alternate production channels, notably cable television (*My Name is Bill W.* [1989], *Life of the Party* [2005]).

Genres

In American film studies, there are some genres that lend themselves specifically to the exploration of alcohol use due to settings that strongly feature alcohol. These include film biographies of alcoholic artists (*Lady Sings the Blues* and *W. C. Fields and Me*); Prohibition-era gangster movies (*Little Caesar* [1931] and *Scarface*); film noir detective movies (*The Thin Man* [1934], *The Maltese Falcon* [1941], *Double Indemnity* [1944], *The Big Sleep* [1946]); and Westerns replete with saloons, alcoholic gunfighters, town drunks, and **whiskey** (*Stagecoach* [1939], *High Noon* [1952], *Unforgiven* [1992]).

Further, three versions of the classic alcoholism story now exist as new American film subgenres of the love story. Notably, romantic comedies portray two possible scenarios: alcohol is "bad" but is a source of humor based on broad slapstick (*The Cure*); or alcohol is "neutral," a problem for other people but not necessarily for the person who drinks (*Harvey* [1950], *Arthur* [1981]). In both subgenres, the alcoholic character ends up with the love object (rabbit or human) in spite of the deleterious presence of alcohol in his life.

In melodramatic tragedy, the main character heroically struggles with an alcohol "problem," but the character is not successful by the end of the movie: Alcoholic heroes either try and fail to solve their alcohol problem, in which case they end up separated from or losing their primary love interest; or they do not try to solve their problem at all and end up taking their own lives. The various versions of *A Star Is Born* (1937, 1954, 1976) and Chaplin's *Limelight* (1952) follow this narrative arc.

Finally, in the melodramatic alcoholism genre story of suffering the disease and receiving redemption via the rehabilitative cure, alcoholic heroes struggle for a now-classic Hollywood happy ending—via AA in *8 Million Ways to Die* (1986) and *My Name is Bill W.*; or via alternate treatment as in *The Betty Ford Story* (1987).

Narratives

In American film narratives, alcohol takes on certain values: Positively, alcohol is either a forbidden pleasure, or it is an almost medicinal antidote to a stressful or dull job, relationship, marriage, or life. Negatively, alcohol is an object that problematically stands in the way of happiness in career, love life, marriage, and/or family; and, most significantly, it is a disease that can be treated with effort and possibly even cured.

In American films, drinkers are either the happy drunks of romantic comedy, or they are the tragic and flawed alcoholic heroes of drama and tragedy. Drinking itself is a cultural behavior that exists only in two extreme forms: complete abstinence and teetotalism, or excessive consumption requiring salvation and redemption via government legislation (in the case of Prohibition and repeal) or via an anonymous but democratic mutual aid society of fellow problem drinkers (in the case of AA).

Culturally, Americans define themselves as a people who like to drink a lot but who do not like alcoholics or alcoholism. National debates about drinking therefore tend to read like dualistic morality plays. In American films and American **politics**, there is no apparent middle ground of responsible drinking in moderation; this middle ground exists, to be sure, but it is not celebrated culturally or portrayed cinematically like it is in the national cinemas of France and Italy. (*See also* **Arts.**)

Further Reading

Cornes, Judy. *Alcohol in the Movies, 1898–1962.* Jefferson, NC: McFarland, 2006.

Denzin, Norman K. *Hollywood Shot by Shot: Alcoholism in American Cinema.* Piscataway, NJ: Aldine Transaction, 2007, 2004, 1991.

"Drugs and Alcohol in the Movies." University of California at Berkeley Moffitt Library Media Resources Center. http://www.lib.berkeley.edu/MRC/drugs.html.

McIntosh, William D., Doris G. Bazzini, Stephen M. Smith, and Penny S. Mills. "Alcohol in the Movies: Characteristics of Drinkers and Nondrinkers in Films from 1940 to 1989." *Journal of Applied Social Psychology* 29.6 (June 1999): 1191 (9).

Wedding, Danny. "Alcoholism in the Western Genre: The Portrayal of Alcohol and Alcoholism in the Western Genre." *Journal of Alcohol and Drug Education* 46, no. 2 (Winter 2000): 3–9.

Karen Eilene Saenz

FOOD AND DRINK CULTURE

Alcohol and Structured Meals

In many cultures, alcoholic beverages are considered food from a nutrition perspective, and in other cultures, food and drink are inseparable. This is rarely the case in the United States. Although there are individuals who regularly consume alcoholic beverages, such as **beer** and **wine**, with their meals, it is more common to see people drinking soda or coffee. In the United States, there is little codification and no real social norm that indicates what alcoholic beverages are appropriate at what meals. The exception, perhaps, is breakfast. It is rare to find individuals who consume alcohol at breakfast. Some believe that consuming a drink in the morning after a hard night of drinking, known as the **hair of the dog**, helps cure a **hangover.** Brunch is perhaps an exception to this rule: Bloody Marys and mimosa **cocktails** are frequently consumed with this weekend meal that usually falls somewhere between breakfast and lunch.

Alcohol is generally consumed by adults occasionally at lunch and more frequently along with the evening meal. Alcohol at lunch is often associated with leisure; for example, "ladies who lunch" are well-off women who do not work and can be found lunching and imbibing a glass of wine at noon. There seems to be a general stigma with drinking at lunchtime in the United States these days; it is largely seen as unproductive and decadent, particularly in these economic times. In addition, **workplace drinking** or working while intoxicated is normally heavily reprimanded, particularly in blue- and white-collar jobs.

In restaurants, it is common for people to order cocktails at the beginning of a meal, and this is sometimes accompanied by appetizers or lighter fare. Often people order **beer** or **wine** with their main course; however, it is not unheard of to drink a mixed drink containing hard alcohol with the main course. In some parts of the United States, some people (frequently men) drink **bourbon** or other forms of **whiskey** at a meal. Dessert can be accompanied by a sweet after-dinner drink that can range from Kahlua with coffee to port. The general order of food and drinks outlined here is not extremely codified compared with that of other cultures, and the order of food and drinks can vary wildly.

Drinking wine with meals has a number of connotations. It can demonstrate a certain degree of cultural capital: wine is generally associated with upper-class

Eating and drinking are two important Super Bowl traditions. Americans have developed recipes for special finger foods that go particularly well with beer and are easy to eat while watching the game on television. (Lisafx/Dreamstime)

culture, and displaying knowledge of wine can be a **class** identity marker. How beverages are "read" as an identity marker can often depend on the context. What drinks are chosen in what context can also be a gendered choice. For example, white or rosé wine is often seen as effeminate, particularly if the wine is sweet. Likewise, fruity cocktails may also be associated with female tastes. Whether at a cocktail party or at dinner in a restaurant, gender norms and social expectations can heavily influence what people choose to drink. Douglas (1972) demonstrated that if we look carefully at the ways in which meals are structured, we can see patterns that can reveal a great deal about social relations: hierarchy, inclusion, and boundaries as well as the transgression of these boundaries. The same largely holds true with drinks; however, it is very difficult to find one unified code for eating and drinking in the United States, because of the cultural diversity of the population.

Scholars studying trends in American eating and drinking habits have often focused on specific ethnic or racial groups to discern cultural norms. Many recent immigrants still hold true to their "traditional" eating and drinking norms, whereas ethnic groups may invent their own food-and-drink order based on the availability of abundant food and drink in the United States. Age may also be an important factor in food and eating trends as eating has become increasingly less formal in the United States, with fewer families sitting down to enjoy a meal all together. Research has shown that children in families who eat meals together are less likely to engage in high-risk behavior such as **binge drinking** (Videon and Manning 2003). Many academics believe that part of the problem with Americans' sometimes-dysfunctional drinking habits comes from this divorcing of meals from alcohol culture, in particular, the commensality of family meals. It is believed that "normal" drinking behavior can be learned in these familiar social settings where social norms are controlled and reproduced.

Occasions for Eating and Drinking

Barbecues and picnics are popular American traditions that often involve eating and drinking. At these events, guests will generally bring a dish and something to drink. Sometimes the host will supply both food and drinks. Drinks can vary from beer and wine to cold fruit drinks that can be spiked with alcohol. Picnics and barbecues can be family or community events, and in these cases, the overconsumption of alcohol is generally frowned upon. There is usually as much emphasis on eating and socializing as there is on drinking. Games or **sports** activities might also be included as part of these gatherings.

Sporting events are also occasions when specific food is consumed with specific alcohol. For example, frequently part of the ritual of going to a baseball game is eating a hot dog and drinking beer while sitting in the stands watching the game. American football has a number of elaborate drink and food rituals, including tailgate parties in the parking lot before the game. These parties feature large quantities of beer and snacks. Some people even bring out their barbecues for these pregame occasions. The Super Bowl is the biggest football event of the year, and people often have parties while watching the game. It is common to bring and serve food at Super Bowl parties. Most of the food is finger food, and rarely is there anything that requires utensils to eat. Some popular Super Bowl dishes include clam dip, chili, pulled pork sandwiches, hamburgers, bean dip, and pigs in a blanket. Beer is usually the beverage of choice at these occasions.

Snacks

Alcohol may play only a minor role in structured meals. Most Americans love snacks, and it is not uncommon to find a bowl of peanuts on a bar, elaborate sandwiches at a cocktail party, or cheese served with wine.

Although studies have found that alcohol consumption increases appetite in some drinkers (Veenstra et al. 1993), "Do you skip meals while drinking?" is one of the questions frequently asked when assessing **alcoholism**. Eating something before or during the consumption of alcohol is generally advisable: food can slow the absorption rate of alcohol. This is perhaps one of the reasons why some interesting food traditions have been invented around cocktail culture.

Many **bars** often serve salty snacks such as peanuts or potato chips to make patrons more thirsty. Bars and **pubs** have also developed a whole genre of "pub food." These are usually highly caloric snacks that can be shared. Chicken wings, chips with dip, and potato skins are all examples of typical American bar food. These foods are also served to keep people at bars drinking rather than have customers wander off to restaurants in search of food. At receptions and **cocktail parties**, refined forms of finger food have developed. Again, food is usually offered to keep patrons from getting too inebriated. These events are often held in the early evening and before dinner. Food must also be served to sate the guests' hunger and keep them from leaving early in search of dinner. Common cocktail foods include bite-sized sandwiches, cheese, olives, and *petits fours*. Most importantly, it must be possible to eat these foods with one hand, because most likely the guests will be standing and have a drink in the other hand. For this reason, much of this food is served on toothpicks.

General Trends

Eating while drinking alcohol is quite common in the United States. However, drinking during structured meals seems to be less codified or dictated to by cultural norms than in the past. The individualism that pervades American food choices also seems to shape beverage choices at the table; it is not uncommon for guests at the same table to all choose a different type of drink (alcoholic and nonalcoholic). Many have pointed to this dominance of individual choice as an example of the way in which American commensality has been breaking down since the 1950s. Dining is no longer a shared experience, because each individual eats and drinks something different. Previously, this was most common in restaurants, but now this trend is increasingly frequent in the home—that is, when a family actually eats together at the same time at the same table. Nutritionist and psychologists have warned that this is one of the causes of poor eating habits and antisocial drinking habits. The American dinner table is rarely a place where cultural norms are reproduced these days.

Although eating and drinking culture in the United States is not highly codified, there is a very rich and ethnically varied culture of food and drink. There are many occasions when food and alcohol are inseparable, and Americans have certainly invented their own food and drink traditions that are an important part of social life.

Further Reading

Barr, Andrew. *Drink: A Social History of America*. New York: Carroll & Graf, 1999.

Douglas, Mary. "Deciphering a Meal." *Daedalus* 101, no. 1 (1972): 61–81.

Fulkerson, J., et al. "Family Dinner Meal Frequency and Adolescent Development: Relationships with Developmental Assets and High-Risk Behaviors." *Journal of Adolescent Health* 39, no. 3 (2006): 337–45.

Veenstra, J., et al. "Alcohol Consumption in Relation to Food Intake and Smoking Habits in the Dutch National Food Consumption Survey." *European Journal of Clinical Nutrition* 47 (1993): 482–89.

Videon, Tami M., and Carolyn K. Manning. "Influences on Adolescent Eating Patterns: The Importance of Family Meals." *Journal of Adolescent Health* 32, no. 5 (May 2003): 365–73.

Rachel Black

FREE DRINKS

Free drinks are customarily provided at certain commercial and social events, ostensibly for purposes of promoting increased event attendance. As such, free drinks constitute an apparently complimentary "gift" that creates a social bond between a giver ("host") and a receiver ("guest") with an implied obligation for the guest to reciprocate fairly at some unspecified time in the near future. Because alcoholic drinks are commodities with positive value in a market economy, the free drinks gift exchange is best understood as an example of informal economic reciprocity between parties. In other words, free drinks are not really free.

In a typical exchange, for example, a bar or nightclub ("host") provides free drinks ("gifts") to a patron or class of patrons ("guest"). Superficially, the host appears to be altruistic, benevolent, and sociable; in actuality, the host expects to accrue a return of comparable or greater value in exchange for the free drinks. This accrual may be returned with future sales or profits, which have a tangible fiscal value. Or, the gift may also result in the intangible receipt of "goodwill," defined as a positive attitude of or reputation for kindness, friendliness, or benevolence. Goodwill is valued for its immediate social benefit as well as for an implied potential for fiscal return in the future.

Some common examples of hosts who may provide free drinks or samples primarily for fiscal benefit include **bars** and nightclubs at "Ladies Nights" and similar promotional events; casinos (as "comps" for gamblers); liquor retailers and winery, brewery, and distillery tasting rooms (as "free tastes" for customers); realty firms (as "refreshments" for open-house visitors); and museums and galleries (as "refreshments" for exhibition openings).

Some common examples of hosts who may provide free drinks for social benefit include university groups (at parties for potential recruits), employers (at parties for their employees during the winter holidays), and the bride's family (at traditional American wedding receptions for wedding attendees).

Additionally, free drinks may also constitute a gift in a more generalized reciprocal exchange between two or more guests in a bar or nightclub who are close friends or kin. In these cases, the primary benefit of the exchange is the social closeness earned in the context of social bonding or friendly game playing. Common examples include drink purchase by one guest for another in "buying a round" or "winning a round."

Finally, a form of negative reciprocity may obtain in the practice of "bar betting," wherein a patron aggressively attempts to secure more than his fair share of free drinks via confidence games and tricks. (*See also* **Bar Bets; Drinking Games.**)

Further Reading

Gregory, Christopher A. *Gifts and Commodities*. London: Academic Press, 1982.

Mauss, Marcel. *The Gift: Forms and Functions of Exchange in Archaic Societies*. London: Routledge, 2000.

SmartBar Drink Token Company. "Bar Promotions and Ideas from SmartBar: 18 Bar Promotions with Drink Tokens." http://www.gosmartbar.com.

Karen Eilene Saenz

G

GIN

Gin is a distilled, clear liquor made from grain such as wheat or rye and flavored with juniper berries, thus deriving its name either from the French word, *genievre*, or *jenever* in Dutch. The drink was developed in the seventeenth century by the Dutch physician Franciscus De la Boe, also known as "Sylvius," a professor at the University of Leiden. For centuries, juniper berries were believed to have medicinal qualities, and at one time they were even considered a cure for the bubonic plague. The oil of the berries was also used for stomach ailments and headaches. Sylvius created the alcohol as a remedy for kidney problems, using grain liquor infused with the juniper. Because grain alcohol was quite inexpensive, the nature of the concoction added to its general appeal.

Spreading rapidly through the Low Countries of Holland and Belgium, gin became popular in England as a result of British soldiers who favored the drink. Gin also became known as "Dutch Courage" and was associated with English and Dutch Protestant **politics** that heavily taxed the wines of Catholic France and thus stimulated the import of gin. By the early eighteenth century, consumption of gin in England reached the millions of gallons. Its low cost and easy availability led to an upsurge in public drunkenness, especially among the poor, and in 1736 the English Parliament outlawed the liquor. This ban was reversed in 1742 because the impurity of illegal gin presented grave health concerns. The "Gin Craze" gave rise in the eighteenth century to a number of anonymous poetical pamphlets. These penny publications sold on the streets took pro and con views of gin and social politics. At this same time, artist William Hogarth created his notorious engravings of "**Beer** Street" and "Gin Lane," showing the depraved drunkenness engendered by gin. Gin had a brief revival among the upper classes during the Industrial Revolution but, by the late nineteenth century, was again considered a drink favored by the poor and the unsophisticated.

In 1870, the first manufactured gin in the United States was introduced by the Fleischmann distillery in Cincinnati, Ohio. A few decades later, gin moved from its stature as a lowbrow, working-class drink to social esteem when it began to be used in **cocktails**. Its distinctive clear, dry taste made it compatible with fruit juices, bitters, club soda, or tonic water. The popularity of gin cocktails in the United States surged in the years leading up to **Prohibition,** so much so that illicit "bathtub gin" **distilling** became a cultural facet of the era. Bathtub gin was not distilled as was juniper berry–infused manufactured gin, but rather the grain alcohol and berries were steeped together. The result was particularly unpalatable; the very dry homemade liquor was used in a cocktail that added other flavors. During Prohibition, bathtubs actually were used sometimes to create the gin, thus giving this version its name. However, occasionally wood alcohol, which could cause blindness or death, was substituted for grain alcohol.

There are several classifications of gin, primarily the traditional London Dry Gin; Plymouth Gin, which is aromatic and clear; sweetened gins; and *genever*, this style reaching its greatest expression in Belgium and Holland. Distilled from a malted grain mash, this gin is aged and can be infused with a nearly endless list of ingredients. For example, a noted Antwerp bar offers over 200 varieties of *genever*. In the United States, London Dry Gin is the most popular type for what is the world's largest market for the liquor. The American-manufactured version of this dry gin is also called "soft gin" because it has a lower proof than the English versions. In recent years in the United States, boutique manufacturers of special gins such as Philadelphia's Bluecoat brand have garnered appreciation and growth in the upscale spirits market. Many of these special gins are entered annually in the Great American Distillers Festival as representatives of fine distilling in the United States.

Further Reading

Gately, Iain. *Drink: A Cultural History of Alcohol*. New York: Gotham Books, 2008.

Lender, Mark Edward, and James Kirby Martin. *Drinking in America: A History*. New York: The Free Press, 1987.

Lord Kinross. *The Kindred Spirit: A History of Gin and of the House of Booth*. London: Newman Neame, 1959.

Kevin Grace

H

HAIR OF THE DOG

A term that traces its earliest common usage to sixteenth-century England, "hair of the dog" refers to curing a **hangover** by ingesting additional alcohol in the belief that the result of overindulgence the night before can be tempered. A line recorded from 1546 states, "I pray the leat me and my felow haue a heare of the dog that bote us last night." Subsequently, similar phrases can be found in literature from the seventeenth century to the present, and in everyday discourse in cultures throughout the world. One purported origin of the term dates to ancient Greece, where medical practices used cures derived from the source of the ailment. Thus, in "hair of the dog," references have been discovered of the notion of sympathetic magic that dog bites that result in injury or rabies (hydrophobia) can be cured by placing the hair of the attacking dog in the wound.

In contemporary American culture, expressing the need for some "hair of the dog" is often used either to elicit sympathy from one's companions or is extended in sympathy to someone overtly suffering from the headaches and nausea symptomatic of a hangover. It is often used in jest or in sarcasm. As the body processes alcohol toxins and suffers dehydration, there is some popular belief that fresh consumption of alcohol will temporarily reduce the ill effects of overdrinking, though the additional alcohol would also have to be processed. In studies of Irish drinking culture, for example, the term is also used to indicate a cycle of **alcoholism**. (*See also* **Hangovers**.)

Kevin Grace

HANGOVERS

A hangover is a set of symptoms experienced after heavy alcohol drinking, commonly including thirst, headache, nausea, diarrhea, fatigue, and "the shakes." Emotional effects include remorse and anxiety. The hangover generally begins after a period of sleep and can persist for many hours after alcohol has left the bloodstream. Also known as "veisalgia," the hangover has been subject to numerous clinical studies in recent decades. There is ongoing debate about its exact nature—its relationship to alcohol withdrawal, for example.

Commonly agreed are the impacts of alcohol as a diuretic: dehydration, headache, and dizziness. It is known to irritate the stomach lining, causing nausea, stomachache, and diarrhea. Disturbed sleep has been linked to the overproduction of glutamine, a natural stimulant, to compensate for the inhibition of production while drinking (tremors may also be related to this). Congeners (by-products of drink preparations) may be a significant variable in hangover severity. "Dark" drinks with more congeners, such as brandy, **wine** (especially red), and **whiskey**, are associated with more severe effects, in contrast to "clear" drinks such as **gin** and **vodka**. Research continues into the significance of gender, age, family history, and drinking habits. A minority of people appear to be immune.

Abstention and light drinking are the surest preventatives. Current advice also includes consuming food beforehand (to slow alcohol absorption) and lining the stomach with milk; alternating alcoholic beverages with soft, still drinks, and drinking water before going to sleep. Most cultures have a rich folklore regarding hangovers. Well-known remedies are egg-based combinations (e.g., "prairie oyster"), the fried breakfast, and the alcohol-based **hair of the dog**. Unlike many traditional "cures," eggs have survived some clinical scrutiny. Containing cysteine, they may combat the buildup of acetaldehyde in the liver. Complex carbohydrates are recommended to fight low blood sugar. Central to recovery is drinking water and the passage of time.

Many people will experience hangover at some point, even usually moderate drinkers. This has wide consequences. Lost productivity, annually, from all alcohol-related illness was estimated at $68 billion in the United States in 1998. In England in 2004, the estimated annual cost of alcohol-related absenteeism was £1.8 billion.

This term is fairly recent. The earliest reference to "hang-over" in the *Oxford English Dictionary* is taken from Gideon Wurdz's 1904 *Foolish Dictionary*, though it was already in use in the 1890s. Representations of hangovers abound in popular culture: see, for example, Charles Jackson's novel *The Lost Weekend* (1944), made into the 1945 Billy Wilder movie, and Patrick Hamilton's 1941 novel *Hangover Square* and its 1945 film version. The memory "blackout" sometimes accompanying a hangover is central to *Remember Last Night?* (1935), based on Adam Hobhouse's *The Hangover Murders*, and the 2008 film comedy *The Hangover*. (*See also* **Blackouts**.)

Further Reading

Stephens, R., et al. "A Review of the Literature on the Cognitive Effects of Alcohol Hangover." *Alcohol and Alcoholism* 43 (2008): 163–70.

White, A. M. "What Happened? Alcohol, Memory Blackouts, and the Brain." *Alcohol Research and Health* 27 (2003): 186–96.

Wiese, J. G., et al. "The Alcohol Hangover." *Annals of Internal Medicine* 132 (2000): 897–902.

Vanessa Taylor

HAPPY HOUR

Happy hour can be one singular hour in the day, but is more generally encompasses a few hours spanning the late afternoon into early evening during weekdays. These hours tend to fall between the end of the workday and the beginning of the dinnertime meal. **Bars**, lounges, and restaurants offer specials and reduced prices on drinks to boost business during this often slow period. This time of day has become the socially accepted hour in which to begin drinking alcohol, recalling the popular phrase, "It's 5 o'clock somewhere."

The origin of the phrase "happy hour" may go back as far as the 1700s, when it was used to refer more specifically to an "hour of happiness," or rather, playtime for children. This term was later applied to adults on board American navy ships during World War I to describe a scheduled amount of time for entertainment activities such as boxing and wrestling matches. These activities were usually accompanied by refreshments, most likely alcoholic in nature. The idea of a set time period for relaxation and fun soon spread onshore—ironically, as **Prohibition** bans came into effect. Public restaurants and bars were banned from serving alcohol. Therefore, diners would drink at home or in **speakeasies** (private and illegal bars) in the hours before eating dinner, also known as cocktail hour.

The first printed references of happy hour in regards to reduced prices and drink specials are found in 1950s newspaper advertisements and articles. As the years passed, bargain happy hours naturally gained popularity. In the 1980s, two-thirds of all **beer** consumed was between 4:00 and 8:00 p.m., creating what advertisers for Miller beer called "Miller Time."

As happy hours around the country multiplied in the 1980s, state government officials began to ban them in hopes of curbing **binge drinking, driving under the influence (DUI)** and **underage drinking**. Massachusetts was the first to do so in 1984. As recently as 2008, the Minneapolis city council considered banning drink specials in establishments around the University of Minnesota. In addition, the Iowa City, Iowa, council met the same year to discuss a law to keep drink prices the same at all hours of the day.

Regardless of the backlash of happy hour drinking, it is still thriving all over the country. Hundreds of Web sites display happy hour drink specials and include search engines to find the best happy hour in a specific area. Deals include but are not limited to two-for-one pricing, half-off discounts, and free appetizers. (*See also* **Internet**.)

Further Reading

Babor, Thomas. *Alcohol: Customs and Rituals*. New York: Chelsea House, 1986.

Harsanyi, David. *Nanny State: How Food Fascists, Teetotaling Do-Gooders, Priggish Moralists and Other Boneheaded Bureaucrats Are Turning America into a Nation of Children*. New York: Broadway Books, 2007.

Packer, Matt, Johnny Acton, and Tania Adams. "Happy Hour" In *Origin of Everyday Things*, ed. Johnny Acton, 107. London: Think Publishing, 2006.

Whitney Adams

HEALTH EFFECTS OF ALCOHOL

Alcohol, legal in most societies, is a central nervous system depressant, and its abuse can have extreme consequences on health and society that are often overlooked or ignored. Alcohol abuse can result in such health problems as cirrhosis of the liver, stroke, cancer, **fetal alcohol syndrome**, heart failure, and sexually transmitted diseases, as well as driving accidents, unwanted pregnancy, and violence. The overindulgence in alcohol has been regarded as the origin of many social ills such as increased violence, increased likelihood of legal problems, crime, and increased problems with social relationships. So much so have the social ills been recorded in the United States that **temperance** movements of the nineteenth and early twentieth centuries played on and often exaggerated these ill social affects and occasional tragedies. Such early-twentieth-century social activists as Richmond Pearson Hobson, a leading moral entrepreneur of his day, called alcohol the "great destroyer" and portrayed the need to rid the United States as a battle between good and evil (Faupel et al. 2004). Since the time of the Temperance Movement, alcohol has been considered a major cause of deviant behavior. With the ratification of the Twenty-first Amendment, which repealed **Prohibition** and established a more tolerant social climate toward public drinking and drunkenness, alcohol's abuse triggered more visible disruptive behavior. Recent alcohol control measures, including legislation, education in schools and colleges, and workplace employment programs to increase public safety and order, are based on evidence rather than moral crusades or social outcries for "zero tolerance." The combination of these historical factors and attitudes, the social perception of the ritual of alcohol consumption that characterizes the conditions, social institutions, public institutions, and social environments in many cultures places alcohol consumption—sometimes its overconsumption—at the center of community life. While the effects on social behavior and the possible actions resulting from the impaired judgment that alcohol brings are just as important, the focus here is upon the health effects of prolonged consumption of alcohol on the human body. Most notable are the effects of alcohol on the liver, the digestive tract, and the heart.

The Liver

The liver is most commonly thought of when discussing the effects of long-term alcohol consumption. When alcohol enters the body, it is digested and puts extra pressure on the liver. The liver strains to metabolize alcohol and is often damaged.

Fatty liver is a condition where the liver accumulates fat because of heavy drinking. Common symptoms include dilated peripheral blood vessels, reddening of the palms, tendon contractions of the hands, and parotid gland swelling. Usually more serious than fatty liver is alcoholic hepatitis. Symptoms include fluid in the abdominal cavity, gastrointestinal hemorrhage, and hepatic coma resulting in severe damage of the liver, severely decreasing its functionality. Perhaps the most serious affliction to come from alcohol abuse is cirrhosis of the liver. Part of what makes this disorder so dangerous is that it goes undetected in as many as 40 percent of people who have it. Cirrhosis involves a decrease of total blood flow and restricts it coming out of the liver, which causes portal hypertension.

Digestive Tract

The digestive tract also suffers from long-term alcohol abuse: Much like the liver, prolonged exposure to significant amounts of alcohol affects the natural processes of the stomach and digestive tract. Before consuming alcohol, the body creates a barrier that can mitigate the effects of occasional alcohol consumption. However, after chronic alcohol consumption, much of that barrier appears to be lost, so that systemic effects of alcohol are exacerbated.

The pancreas is also severely affected by alcohol. Heavy alcohol consumption is the main cause of chronic pancreatitis. The abdominal pain caused by this disease is severe and, if chronic, can sometimes be relieved by surgical removal of the pancreas. This condition can result in permanent damage to the pancreas; attacks of pain can recur even if drinking has ceased. In fact, clinical studies suggest that those who abstain from alcohol after an acute attack have a good prognosis and a survival rate of 90 percent.

The Heart

Alcohol abuse has been linked to adverse effects on the cardiovascular system. It has been found to affect the heart muscle itself, producing cardiomyopathy (degeneration of the heart muscle) and cardiac arrhythmias. Chronic alcohol consumption is also associated with a significant increase in hypertension and may play an important role in ischemic heart disease (deficient blood circulation to the heart) and cerebrovascular disorders, including stroke (U.S. Department of Health and Human Services 1990, 117). Along with directly affecting the heart, alcohol use (as well as alcohol withdrawal) has been proven to raise blood pressure up to three times higher than in the general population (Knight and Longmore 1994).

Alcoholic cardiomyopathy is another serious heart condition associated with heavy drinking. The symptoms are commonly chest pain, a proneness to fatigue, abdominal discomfort, swelling from edema, and palpitations and arrhythmias. The condition can prove deadly if the person continues to drink. Concerning coronary heart disease, evidence points to a higher mortality rate among nondrinkers than among those of who drink four or more drinks a day. These findings have started many ethical debates about any possible implication that drinking can help prevent heart disease. While all empirical evidence suggests that a few drinks a day can reduce the risk of coronary disease, the many other risks of frequent alcohol consumption must be taken into account.

Alcohol affects the human body in a wide variety of ways. Because of its chemical makeup, the human body digests and metabolizes it differently, resulting in an increased pressure on different systems such as the liver, digestive tract, and heart. As a result, prolonged consumption of alcohol results in a wide variety of afflictions that damage and, in some cases, destroy these natural systems. Once diagnosed, some of these disorders can be reversed if alcohol consumption ceases immediately, but almost every one causes permanent damage that can significantly lower the lifespan of a person if alcohol is ever consumed again.

Further Reading

Faupel, Charles, Alan Horowitz, and Greg Weaver. *The Sociology of American Drug Use.* Boston: McGraw Hill, 2004.

Knight, Robert G., and Barry E. Longmore. *Clinical Neuropsychology of Alcoholism.* Hove, UK: Lawrence Erlbaum Associates, 1994.

Town, M., T. S. Naimi, A. H. Mokdad, and R. D. Brewer. "Health Care Access among U.S. Adults Who Drink Alcohol Excessively: Missed Opportunities for Prevention." In *Preventing Chronic Disease* (2006). http://www.cdc.gov/alcohol/publications .htm (accessed August 26, 2009).

U.S. Department of Health and Human Services. "Seventh Special Report to the U.S. Congress on Alcohol and Health from the Secretary of Health and Human Services." Washington, DC: U.S. Department of Health and Human Services, 1990.

DeMond Miller and Joel Yelin

HOME-BREW

Home-brew refers to the small-scale production of **beer**, and to a lesser extent **cider**, mead, **wine** or other alcoholic beverages for personal consumption. There are an estimated 1.5 million home-brewers in the United States, and the number is steadily rising. Home-brewing has a long tradition. Indeed, the first beer brewers and winemakers were themselves home-brewers, producing these beverages not for commercial purposes, but for personal consumption and free **distribution** to friends and family. However, it is only in more recent years that the popularity of home-brewing has risen, becoming a subculture throughout the United States.

Home-brewing was the catalyst for the craft beer revolution in the United States, and its rise in popularity in recent years has mirrored the rise in small craft breweries. The craft beer movement began when home-brewers, unsatisfied with the monopoly of homogenous, mass-produced beer, began to open their own breweries. American home-brewing served as a training ground for **microbreweries**, regional craft breweries, and brewpubs throughout the country.

Although home winemaking was legalized after the repeal of **Prohibition**, home-brewing remained outlawed due to a clerical error until 1978 when the restrictions were repealed, giving individual states the capacity to restrict the domestic production of beer. The rise of home-brew culture is often attributed in large part to Charlie Papazian, the author of *The Complete Joy of Home-Brewing* (1984), who founded the Association of Brewers several months after the repeal. Papazian's writings and efforts have helped thousands of Americans get started as home-brewers.

Home-brewers have access to the same raw ingredients as commercial brewers. There are currently more than 1,500 home-brew retailers who supply high-quality specialty grain, hops, and yeast. Local home-brew stores throughout the country and online retailers make possible the production of virtually any beer style on a small scale.

The subculture of home-brewing in the United States consists of a community that shares a common sense of purpose. Home-brewers throughout the country meet through **Internet** forums, home-brew festivals, and clubs, sharing information on **brewing** technique and recipes. Most home-brewers share the desire to educate the general public in an attempt to elevate their image of and appreciate for craft beer. The literature and media surrounding home-brewing are vast; the many radio shows, pod casts, Web sites, and blogs on the Internet provide home-brewers with invaluable information.

There are over 600 home-brew clubs in the country. While most are small, the American Home-Brewers Association (AHA)—a division of the Brewers Association founded in 1978 by Charlie Papazian in Boulder, Colorado—boasts about 25,000 members. Although most home-brewers are avid beer drinkers, they also tend to hold a respect for their craft that goes beyond consumption and that is connected to the greater concerns regarding the integrity of beer.

Further Reading

Palmer, John. *How to Brew: Everything You Need to Know to Brew Beer Right the First Time*. Boulder, CO: Brewers Publications, 2006.
Papazian, Charlie. *The Complete Joy of Home-Brewing*. New York: Avon Books, 1984.

Matthew Russell

HOOCH

Hooch or moonshine, also known as "white lightning" and "mountain dew," is a distilled spirit made from corn. Common to the Appalachian region of the Southern United States, moonshine has been around since colonial times. Folklore traces its origins to the British Isles, and Scottish and Irish immigrants brought this tradition to the American South. The seventeenth- and eighteenth-century method of making liquor from corn using a copper still died out elsewhere in the United States with industrialization, mass manufacturing, and increasing urbanization in the nineteenth century. Yet, the mountains of Appalachia provided a home for moonshine well into the 1960s, when Georgia, Tennessee, North Carolina, and South Carolina revenuers still found operating stills and disabled them, sending their proprietors off to jail for the illegal, unlicensed manufacture and **distribution** of homemade corn **whiskey**.

Those making moonshine might have used a traditional recipe, which required an 80-gallon still, a 60-gallon barrel, a half bushel of malt made from sprouted corn that was

A moonshiner called "John" stirs mash in one of the 300-gallon wooden vats at his still located in the foothills of North Carolina. The still is capable of producing 400 gallons of moonshine every four to five days. (AP/Wide World Photos)

dried and ground into meal, four bushels of corn, and a half bushel of coarsely ground rye (Dabney 1998). These ingredients were scalded, mixed together, and made into a dough, which was allowed to rest for 24 hours. Then, the dough was put into the barrel and covered with water. The natural **fermentation** process took place for 18 days or longer until the cap of foam broke apart, making a mash, the "still **beer**," which was boiled in the still's pot at a high temperature, usually all night until the preferred strength of the drink was achieved. While this process was taking place, the distiller had to be present and alert to oversee the maintenance of a proper temperature and to troubleshoot any problems with the still or with law enforcement.

Moonshine manufacturing was always a cottage industry. Making whiskey from corn or brandy from apples, peaches, cherries, and other local fruits provided a supplemental income for Southern subsistence farmers living in the mountains. With limited arable land and abundant fruit trees, these mountain men made small batches of potent spirits, initially for home use and for medicinal purposes but, when the economy was bad, for sale to strangers. During the Great Depression of the 1930s, for example, a bushel of corn sold at market only commanded a few cents, but that corn made into moonshine produced serious income. In north Georgia, for example, some families openly trace the origin of their wealth, and their immediate ancestor's upward mobility, from dirt farmer to town merchant in the mid-twentieth century to moonshine manufacturing. Illegal profits were channeled into legitimate businesses.

In the antebellum South, these homegrown distillers were respectable members of the community, even when they defied the government's attempts to tax their alcoholic wares. Moonshine was an important commodity in eighteenth- and nineteenth-century field hospitals. It was used before the discovery of anesthesia, to calm patients undergoing surgery and amputations. It also had antiseptic properties for cleaning wounds and provided a boost to the foot soldiers going into battle.

Special jugs for holding this whiskey were created in the north Georgia mountains and in Edisto, South Carolina. Large pottery jars thrown on a potter's wheel, these containers were decorated by hand to resemble distorted human faces with grimacing mouths full of crooked teeth and bulging eyes. Today, they are called *face jugs*, and anthropologists have traced their motifs to West African influences, hybridized with British stoneware pottery. The faces, though, were made to scare children so that they were not tempted to lift these tall jars and take a sip of the strong corn liquor inside.

Moonshine continued in the South for such a long time, past **Prohibition**, due to the fact that local ordinances often made the counties "dry." This term meant that the sale and public consumption of alcoholic beverages were illegal. However, moonshine, an illegal substance, continued, despite these ordinances, and supporters of the ordinances were often fundamentalist Protestants and their **temperance** predecessors. Regarding distribution of moonshine, the mountaineers had their own system in the 1920s and 1930s, with fast cars that were loaded with jugs of homegrown whiskey and sent at dizzying speeds into urban centers, like Atlanta, Georgia. The cars had to be fast to outrun the revenuers, the government tax agents, who were always trying to find the stills and shut them down. Southern folklore attributes the rise of stock car racing, where older cars are retrofitted with larger and faster engines, and its commercial descendant, NASCAR, to moonshine running.

Many local history museums throughout Appalachia have stills in their collections, illustrating the variety of shapes and sizes of the moonshine-making technology. Several examples can be seen at the Georgia Mountains History Center at Brenau University in Gainesville, Georgia, as well as in Franklin County, Virginia. In Franklin County, historic preservationists have documented turnip-shaped boilers, used until the 1930s. That portion of the still was made of hammered and riveted copper sheets into the squat shape of a root vegetable. The blackpot submarine still, used in the 1920s, was made from wooden boards and sheets of steel. It was durable and had a modernist look. Steam stills were larger than their submarine- and turnip-shaped counterparts. Used in the Blue Ridge Mountains of Virginia, the steam stills worked fast and never scorched the mash, because of the position of the flame.

Mountaineers swore that the moonshine from steam stills also had a superior taste than that made in other types of stills. In the mid-twentieth century, some stills were constructed of recycled car parts, including radiators and the sheet metal taken from junked automobiles. Toxicity was a feature of moonshine manufactured in these recycled units. Lead and other heavy metals were a danger, providing fodder for a campaign of public awareness, which finally shut down the moonshine industry in the 1960s.

Further Reading

Burrison, John A. *Brothers in Clay: The Story of Georgia Folk Pottery*. Athens: University of Georgia Press, 2008.

Carr, Jess. *The Second Oldest Profession: An Informal History of Moonshining in America*. Engelwood Cliffs, NJ: Prentice-Hall, 1972.

Dabney, Joseph E. *Mountain Spirits: A Chronicle of Corn Whiskey from King James' Ulster Plantation to America's Appalachians and the Moonshine Life*. New York: Scribner, 1974.

———. *Smokehouse Ham, Spoon Bread, and Scuppernong Wine: The Folklore and Art of Southern Appalachian Cooking*. Nashville: Cumberland House, 1998.

"Moonshine: Blue Ridge Style." Martinsville, VA: Blue Ridge Institute and Museum of Ferrum College, 2009. http://www.blueridgeinstitute.org/moonshine/index.html (accessed April 24, 2010).

Stewart, Bruce E. "Moonshine." In *The New Georgia Encyclopedia*. Athens: University of Georgia Press and the Georgia Humanities Council, 2005. http://www.georgia encyclopedia.org/nge/Article.jsp?id=h-2580 (accessed April 24, 2010).

Pam Sezgin

I

INTERNET

The Internet has revolutionized communications and the sharing of information. The World Wide Web has also had a major impact on the culture of alcohol in America from health knowledge and political campaigns against **driving under the influence** to popular culture and the sale of alcohol.

The Internet has become a powerful tool for groups such as **Mothers Against Drunk Driving (MADD)** and the National Institute on Alcohol Abuse and Alcoholism that try to raise awareness about the dangers of alcohol abuse. Campaigns are easily organized and disseminated online, and fund-raising activities are also facilitated by the Internet. It is easy for anyone to look up data and reports about alcohol consumption and abuse in the United States. This is an important source for alcohol education and awareness.

The Web also contains a lot of popular culture information related to alcohol. One can find the rules to the game of **beer pong** online and read about the game's history and many variations. In addition, some sites offer recipes for **cocktails** and **shooters**. Discussion boards associated with these sites are virtual spaces where drinkers and bartenders can discuss the merits and pitfalls of different drink preparations. Online communities are also places where events and parties that focus on drinking are organized. It is easy to find others who have similar interests in alcohol.

The Internet is giving a voice to amateur **wine** critics to express their views and opinions about wine. This democratization of wine reviewing has the potential to change the shape of not only print media, but also the wine trade as a whole. The power of professional wine critics and writers is slowly being diffused by the presence of thousands of blogging wine enthusiasts who either recommend or pan the bottles of wine they are drinking.

Perhaps the most revolutionary aspect of the Internet when it comes to alcohol in American is the online sale of alcohol. This has been a heavily disputed issue throughout the United States, and Internet sales have serious political and economic repercussions for all parties involved. Each state has been left to decide its own ruling on this topic. At present, 15 states have made reciprocal arrangements for the shipment of wine. Many lawmakers fear that out-of-state shipment of wine undermines individual state authority and taxation. The online sale of alcohol is seen as a conflict with the Twenty-first Amendment that ended Prohibition but gave states the authority to regulate the sale of alcohol. Internet sales make it possible for small wine producers to reach a wider consumer base and give consumers an opportunity to access products outside of mainstream distribution channels. However, it is feared that the shipment of wine will make it possible for minors (under the age of 21) to buy alcoholic beverages. In states where the online sale of alcohol is permitted, this sales segment continues to grow.

Further Reading

Duffy, Daniel. "Internet Alcoholic Beverage Sales." January 14, 2004. http://www.cga.ct.gov/2004/rpt/2004-R-0074.htm.

McCullagh, Declan. "The Uncorking of Online Alcohol Sales." *CNet News*, December 7, 2004. http://news.cnet.com/The-uncorking-of-online-alcohol-sales/2100-1028_3-5479316.html.

Rachel Black

INTERVENTIONS

The term intervention refers to a strategy in which a substance abuser is confronted by those who have been negatively affected by their actions while using alcohol or other drugs. It involves a preplanned dialogue between the alcoholic and the significant people in the addict's life. It also enlists the aid of an interventionist, who is often in the addiction recovery process, to facilitate the course of action. Normally during this confrontation, an ultimatum is given by the assemblage to the abuser to complete treatment, or social support will be withdrawn.

Vernon E. Johnson, founder of the Johnson Institute, a substance abuse treatment program, promoted the intervention, often called the Johnson Method of Intervention, as part of his overall treatment plan. Johnson adopted the disease model approach to substance abuse by seeing **alcoholism** as a disease with similar progressive traits as other medical conditions. Three factors must be accepted in this perspective: (1) addiction is a progressive disease requiring early intervention; (2) the illness is chronic, and the goal is to arrest rather than to cure the user; and (3) the addiction must be seen as primary, with its own distinctive symptomatology. A key component of this symptomatology involves the cognitive distortions that maintain the user's self-destructive behavior.

In spite of the cognitive distortions, often termed "denial" in substance abuse treatment parlance, Johnson believed that no matter how sick, the alcoholic will respond to information that is presented in a form that can be accurately received; in other words, the person need not hit "rock bottom" before seeking treatment. That is the basic tenet of the intervention process in this model. Certain factors will make the intervention process effective: (1) persons meaningful to the addict (such as family members, friends, clergy, and others) must present factual evidence of the negative effects of the addict's behavior due to the influence of alcohol; (2) the complaints presented must be specific rather than vague or general and based on true observations rather than opinion or hearsay; (3) the tone of the discussion should be one of concern and nonjudgmental, and the facts should be clearly presented; (4) the facts should be tied specifically to alcohol-related behavior rather than other personality issues; (5) the complaints should be detailed to confront the alcoholic—video or audio tapes of the drinking behavior will help reinforce this evidence; (6) the user should receive encouragement to become receptive to treatment possibilities; and (7) the user is given a choice to enter a treatment program or to risk a lack of support from the addict's significant others.

The intervention, often dubbed a "tough love" strategy because of its requirement that resources will be withdrawn if treatment is not sought by the alcoholic, has become a part of popular culture and is increasingly seen in **films** and **television** shows. The model has even received its own reality television series, a testament to the interest it has garnered in recent years.

Further Reading

Johnson, Vernon E. *I'll Quit Tomorrow*. New York: Harper and Row Publishers, 1973.
———. *Intervention: How to Help Someone Who Doesn't Want Help*. Minneapolis, MN: Johnson Institute Books, 1986.

Leonard A. Steverson

K

KEGGERS

A kegger is a party that is centered on kegs of **beer** and can often be defined as large in size, wild in nature, and lacking in artifice. It can be considered a proto-typical symbol of the hedonistic culture of the American undergraduate, particularly in fraternities.

The essential feature of the kegger is, of course, the keg of beer. The larger half-barrel kegs—which hold 14 to 16 gallons of beer—are most commonly bought. There is some debate around how many kegs must be present to make a party a true kegger. Conversely, the presence of a keg is not the sole qualifying variable.

Keggers can be simple social mixers. In addition, some keggers can turn into makeshift venues—acting like temporary, unlicensed **bars** where organizers typically charge a small entry fee for admission (or a "cup fee").

These parties also differentiate themselves from other gatherings in that they have their own codes of etiquette and protocol. For example, cutting in line for the keg, hovering excessively around the keg, and giving away fee cups are just a few examples of counter-social behavior. Conversely, other traditions are celebrated—such as the anointing of a "keg master," the person to first tap the keg; the "kicking of the keg," the moment when it is fully consumed; and "the keg toss," the act of hurling an empty keg. (*See also* **College Drinking Culture**.)

Further Reading

Bruce, Dennis. *Party thru College: The Official Party Animal's Guide to College: A Complete Manual on How to Waste Your Student Loans on a 4-year Self-indulgent Journey to Nowhere.* Philadelphia: Venture House Press, 2009.

Ben Applebaum and Michael P. Ferrari

KOSHER WINE

Kosher **wine** meets the religious dietary requirements for Jews who keep kosher. Kosher wine plays a pivotal role in many aspects of Judaism and Jewish culture, such as during the ceremonies related to the Sabbath, Festivals (Passover), and life-cycle events. Indeed, there is a special blessing within Judaism recited before the consumption of wine. Historically, kosher wine was also used in the First and Second Temples of Jerusalem during the Biblical period. Wines produced by non-Jews were not considered appropriate for use in the Temple during the Biblical period, which created a tradition of standards as to how wine should be produced and handled in order to be kosher. An additional essential element of these standards is that kosher wine be physically made by Sabbath-observing Jews. Other grape-based beverages, such as grape juice, brandy, and cognac, are also considered to be as sacred within Judaism as wine and, therefore, must be made according to the same standards. In contrast, **beer** and hard liquor do not have the special status within Judaism.

All species of grape can be used for producing kosher wine. In colder climates, such as in Eastern Europe, Jews often made wine from raisins because fresh grapes were unavailable. Kosher raisin wine follows a similar production process as regular kosher wine. After the grapes are harvested, they are brought to the winery for

During the Passover Seder, four cups of wine are consumed at various points in the meal. Each cup represents one of the four deliverances promised by God. Of course, the wine must be kosher. (Papabear/Dreamstime.com)

pressing, and it is from this point forward until the final bottling of the wine that Sabbath-observant Jews must be involved in the production of the wine and its supervision in order to be considered kosher. The Sabbath-observant Jew involved with this process is called a *mashgiach*. If the winery is a facility not exclusively devoted to the production of kosher wine, the mashgiach will clean and sterilize the equipment in a process known as *kashering*. Contrary to some popular beliefs, a rabbi does not hover above the wine and bless it to make it kosher. After the pressing of the grapes for juice, sometimes the juice is pasteurized for a special kind of kosher wine called *mevushal*. Mevushal kosher wine may be handled by a non-Jew and still be considered kosher. Many kosher wine connoisseurs believe that the mevushal process affects the flavor of the wine, with some preferring it. When sold in the store, kosher wine is almost always denoted as either being mevushal or non-mevushal on the label. If the label does not state either way, the wine is presumed to be non-mevushal. Often non-kosher winemakers will use animal-based gelatin to clarify the wine. Regular animal-based gelatin is not kosher (it would have to come from a kosher animal slaughtered in the kosher way), so kosher wine does not use this process. Kosher wine is therefore always vegan. Kosher wine that does not use grapes, such as fruit wines, have a different set of rules and, within the religious-cultural framework of Judaism, are considered to be in the same non-special category as beer and liquor.

Kosher wines are made all over the world, including Israel, the United States, France, Italy, Spain, Portugal, Australia, Argentina, Chile, and South Africa. The most significant states for the production of kosher wine in the United States are California and New York, where there are wineries and vineyards exclusively devoted to the production of kosher wine. Wineries in other states, such as Michigan, have been known to have had special runs on kosher wine in the past. During American **Prohibition** (1920–1933), some wineries and vineyards survived the period by producing kosher wine, since it fell under the exemption of sacramental wine protected by freedom of religious expression. Traditionally in the United States, kosher wine was considered to be very sweet and very red. This changed during the twentieth century to not only include white and dry wines, but all sorts of varieties including Chardonnay, Cabernet, Merlot, Syrah, and Riesling, as well as specialty wines like port, sherry, marsala, and **champagne**. Due to popular demand, certified organic kosher wine is also available. In recent years, kosher wines have won awards at significant competitions, such as the World Wine Championships. Despite its reputation in the United States of being very red and sweet, such as those produced by the popular Manischewitz and Mogen David brands, what makes a wine kosher is the way it is made according to Jewish dietary laws. In respect to taste and varieties, kosher wine is no different from any other wine. (*See also* **Religion**.)

Further Reading

The Grapevine: Kosher Wines and Spirits. London: The Grapevine, 2007.

Rosenberg, Maurie. *L'chaim: User's Guide to Kosher Wines 1.0.* Charleston, SC: BookSurge, 2006.

Barry Stiefel

L

LAST CALL

In response to liquor laws, "last call" has become ubiquitous in public establishments throughout the world as an announcement that final alcohol orders must be placed before closing time. It is commonly regarded as the final legal chance to drink for the evening or for an event, though drinkers may often buy package liquor or **beer** in businesses where no on-site drinking is permitted. In British **pubs**, the phrase is often "last orders." The manner in which "last call" is announced varies according to local and individual custom. For instance, in some **bars** or pubs, the owner or bartender may just announce it in a loud voice, while in others the house lights may be flashed, or a loud bell may be rung. The time of "last call" is determined by applicable legal statutes for the locality, and is aimed at reducing alcohol abuse and crime resulting from overconsumption.

"Last call" has also entered the everyday lexicon as indicating the final chance to do something. In recent years, the practice has become part of sporting events, particularly in the United States where alcohol at baseball games cannot be purchased after the seventh inning of play, or in basketball games after the third quarter of play. Again, the intent is to minimize potential problems as well as liability on the part of vendors or concession managers. A popular phrase in the United States has arisen in conjunction with "last call," that is, "You don't have to go home, but you can't stay here."

Kevin Grace

LIQUOR BOARDS

Liquor boards are public entities that control the import, wholesale, and/or retail sale of alcohol—mainly **wine** and spirits—throughout a given jurisdiction. Eighteen U.S. states and all Canadian provinces and territories, with the exception of Alberta, rely on such a monopolistic system. Other jurisdictions rely on a liquor commission to regulate the trade of alcohol on their territories.

Created in 1921, the first liquor board in North America was the Commission des liqueurs du Québec, the ancestor of today's alcohol monopoly in Quebec, the Société des alcools du Québec. At the time, Quebec was the only territory that did not prohibit the sale of alcohol. To justify the creation of its liquor commission, the Quebec government argued that it was better to control alcohol sales and derive fiscal revenue from them, rather than leaving them in the hands of organized crime.

The fiscal argument remains central for states and provinces that maintain the liquor boards to this day. Conversely, critics of the liquor boards complain vigorously that the use of alcohol sales by governments as an important source of revenue causes prices to be unnecessarily high, while also limiting consumer choice.

The origin of state liquor boards is found in the Twenty-first Amendment to the U.S. Constitution, ratified in December 1933. While the amendment repealed **Prohibition** at the national level, it also stated that "the transportation or importation into any State, Territory, or possession of the United States for delivery or use therein of intoxicating liquors, in violation of the laws thereof, is hereby prohibited." This essentially gave states complete control over alcohol and resulted in a remarkably complex legal framework, varying from state to state in many respects. The sale of **beer**, wine, and spirits can, for example, take place through a single or two or three different channels, in public or private outlets, depending on local laws. While all of the states that have liquor boards act as sole wholesalers of distilled spirits, only Alabama, Idaho, New Hampshire, Oregon, North Carolina, Pennsylvania, Virginia, Washington, and Utah sell wines and spirits in state-controlled retail stores.

In recent years, liquor monopolies in the United States have come under increasing challenge, especially with regards to sales of wine. In a 2005 decision (*Granholm v. Heald*), the Supreme Court ruled that laws that allowed a state's wineries to ship directly to consumers within the state, while prohibiting wineries in other states to do so, were unduly limiting interstate commerce and thereby unconstitutional. This has led to an opening up of interstate wine-shipping laws, although conditions governing these sales still can vary. With modern transportation, the lack of control along state or provincial borders also makes it difficult, if not impossible, to prevent customers from driving to another jurisdiction to purchase alcohol. So while liquor boards retain a large amount of control over alcohol sales, the system is by no means watertight.

Rémy Charest

LIQUOR LICENSES

Liquor licenses are permits authorizing the retail sale of alcohol by a private business, whether a store, a restaurant, or a bar. Their administration is derived from the same post-**Prohibition** legal framework that oversees the sale of alcohol as a controlled substance and that led to the creation of **liquor boards**. Although states have the authority in this matter, municipalities also play a role in some jurisdictions, adding their own regulations to the state laws. Licenses are granted according to requirements of public safety and public interest. This means that obtaining a liquor license is linked to the applicant's legal standing and reputation and their anticipated capacity to respect the conditions of the license and respect all laws and by-laws, from hours of operations to the sale of alcohol to minors, fiscal laws, and the criminal code. In theory, this control is supposed to keep alcohol sales out of the hands of criminals, and especially of organized crime. However, police operations routinely lead to the revocation of liquor licenses, especially of **bars** and adult entertainment businesses, because of criminal activities such as prostitution and drug sales, showing a difficulty in severing the connection between alcohol and other less reputable dealings. Because liquor licenses are granted in limited numbers, they can be very lucrative business tools and thereby become highly valuable commodities themselves. Numerous consultants and firms specialize in helping businesses buy or sell liquor licenses, which demonstrates the amount of legal complication related to the licenses, as well as their commercial value.

Rémy Charest

LIQUOR STORES

A liquor store is a retail establishment where alcohol is sold by the bottle to individual customers of legal drinking age, to be consumed in another location—as opposed to **bars**, for example, where drinking is expected to take place on the premises. The types of alcoholic beverages sold in liquor stores vary according to the particular jurisdiction where they are located. Distilled spirits are always part of the list, although **wine** may also be included and, to a lesser degree, **beer**. The nature of the beverages sold in liquor stores of a state or province is directly related to what is allowed to be sold in other outlets, like supermarkets or convenience stores. Although liquor stores of one sort of another exist practically everywhere around the world, they are part of a regulated system in just about every part of Canada and the United States. In the states and provinces where a state monopoly is in effect, distilled spirits and, to a lesser degree, other alcoholic beverages are sold through state-owned liquor stores or private stores holding a state-delivered liquor license. In popular culture, liquor stores may hold as much of a place as a crime scene than as a commercial outlet, as liquor store robberies take place at a remarkably high rate in crime **literature**, **films**, or **television** shows. (*See also* **Liquor Boards; Liquor Licenses.**)

Rémy Charest

LITERATURE

Historically, writers have discussed alcohol in medical and spiritual terms as well as in more everyday social contexts. Given the large role alcohol has played in Western culture, it is unsurprising that the subject often comes up in literature. Writers have mentioned drinks and drinking in numerous ways. Alcohol appears as a muse, a devil, a simple beverage, and everything in between. In addition to appearing in literature, alcohol has had a dramatic effect on the production of American literature. On the one hand, the impact of the **Temperance** Movement and **Prohibition** on American culture was often expressed in popular culture. On the other hand, alcohol has influenced many of America's greatest authors rather directly.

Alcohol makes for an extraordinarily versatile literary device. Alcohol, not only as a subject but as a storytelling tool, has been used across genres, in fiction and nonfiction, entertainment, high art, and argumentative prose. Alcohol is the defining feature of many stock characters in the canon of American literature. Bootleggers and drunks consistently appear alongside authorities that restrain them or communities that idolize them. Alcohol can convey wisdom or forgetfulness, masculinity or reckless abuse of power. It may be formal or informal, the **wine** in a sacred religious ritual or a can of cheap **beer**. American writers have praised alcohol, condemned it, derived inspiration from it, and died from abusing it.

Before 1800

The great writers who numbered among the founding fathers of the American Revolution discussed alcohol in writing both as a practical political matter and as a cultural feature of the new American republic. John Hancock made a sizable fortune from smuggling goods, particularly liquor, and smuggling was a

Drink played an important role in the life and literature of the prominent American writer Ernest Hemingway. (Library of Congress)

profitable response to British taxes on products such as Caribbean **rum**. Ben Franklin is quoted as saying that "God himself made beer so we can be happy." However, many notable early American writers disapproved of drinking. Spiritual revivals in the 1700s led to the creation of literature that was either directly spiritual or allegorical. These writers and preachers, such as the fiery Jonathan Edwards and Cotton Mather, denounced the grievous sins associated with drinking. From these and many early temperance writers comes the phrase "demon rum," referring to the spirit most common in colonial times because of the sugar plantations of the Caribbean.

1800s

Literature from the 1800s is filled with references to liquor and authors who tasted their fair share. Washington Irving's story of Rip van Winkle features a colonial sailor of Dutch descent who drinks liquor offered to him by the ghosts of his former shipmates. After he drinks, he sleeps for so long he misses the American Revolution. Rough-and-tumble stories of the American frontier also mentioned alcohol in various contexts as either a welcome drink or a motivator of wild and dangerous behavior.

American literature often followed European trends, which had cultural validity in the United States. Charles Dickens's London had its American equivalents as the culture of drinking pervaded major cities, either celebrated as part of a lively popular culture or denounced as a source of urban poverty. Popular literature associated alcohol with various stereotypes. The general town drunk was a popular stock character. Pap Finn, father of Huck in Mark Twain's *The Adventures of Huckleberry Finn*, is a particularly strong example. A variation on the character is the wise old man found in the tavern or on the frontier with sage words and a full bottle.

Ethnic stereotypes in the 1800s included racist depictions of nonwhites. These images characterized **Native Americans** and **African Americans** as prone to drink and to succumb to wild, drunken behavior. Irish and German immigrants were also depicted as habitual drunks. This stemmed from a combination of anti-immigration sentiment, the actual role of alcohol in these cultures, and the Protestant stereotype of Catholics as excessive drinkers.

Another aspect of American literature similar to trends in Europe is the depiction of vivid and surreal scenes influenced by intoxication. Wine and liquor were trumpeted for their inspirational value, empowering the drinker to stretch his mind and achieve greater creativity. **Absinthe**, surrounded by many legends, was one such drink. While absinthe, the green fairy, has its own special place in literature and popular culture in general, its actual role in the creative process is debatable. Recent tests have shown that the chemical in absinthe that causes hallucinations does not actually survive the distillation process in any significant amount. Closer inspection of drinking practices suggests an alternate explanation for absinthe's allure: it was often consumed with laudanum, an alcoholic medication containing opium and a touch of morphine. While absinthe is most often considered part of a Bohemian subculture in nineteenth-century Europe, this culture impacted the United States as well. In particular, Bourbon Street in New Orleans features a historic landmark, The Old Absinthe House, which opened in 1874 and currently houses a museum dedicated to the absinthe phenomena in the United States and famous visitors such as Oscar Wilde, Mark Twain, and Franklin D. Roosevelt.

The American poet Edgar Allan Poe is known for his stories of mystery and macabre scenes. However, he also mentions alcohol often, and it plays a significant role in his story "The Cask of Amontillado." In this story, a habitual wine drinker is tricked into a cavern full of wine barrels with the promise of fine wine, then chained and trapped by a wall the murderer builds while his victim recovers from drink. Poe himself is an excellent example of alcohol's influence on American writers as well as the stern proclamations of the Temperance Movement. Poe died in a Baltimore street following a night of strong drinking at a political rally. He was one of the first and most famous authors whose alcohol abuse became part of his legend.

Numerous other American writers are closely associated with alcohol because of their own drinking or the way they wrote about alcohol. For many writers, including Mark Twain and William Faulkner, alcohol was closely related to the culture they grew up in and were trying to depict. **Alcoholism** was a common problem for Faulkner's characters in a manner that has become archetypical in depictions of the American South. Later, in the twentieth century, the drinking habits of the Old South and Wild West were used in pulp fiction and the Western genre of literature and film to identify tough guys and bad guys. In these characterizations, strong protagonists consume stout drinks without losing their composure, while cruel villains drink excessively, leading to wild behavior and often their demise at the hands of the sober hero.

Twentieth Century to the Present

In the twentieth century, alcohol's role in literature has taken several turns. Prohibition created a subculture of illegal drinking and popular literature. Prohibitionist pamphlets and moralist stories have literary value in their own right; however, Prohibition also produced modern American detective and gangster stories. These works described a seedy criminal underground fueled by illegal alcohol. They also reflected the ambivalence of many Americans to the prohibition experiment. Archetypes in these genres include clean and sober or morally corrupt policemen, shining knights of law enforcement or participants in the illegal liquor trade. Villains were bootlegging gangster businessmen, inspired by men like Al Capone, or ruthless gun-toting enforcers. In the middle of it all stood morally ambivalent protagonists, fighting the cruel excesses of crime but not averse to a drink. Like much of the American public, these people were caught in the middle.

In the early twentieth century, the pressures of a modernizing economy and the terror of World War I contributed to uncertainty in European and American society. After the war, a number of American writers and artists stayed in or moved to Europe, particularly Paris, participating in postwar political upheaval and artistic development. This "Lost Generation" of writers included Ernest Hemingway, F. Scott Fitzgerald, Ezra Pound, and John Steinbeck. These authors focused on many of the hypocrisies, paradoxes, and sad realities of modern life. Many of their characters turned to drink from desperation or as a means of escape. In many cases, life imitated art. Fitzgerald and Hemingway in particular were notorious alcoholics. Fitzgerald's characters often dealt with the inability of wealth to secure happiness and with the depressing artificiality of high society. His Jay Gatsby supposedly made his fortune as a bootlegger. Hemingway's contributions are wide ranging and deep, from the horror of war to the death frenzy of Spanish bullfights.

The simple rituals of alcohol consumption are a common feature in twentieth-century writing after the repeal of Prohibition. The neighborhood bar, the evening glass of wine, and the strong drink after a hard day's work are all staples of modern fiction. Alcohol has also been part of literature's commentary on modern capitalist society. Heavy drinking was part of the counterculture, though drugs and politics receive most of the attention. Meanwhile, social commentary in American literature lamented the alcoholism of the working class while condemning the extravagance of capitalists and the superrich who are caricatured drinking **champagne**, martinis at business lunches, and brands of liquor made expensive solely by being fashionable, thus playing a part in the construction of stereotypes and social norms.

Another aspect of alcohol in literature is its association with sensuality and sex. Romance novels, an often disdained but well-selling genre, use this convention to great effect with their overwrought prose. However, alcohol has been used to convey sophistication, poise, elegance, and even adds a risqué touch. This style is appealing, and historically, it evokes a time when women engaging in vices such as drinking and smoking in public was taboo and considered a sign of the decadence of modern cities or the roughness of rural communities.

Recent decades have seen alcohol lose much of its controversial taboo status. Many writers have taken a more introspective approach to the subject, showing the dangers of alcoholism without the reforming drive of prohibitionists. Hearkening back to the Lost Generation, American authors from the popular fiction of John

"Here's to alcohol, the rose colored glasses of life."

—F. Scott Fitzgerald, *The Beautiful and the Damned*, 1922.

"Our national drug is alcohol. We tend to regard the use of any other drug as a special horror."

—William S. Burroughs, *Naked Lunch*, 1959.

"Drinking is an emotional thing. It joggles you out of the standardism of everyday life, out of everything being the same. It yanks you out of your body and your mind and throws you against the wall. I have the feeling that drinking is a form of suicide where you're allowed to return to life and begin all over the next day. It's like killing yourself, and then you're reborn. I guess I've lived about ten or fifteen thousand lives now."

—Charles Bukowski, *London Magazine*, December 1974–January 1975

"I hate to advocate drugs, alcohol, violence or insanity to anyone, but they've worked for me."

—Hunter S. Thompson, *Life*, January 1981.

"There is a terrible sameness to the euphoria of alcohol and the euphoria of metaphor."

—John Cheever, personal letters

Grisham to the complex literature of Phillip Roth continue to examine troubled personalities who turn to alcohol for relief. Hunter S. Thompson's books are filled with men and women trapped in unsatisfying or unstable lives, resorting to substance abuse. And, despite the images of drug use Thompson was known for, alcohol is often the vice of choice. American writers are not necessarily alcoholics, but they have a definite grasp of alcohol's role in American culture. (*See also* **Arts.**)

Further Reading

Gately, Iain. *Drink: A Cultural History of Alcohol*. New York: Gotham, 2008.

Gilmore, Thomas B. *Equivocal Spirits: Alcoholism and Drinking in 20th Century Literature*. Chapel Hill: University of North Carolina Press, 1987.

Lender, Mark Edward. *Drinking in America: A History*. New York: The Free Press, 1987.

Pegram, Thomas D. *Battling Demon Rum: The Struggle for a Dry America, 1800–1933*. Chicago: Ivan R. Dee, 1999.

Rorabaugh, W. J. *The Alcoholic Republic: An American Tradition*. New York: Oxford University Press, 1979.

Michael Lejman

M

MADEIRA

Often called the "American **wine**," Madeira is a fortified wine produced on the island of Madeira. This island, a Portuguese possession, is 625 miles from the coast of Portugal in the Atlantic Ocean, an important stopping point for ships crossing the Atlantic or heading to Africa from the seventeenth to the twentieth century.

One of the most resilient and long-lasting wines in the world, Madeira is called *vinho da roda* (wine that travels). Early on in the production and export of this wine in the second half of the seventeenth century, it was noted that this wine improved on the return voyage from Africa. Like port, Madeira wine did not start off fortified. Alcohol from distilled cane sugar was added to stabilize the wine for shipping. Not only were Madeira wines fortified to help them endure long sea voyages, they were heated during shipping, causing oxidation. The process of heating the wine gave these wines even greater endurance. This heating process, *estufagem*, is still used in modern Madeira-making practices.

In the seventeenth century, the initial Atlantic colonies in North America became an important market for Madeira (Robinson 2006). By the eighteenth century, the American colonies were buying a quarter of all the wine produced on the island of Madeira. Initially it was not possible to grow grapes that would produce quality wine in America, and wine had to be imported. Therefore, wines such as Madeira were precious and expensive in the colonies. Madeira became an important status marker—only the rich and influential could afford to buy this luxury import.

Madeira has an important place in American history; in 1776 it was the wine used to toast the Declaration of Independence.

Further Reading

Hancock, David. *Oceans of Wine: Madeira and the Emergence of American Trade and Taste*. New Haven, CT: Yale University Press, 2009.

Robinson, Jancis, ed. "Madeira." *The Oxford Companion to Wine*. 3rd ed., 416–19. Oxford: Oxford University Press, 2006.

Tuten, James. "Liquid Assets: Madeira Wine and Cultural Capital among Lowcountry Planters, 1735–1900." *American Nineteenth-Century History* 6, no, 2 (June 2005): 173–88.

Rachel Black

MARDI GRAS

Mardi Gras (French for "Fat Tuesday") is the day before Ash Wednesday and is often used as synecdoche to refer to the entire season of Carnival (from Twelfth Night, January 6, until Ash Wednesday), or especially to the last weeks of Carnival, when the majority of the season's parades and events in New Orleans are scheduled. Though the first Mardi Gras celebration in the United States was held by the French settlers of Mobile, Alabama, in the early eighteenth century, and the season is observed in a variety of forms throughout the Catholic world, in the United States, the day is virtually synonymous with New Orleans.

Louisiana in general and New Orleans specifically are neither as overwhelmingly French nor as overwhelmingly Catholic as the average American thinks; even before Katrina, French Americans made up less than a fifth of the population, and Catholics about a third of it. But the city's French-Catholic self-image has been as important a part of its identity for the newcomers who, after two centuries of American possession and interstate migrations, have diluted the settlers' demographics as for the nth-generational descendants of those settlers. Just as the city has developed under a complex variety of influences, Mardi Gras itself has become a French-Catholic celebration of neither Frenchness nor Catholicism.

Bourbon Street is the center of the New Orleans Mardi Gras. Bars line this famous street, and it is not uncommon for those joining the crowded street party to ask for their drinks to go. (iStockPhoto.com)

Louisiana has long stood out from the rest of the United States when it comes to its drinking culture. One of the last states to raise the drinking age to 21, it lowered it to 18 twice while legal mechanics worked themselves out. There are a number of exceptions to that drinking age: though minors cannot purchase alcohol, they are permitted to consume it at home or in the presence and with the consent of a parent or legal-age spouse. This is typically ascribed to the state's French heritage, and the practice of teenagers drinking **wine** at dinner with their parents. Though they may not drink without the presence of a parent, 18-year-olds are legally allowed in **bars**—many visiting college students do not realize this and tend not to be informed when bribing a bouncer for entrance, with a folded-up bill or a lifted-up shirt. Twenty-four-hour bars are common in Orleans and Jefferson parishes and are virtually the default in tourist areas.

Furthermore, Louisiana has no open container laws, and the city of New Orleans (among others) explicitly allows open plastic containers, which has led to two unique local traditions: the drive-through daiquiri shop, which serves dozens of flavors of alcoholic frozen slushes in plastic cups and gallon jugs; and the go-cup, a plastic cup to pour one's drink into as one leaves the bar. Naturally, particularly around Mardi Gras when the "population" swells to twice its off-season size, a number of marked-up commemorative and collectible go-cups are available. Plastic cups are also among the common throws at parades.

New Orleans is also the birthplace of the Sazerac and the Ramos **gin** fizz, two old and revered **cocktails** much loved by the cocktail revivalists, and is home to the annual Tales of the Cocktail convention, held at the end of the summer and celebrating in many ways the opposite of Mardi Gras's drinking culture, with an emphasis on well-made cocktails and recreations of traditional ingredients, rather than plastic cups of **beer** and frozen concoctions. For years, when **absinthe** was not legally available in the United States, New Orleans was rumored to be a place where it flowed freely. In most cases, tourists being served the forbidden green fairy were actually given Herbsaint, a locally made Pastis.

Though it is the city's principal tourist attraction, Mardi Gras is simultaneously a celebration of deeply local concern. There are both public and private activities conducted to celebrate Carnival. While many krewes (social clubs) parade in public, with elaborate floats following particular themes, and in some cases celebrity involvement (the Krewe of Bacchus in particular appoints a celebrity king every year, with recent kings including Val Kilmer, Hulk Hogan, James Gandolfini, and Michael Keaton), other krewes eschew parades and hold private balls, typically attended by members of old New Orleans families, with few if any outsiders. Notable non-parading krewes include the Twelfth Night Revelers, whose ball signifies the commencement of the season, and the High Priests of Mithras. The most famous parading krewes are Rex and the Zulu Social Aid and Pleasure Club, both of which arrive in the French Quarter ceremonially by boat on Lundi Gras (the day before Mardi Gras) and hold their parades the following day. Rex is an old krewe, still using nineteenth-century wagons as the basis for its floats, and has held more parades than any other krewe. The annually chosen monarch of the krewe, Rex himself, is always a prominent member of the local community, while his consort the Queen of Carnival is chosen from among the season's debutantes. Rex and the Queen are selected during the previous spring, and keep their identities secret until Lundi Gras.

Zulu's traditions are a combination of irreverence toward Rex and the other formal krewes of upper-class New Orleanians (from which blacks were originally excluded) and Mardi Gras's unique ethnically charged identity play. Carnival revolves around masks to a great degree; masked parades and masked balls. Zulu dresses its members in heavy blackface (despite most of its members being black), with stereotypical African garb-like grass skirts. This has caused controversy over the years, but there was always a design to it: as Rex is about pomp and circumstance, Zulu mocks it, by holding its parade on the same day, crowning its own monarch, and intentionally acting like a group of savages putting on airs.

A similar tradition that makes some nonlocals uncomfortable is that of the Mardi Gras Indians—a group (not a krewe) of blacks dressed as Native Americans in elaborate ceremonial apparel. The Mardi Gras Indians are organized into nearly 40 tribes, and parade for Saint Joseph's Day as well as Mardi Gras. The origin of the Indians is not clear, though they date from the middle of the nineteenth century or earlier, and seem to represent either a fascination with Indian culture and dress, or an affinity blacks may have felt with the area's other minority. Sugar Boy Crawford's 1953 song "Jock a Mo"—better known as "Iko Iko"—is about the ritual parade "fight" between two tribes of Mardi Gras Indians.

What makes New Orleans Mardi Gras parades different from parades in most American cities is the throws. Every krewe spends a large amount of money on buckets of strings of beads, doubloons (custom-made aluminum or wooden coins), plastic cups, Moon Pies, stuffed toys, and other things to be thrown from the floats into the crowd, and "Throw me something, mister!" has become a phrase as associated with the season as the French "*Laissez les bon temps rouler*" (Let the good times roll). This is a practice that goes back to the nineteenth century; since the 1990s, more and more unusual throws have been used, often unique to each krewe.

The city's reputation for revelry expands to include outright decadence during Carnival, but toplessness and extreme drunkenness are tolerated only in the French Quarter—where female flashers typically congregate on balconies, since the crowds are too thick at street level—and to a lesser degree along certain portions of the parade routes. For many locals, the holiday remains a family holiday, attended by children of all ages; this is especially true outside the city itself, where the ambient level of drunkenness is likely to be more comparable to the Fourth of July or New Years Eve than to the **binge drinking** that characterizes the French Quarter at the heart of Carnival. (*See* **Drinking Age Legislation; Race and Ethnicity.**)

Further Reading

Gill, James. *Lords of Misrule: Mardi Gras and the Politics of Race in New Orleans.* Oxford: University Press of Mississippi, 1997.

Starr, S. Frederick, ed. *Inventing New Orleans: Writings of Lafcadio Hearn.* Oxford: University Press of Mississippi, 2001.

Sublette, Ned. *The World That Made New Orleans: From Spanish Silver to Congo Square.* Chicago: Lawrence Hill Books, 2008.

Tallant, Robert. *Mardi Gras as It Was.* New York: Pelican Publishing, 1989.

Bill Kte'pi

MARTINIS

The martini is an iconic American cocktail. Its standard ingredients are **gin** and dry vermouth with an olive, lemon twist, or onion, served ice-cold. There are numerous variations, chiefly the **vodka** martini. It is distinct from the Italian vermouth martini. Possibly originating as the "Martinez," martini has at least two rival creation stories. The first involves a cocktail invented by Jerry Thomas (barman and author) at a San Francisco bar in 1862, served to a traveler on his way to Martinez, California. The second is set in Martinez itself, about 1870, the drinker being a traveling gold miner. The earliest known Martinez recipe appeared in O. H. Byron's 1884 *Modern Bartender's Guide* (gin and Italian vermouth, curaçao, Angostura bitters). The name "martini" appeared in print in 1888.

The nineteenth-century martini was comparatively sweet, containing "Old Tom" gin, sweet Italian vermouth, and, sometimes, syrup. It became drier in the 1890s, using dry gin and French vermouth. Orange bitters were often included, up to the 1950s. The drink was an established cocktail by 1919 and flourished during **Prohibition**. It is closely associated with the style and popular culture of the 1930s, and was prominent in films of this period; often cited is *The Thin Man* (1934).

The cone-shaped glass with its elegant stem became identified with the martini during the 1930s and 1940s. The 1950s saw a greater emphasis on dryness (more gin, less vermouth), increasing from 3–4 to 8 parts gin to 1 part vermouth. Some omitted vermouth altogether. Vodka martinis became popular at this time, overtaking the gin martini in the 1960s and 1970s. In 1950s Britain, popular counterparts to the American martini were the "Gin and French" (gin, dry vermouth, and a lemon twist) and "Gin and It" (gin, sweet Italian vermouth, and a maraschino cherry).

The martini has suffused American popular culture since the early twentieth century, appearing, for example, in stories by O. Henry and Jack London in the first decade and Ernest Hemingway in the 1920s. It was widely popularized by film versions of British writer Ian Fleming's James Bond novels. The "Vesper" of his *Casino Royale* (1953) combined Gordon's gin, vodka, Kina Lillet, and a slice of lemon peel. The vodka martini, "shaken, not stirred," appeared in *Dr. No* (1958). Martini has long been the drink of urban sophistication, the wealthy, and the upwardly

Even the tools used for making and serving a martini exude elegance and sophistication. (Dreamstime.com)

mobile, as in the Joseph L. Mankiewicz film *All about Eve* (1950) and Patricia Highsmith's 1955 novel *The Talented Mr. Ripley*.

The martini revived internationally in the 1990s in its vodka and gin forms and a multitude of flavored versions. It is currently a feature of marketing strategies. The 1970s TV series *M*A*S*H* (famous for its martinis) was recently re-released on DVD as the "Martinis & Medicine Collection." Authoritative histories of the martini appeared in the 1980s and 1990s. (*See also* **Cocktails; Cocktail Parties.**)

Further Reading

Conrad, Barnaby. *The Martini: An Illustrated History of an American Classic.* San Francisco: Chronicle Books, 1995.

Edmunds, L. *Martini, Straight Up: The Classic American Cocktail.* Rev. ed. Baltimore: Johns Hopkins University Press, 1998.

MartiniArt.com Web site. http://www.martiniart.com.

Vanessa Taylor

MEDICAL USES OF ALCOHOL

Isopropyl, or rubbing alcohol, has been used for some time as a medicine as an antiseptic, anesthetic, and cleansing agent, but the history of ethyl alcohol, or drinking alcohol, as a medicine is considerably more complex. Early Greek and Roman physicians used it as a wound dressing, fever reducer, diuretic, and stimulant. In early Jewish culture, alcoholic beverages were referred to as the "greatest medicine." Prior to the 1800s, distilled spirits were used as a treatment for hepatitis, snake poisoning, and other ailments and were sold in apothecaries' shops.

By the late 1800s, there was a division in the medical community regarding the effectiveness of ethyl alcohol's therapeutic benefits and the appropriateness of prescribing it as a medicine. Some physicians held that the use of the drug was simply deleterious for humans and a contributor to many social ills, therefore not acceptable for use for any medical conditions. Others in the medical community believed that the effects of alcohol abuse were exaggerated in the fervor of the **temperance** activities of the era and continued to use alcohol to treat a vast array of medical conditions.

In the early 1900s, the American Medical Association (AMA) yielded to pressure from temperance groups and rejected the use of alcohol as medicine. In 1915, a physician committee from the AMA voted to remove the substance from the list of approved medications and two years later passed a resolution supporting prohibition of alcohol. Another concern in the medical field during this time involved the appropriate treatment approach for alcoholics: a debate intensified between those who saw **alcoholism** as a disease with characteristics of other physical ailments, and those who saw it as a behavioral issue not to be confused with other conditions for which the medical model applied. During the era of national **Prohibition**, the legal production and trade of alcohol was confined to medical purposes, thus controlled by the medical community.

Alcohol use, at least excessive use, has for some time been often associated with many personal and social maladies including family dissolution, abuse in the home, and crime. However, alcohol does have some positive health benefits if used appropriately. For example, as a sedative, alcohol, in a manner similar to

Valium, can assuage some anxiety problems in patients who are having difficulty coping with certain life stressors. Used in moderation, alcohol can be effective in this circumstance; however, if people begin to use alcohol to cope with ordinary life stressors on a regular basis or as an excuse to indulge, the effects of alcohol as an anti-anxiety agent can become harmful instead of beneficial.

Some studies have also suggested a link between mild alcohol consumption and a lower risk for coronary artery problems. Acting in this manner, alcohol, particularly red wine, can potentially deter heart attacks and heart disease. Also, there is some evidence to suggest that moderate use of alcohol can help decrease the risk of death in middle-aged men. The types of medical conditions that might be diverted (in addition to the heart problems) are cancer and other serious diseases.

Further Reading

Courtright, David T. *Forces of Habit: Drugs and the Making of the Modern World.* Cambridge, MA: Harvard University Press, 2002.

Kuhn, Cynthia, Scott Swartzwelder, and Wilkie Wilson. *Buzzed: The Straight Facts about the Most Used Drugs from Alcohol to Ecstasy.* 3rd ed. New York: W. W. Norton and Company, 2008.

Leonard A. Steverson

MEN AND BOYS DRINKING

The relationship between men, boys, and alcohol is generally framed as one of inappropriate levels of consumption. Historically, men have consumed far larger quantities of alcohol than have women. Men drink more frequently, become more intoxicated, and suffer greater levels of alcohol dependence than women do. Men are less likely than women to be aware of recommendations for safe levels of drinking and are significantly more likely to suffer an alcohol-related death than are women. Further to the inherent dangers of excessive alcohol consumption, there are related dangers such as the behaviors that tend to accompany problem drinking for men. Chief among such behaviors is **violence**: a significant proportion of violence among men happens under the influence of alcohol; similarly, a significant proportion of domestic violence (in which men are overwhelmingly perpetrators) happens under the influence of alcohol.

The relationship between men and alcohol often starts in boyhood. Men tend to start drinking earlier in their lives than do women, and the function alcohol serves in these early experiences differs. In particular, boys are more likely than girls to perceive alcohol as a way through which to become initiated into adulthood: drinking is perceived to make a man out of a boy in ways that are not so apparent with girls on their journey into womanhood. In the early years of drinking, alcohol serves as a bonding agent among young men, lubricating social interaction and creating commonality. As young men become older, attitudes toward alcohol may change: rather than being seen as a way of proving manliness, alcohol may be seen simply as a reason to gather socially, or as a facilitator for meeting potential partners. Whereas drunkenness tends to be considered an integral part of drinking among young men, it is less tolerated among older men, even though remaining common.

Problems occur when a particular type of drinking becomes a defining aspect of manliness. Men are expected to drink in certain ways. Men are expected to opt for certain types of alcohol (traditionally, hard liquor and **beer**, rather than **wine** or sweet drinks) and to drink large amounts, ideally without showing the effects. Such drinking becomes a signifier for manliness. Also, within a largely homophobic society, drinking like a man provides an opportunity for boys and men to assert their heterosexuality.

This type of discussion appeals to what has historically been described as "sex role theory," which suggests that there are certain types of behaviors appropriate to being a man, or that are even an innate part of being male. In more recent years, sex role theory has fallen out of favor and has been replaced by many masculinities researchers with a more fluid understanding of gender. The sex/gender distinction is as follows: sex is biologically determined (one is either born male or female, albeit with occasional cases of intersex/hermaphroditism), whereas gender (masculine and feminine) is socially constructed. In this context, masculinity is defined by society rather than being innate in men, and its meaning can therefore shift with society's values, and even fashion.

When problematic alcohol consumption among men and boys is viewed as a gender rather than a sex issue, it is possible to conclude that there is nothing innate in men that results in problematic alcohol consumption; rather, it is the way society defines masculinity that is problematic. This has become clearer in recent studies that show that different masculinities have different understandings and expectations surrounding the consumption of alcohol: ethnicity, **religion**, and socioeconomic variables, for example, all result in men and boys relating to alcohol in different ways. On the other side of the gender coin, in recent years women and girls have massively increased their alcohol consumption as society has shifted what it considers to be acceptably "feminine."

The most significant way that the problematic relationship between men, boys, and alcohol can be viewed is via the lens of "hegemonic masculinity," which is the type of masculinity to which men are assumed to aspire. Hegemonic masculinity is the form of masculinity that is accepted as the most powerful in society, and it asserts its dominance over those men who either cannot or choose not to adhere to it, such as young, effeminate, or poor men (known as "subordinate masculinities"). The consumption of large amounts of alcohol is an integral part of hegemonic masculine performances, and men may view such consumption as a way of reaping the benefits of being part of the hegemonic order. In short, alcohol consumption becomes a way for men and boys to acquire power. Even when counter-hegemonic masculinities are at work in relation to the consumption of alcohol (such as the ethnicity, religion, and socioeconomic variables), the men who perform them are often still acutely aware of the expectations of hegemonic masculinity, and that they do not meet them.

Many of the problems that are central to the conversation around men and boys drinking are, then, essentially products of how society defines masculinity in relation to power: to solve those problems, it is necessary for society to shift that definition.

Further Reading

Connell, Robert W., and James W. Messerschmidt. "Hegemonic Masculinity: Rethinking the Concept." *Gender and Society* (2005): 829–59.

De Visser, Richard O., and Jonathan A. Smith. "Alcohol Consumption and Masculine Identity Among Young Men." *Psychology and Health* 22 (2007): 595–614.

Lemle, Russell, and Marc E. Mishkind. "Alcohol and Masculinity." *Journal of Substance Abuse Treatment* 6 (1989): 213–22.

Lyons, Antonia C., and Sara A. Willott. "Alcohol Consumption, Gender Identities and Women's Changing Social Positions." *Sex Roles* 59 (2008): 694–712.

Mullen, Kenneth, Jonathon Watson, Jan Swift, and David Black. "Young Men, Masculinity and Alcohol." *Drugs: Education, Prevention and Policy* 14 (2007): 151–65.

Joseph Gelfer

MICROBREWERIES

Microbreweries are breweries with output of fewer than 15,000 barrels of **beer** per year (1 barrel = 31 gallons); however, this distinction is arbitrary in the minds of many American beer consumers. There is little distinction for these buyers between a microbrewery, a regional craft brewery (an independent brewery with an output between 15,000 and 2,000,000 barrels of beer per year), and a brewpub (where beer is produced and consumed on the premises).

The term microbrewery is often synonymous with any establishment that brews "craft beer," which is characterized by artisanal and traditional as well as more experimental **brewing**. It is also defined by a spirit of defiance against the monopoly of light lager made by the multi-national brewing conglomerations. Although there is tremendous variety among craft beer, it tends to have a more full and complex flavor due to the increased amounts of specialty malt and hops. This distinguishes it from the light pilsner style, made with adjuncts such as rice or corn, which dominates the American market.

The rise in interest in craft beer has coincided directly with the "food revolution" in the United States—the burst of interest in more variety, freshness and "sophistication" in food—which began in the mid-1970s and has continued into the twenty-first century. Americans' changing tastes in beer has mirrored their changing tastes in food, becoming more cosmopolitan and diverse, and consumers have become more willing to pay higher prices for fresh, quality, and local products produced by traditional methods.

Since the 1980s, the United States experienced a craft beer revolution, also called the "good beer revolution," characterized by the marked rise of microbreweries, regional craft breweries, and brewpubs throughout the country. Many of these breweries were started by home-brewers who, during the 1970s and 1980s, were the only brewers in the country who brewed alternatives to the beers offered by the major brewing companies. Initially, home-brewers sought to brew alternatives to the mainstream beer, as the English, German, and Belgium beers that inspired them rarely made their way to the United States and were expensive.

Fritz Maytag acquired the Anchor Brewing Company in 1965 and attempted to maintain some of the unique beer traditions of the United States at a time when they were disappearing. This is often cited as one of the foundational moments in the history of the craft beer movement along with the founding of the New Albion Brewery in Sonoma, California, in 1976, which became known as the first "microbrewery" in the country. Although breweries such as these faced many challenges when they began in the 1980s, microbreweries have since become the fastest-growing sector of the brewing industry, and since the early 1990s, the number of breweries in the United States has risen from 44 to nearly 2,000.

The popularity of craft beer attests to the consumers' desire to seek out alternatives to the country's three largest breweries that produce the majority of the country's beer. Indeed, the variety of beer styles currently offered by craft breweries throughout the country is truly astounding. Due almost entirely to these breweries, there are more styles of beer brewed in the United States than in any other country in the world.

Craft beers are often made with traditional ingredients: malted barley, hops, water, and yeast. There is also a sector of craft beer sometimes referred to as "extreme beer" or "extreme brewing" that constitutes beer brewed with greater-than-usual quantities of traditional ingredients, or with untraditional ingredients such as fruits, spices, and herbs. These beers may be aged in **wine** barrels and have higher alcohol content and a higher hop character.

There is also an educational aspect that often accompanies craft brewing. Craft brewers tend to be enthusiastic about their products, and many offer tours of the breweries, beer education classes, and food and beer pairings. Moreover, there exists a veritable community among craft beer brewers and enthusiasts, which the Internet has facilitated.

Craft brewing also shares a strong connection to the **home-brew** movement. Many professional craft brewers began as home-brewers, and there continues to be solidarity between many commercial craft breweries and home-brewers. Commercial craft brewers often share recipes, advice on technique, and even yeast with home-brewers. Commercial craft breweries hold contests for which home-brewers may submit their beers, the winning recipes being brewed and sold commercially through the brewery.

Although there are craft breweries throughout the United States—in Alaska and Hawaii as well as the lower 48—the West Coast (California, Oregon, Washington, and Alaska) contains about 440 microbreweries, one quarter of the country's total. During two consecutive years of the World Beer Cup competition, the state of California won more medals for its beer than any other single country except Germany. The success of American microbreweries has inspired brewers in other countries to open American-style microbreweries.

The craft brewing industry shares a common sense of purpose, and breweries often get involved in their communities through philanthropic acts and sponsorship of events, as well as through attempts to maintain a spirit of integrity and independence. Craft breweries are often leaders in sustainable brewing and business practices, with many embracing "green" brewing techniques with their energy efficiency, water conservation, and waste disposal. Some of the most progressive craft breweries run on wind energy, solar power, and methane gas, which is recycled from the brewing process.

Further Reading

Calagione, Sam. "Extreme Brewing in America." In *Beer and Philosophy: The Unexamined Beer Isn't Worth Drinking*, ed. Steven D. Hales. Malden: Blackwell Publishing, 2007.

Papazian, Charlie. *Microbrewed Adventures: A Lupulin-filled Journey to the Heart and Flavor of the World's Great Craft Beers*. New York: HarperCollins, 2005.

Wells, Ken. *Travels with Barley: A Journey through Beer Culture in America*. New York: Free Press, 2004.

Matthew Russell

MOTHERS AGAINST DRUNK DRIVING (MADD)

Throughout the 1950s and 1960s, newspapers occasionally featured stories about a teen killed in a drunk-driving crash. The teen was often the driver or front-seat passenger, and the story focused less on the perils of drinking and driving and more on the dangers of youth alcohol use. These incidents rapidly increased in the late 1960s and 1970s, as more and more youth and young adults had access to cars in their suburban neighborhoods. However, not all deaths were caused by drinking-and-driving teens. In 1978, New York State mother Doris Aiken established Remove Intoxicated Drivers (RID). RID became the first citizen activist group dedicated to fighting drunk driving among all ages, but it had limited coverage and thus limited impact.

In 1980, Cari Lightner, a 13-year-old girl, was killed in a hit-and-run crash while walking with a friend near her home. The driver struck her from behind and did not look back. The day after Cari's funeral, her mother, Candy Lightner, was notified that the driver who was arrested for killing Cari had been out of jail

Mothers Against Drunk Driving (MADD) national president Millie Webb holds an image of her late 19-month-old nephew Mitchell Pewitt, as she speaks during MADD's 20th anniversary rally outside the U.S. Capitol on September 6, 2000. About 600 drunk-driving victims and activists called on Congress to make a 0.08 percent blood-alcohol content the nationwide drunk-driving limit. Webb lost her nephew Mitchell and a daughter, and she, her husband, and her then-unborn baby were severely injured in a crash with a driver with a 0.08 blood-alcohol content. (AP/Wide World Photos)

for only two days after being arrested for another drunk-driving hit-and-run. In addition, he had three other arrests for drunken driving.

Shortly thereafter, Candy and friends decided to form an organization to combat drunk driving. One suggestion was to call it Mothers Against Drunk Driving or, MADD, to show how they felt. MADD reached out to the press, and quickly spread throughout the country. Chapters formed in small towns and cities alike, with mothers gathering together to protect their children from drunk driving.

One of MADD's first major initiatives was to support President Ronald Reagan's efforts to establish a nationally uniform minimum drinking age at 21. However, MADD's primary success has been to raise awareness of drunk driving as a national public health calamity. MADD advertisements, public service announcements, and campaigns have changed the acceptability of drunk driving and given a face to its victims. MADD efforts increased the number of police checkpoints and roadblocks, spread the use of the **breathalyzer**, and helped to lower state **blood alcohol content (BAC)** policies for "**driving under the influence**" and "driving while intoxicated" standards. Many credit MADD with a significant decrease in drunk-driving fatalities, particularly among young adults.

No longer simply for mothers and victims, MADD has grown into one of the largest grassroots organizations in the United States and now encompasses a wide range of supporters. Some have accused MADD of losing focus and becoming too "neo-prohibitionist." Founded to give a voice to the victims of drunk driving and fight to prevent future tragedies, today's MADD represents a full frontal assault on alcohol misuse and abuse and American drinking culture. Although MADD's goals and scope may have widened, it remains dedicated to its cause of "activism, victim services, and education," so that no family needs to experience the Lightners's loss. (*See also* **Designated Driver; Drinking Age Legislation.**)

Further Reading

Fell, James C., and Robert B. Voas. "Mothers Against Drunk Driving (MADD): The First Twenty-Five Years." *Traffic Injury Prevention* 7 (2006): 195–212.
Mothers Against Drunk Driving Web site. http://www.madd.org.

Joy Newman

MUSIC

Music has long had an association with alcoholic drinks. There is a whole category of European folk music called **drinking songs**. These ballads tell a story, and their lyrics often feature drinking themes. The drinking songs are also performed in **bars** and **pubs**. Irish pubs, whether in Dublin or St. Louis, are known for patron sing-alongs and Celtic bands playing. Bars, nightclubs, and restaurants often have house bands or rotate a schedule of visiting groups who perform for patrons. From swanky hotel bars in large urban centers to small, gritty clubs off of country highways, the careers of many musicians began in these venues.

Today, because so many types of popular music are associated with alcohol consumption and many popular songs refer to drinking, psychologists are concerned. Their assumption is that different types of popular music and the venues in which it is performed encourage **underage drinking, binge drinking**, and alcohol abuse among adolescents, college students, and young adults. One 2008 study analyzed 279 songs identified by a trade journal of the music industry, *Billboard,* as the most popular. Researchers analyzed the lyrics for their references to substance abuse. Alcohol use was the second-most common theme, occurring in 23.7 percent of their sample, after tobacco. Rap music had the most references (77% of their sample), country music followed (36%), R&B and hip-hop were in third place (20%), rock was toward the end of the list (14%), and in last place was pop music (9%) (Primack et al. 2008).

Alcohol played a role early in the development of rock and roll from its rhythm-and-blues roots. This music was promoted in nightclubs in large urban centers such as Chicago, Detroit, and New York and first marketed to African American industrial workers who had gone north during the Great Migration (1910s–1940s). In the 1950s, white youth embraced these genres, and the music venues changed to dance halls and municipal auditoriums. Straight spirits, **cocktails**, and **beer** were served in these venues. The musicians themselves often drank alcohol during performances, but illegal drugs were more their mood-altering substance of choice. From the classic blues singer Billie Holiday to rock and roll's Jimi Hendrix, heroin was more popular than alcohol and, in both these examples, let to fatal overdoses.

The classic rock bands of the 1960s and 1970s performed in festivals such as at Woodstock, where marijuana use trumped beer drinking. Southern rock, though, always kept close to its roots, and strong spirits like **whiskey, bourbon,** and Southern Comfort, Janis Joplin's favorite, were used as well as promoted in song lyrics. Today, though, **wine** and beer are sold at music festivals throughout the United States and served in plastic cups, and drug use is strictly prohibited at these venues. Rap and hip-hop music promote Dom Perignon **champagne** and Benedictine and Brandy. These expensive, exclusive drinks are sold by the bottle in upscale nightclubs, where both patrons and musicians are dressed to the nines and adorned with diamonds.

Country music in contemporary American society has assumed the place of the traditional drinking song and European tavern ballad, as illustrated by Toby Keith's ballad, "I Love This Bar." Country music in the United States springs from an agrarian past that had great ambivalence about alcohol use (Chalfant and Beckley 1977). In this social context, a struggle ensued between a real culture where alcohol had a major role, and an ideal, religious culture tempered by fundamentalist Protestant Christianity's ban on alcohol consumption and the late nineteenth-century **Temperance** Movement.

Even today, despite the rapid urbanization, many counties in the Southern states are still "dry," areas where it is illegal to sell and consume alcohol in public. A 2009 legislative battle in Snellville, Georgia, a once-rural, now densely populated suburb of Atlanta, pitted restaurant owners against religious adherents. The restaurant owners wanted to overturn **blue laws** that still prohibit Sunday sales of alcohol, as they were losing money. Christian religious leaders opposed the repeal, worrying that selling drinks on Sunday violated their faith and would lead to moral collapse.

It is in this cultural context that country music thrives because it articulates the evils of drink that lead to familial tension, financial ruin, and other social problems, while at the same time extolling a trip to Margaritaville or friendship with Captain Morgan, the pleasures of the mood-altering properties of alcohol. Country music is a reflection of ambivalence about alcohol. Some songs like the George Jones classic, "If Drinking Don't Kill Me," and Brad Paisley's "Alcohol" mirror the struggle and the problems that excessive drinking causes. But many others, perhaps the majority, promote drinking or just reflect the country bar culture, small venues in remote areas where most of the singers of this music initially established their careers. Some songs use alcohol as a way to glorify a past and heroic cowboy lifestyle, as in Willie Nelson's "Whiskey for My Men and Beer for My Horses." Many of these songs link drinking to notions of Southern masculinity, but newer songs (1990s–2010) such as Gretchen Wilson's "Redneck Woman," also glorify good-time girls who drink and party in bars without remorse.

Further Reading

Alaniz, Maria Luisa, and Chris Wilkes. "Pro-Drinking Messages and Message Environments for Young Adults: The Case of Alcohol Industry Advertising in African American, Latino, and Native American Communities." *Journal of Public Health Policy* 19, no. 4 (1998): 447–72.

Chalfant, H. Paul, and Robert E. Beckley. "Beguiling and Betraying: the Image of Alcohol Use in Country Music." *Journal of Alcohol Studies* 38, no. 7 (1977): 1428–33.

Primack, Brian A., et al. "Content Analysis of Tobacco, Alcohol, and Other Drugs in Popular Music." *Archives of Pediatric and Adolescent Medicine* 162, no. 2 (2008): 169–75.

Pam Sezgin

N

NATIONAL IDENTITY

In some cultures, alcohol is a deeply embedded part of cultural identity. In others, abstinence rules. Anthropologists have investigated alcohol use by looking at the social patterns involved in drinking, the learned components involved in drunkenness, the meaning of particular drinks in their social contexts, and issues of identity that are involved in drinking cultures (Wilson 2005).

American researchers tend to focus on alcohol abuse and to see it as a global problem, when in fact, that may not be the case (Douglas 1987; Wilson 2005). Ruth Engs (2000) found that, historically, Europe could be divided into two areas based on the type of alcoholic drinks traditionally consumed. The patterns and attitudes that arose still influence perceptions in those cultures about drinking. Engs concluded that Northern Europe had a **binge-drinking** culture related to grain harvesting, from which **beer** was made in ancient times. Ales and beers could not be stored for long periods; they were perishable, so a kind of feast-or-famine attitude toward alcohol consumption resulted. This led to ambivalence about drinking and periods of drinking followed by abstinence (Engs 2000, 1). Southern Europe, Engs discovered, had a vibrant viticulture and a culture of drinking in moderation, with **wine** as an integral part of the diet. These Roman Catholic areas were wine-friendly and avoided the **temperance** movements that characterized the Protestant Northern European countries and their North American counterparts in the nineteenth century (Engs 2000, 4).

National identity, too, is a social construct (Anderson 1991, 5). Since the 1800s, nationalism emerged by building political communities based on notions of communion and comradeship, fraternity, and shared understandings of history, symbols, and governance. It is the youngest form of human social organization, replacing the foraging lifestyle of hunters and gatherers in which humans and their ancestors engaged for several million years; the geographic mobility of tribal pastoralists with their extended kin networks; and about 6,000 years of empires, civilizations that depended upon agriculture and warfare to expand from city-states into regional powers. Nation-states have defined boundaries that are often arbitrary, separating members of the same families and cultural groups because of recent political tensions. The modern notions of the nation-state and nationalism derive in large part from Napoleon and his followers in postrevolutionary France of the early nineteenth century (Holtman 1979).

Specific types of alcohol are associated with particular nations and regions. The United States is known for its Kentucky **bourbon** and its **whiskey** (Jack Daniel's from Tennessee). Mexico has its prized **tequila**. France is famous for its wine, while Belgium is noted for its beer. In the Mediterranean, strong licorice-flavored aperitifs abound: ouzo in Greece, and raki in Turkey, and arrack extends into the Arab world. Japan is known for its **sake**, a rice wine. Ireland has Guinness and Irish whiskey. Poland, Russia, Sweden, and Finland all produce excellent vodkas. Germany is known for its beer, particularly its pilsners. Portugal is a wine-producer: port, **Madeira**, and the Azorean wines. Great Britain is known for its ales, stout, and dark beers and Scotland for its single-malt scotches, its rye whiskey, and Drambouie. Austria is known for its schnapps in many candy flavors, and the Czech Republic for its plum brandy. West Africa is known as a traditional region for palm wine and homemade beers. The Caribbean is known for specialty liqueurs like Curaçao, named after its island home, and the **rums** of Puerto Rico and Cuba. But these distinctions are becoming more matters of brand and marketing. Defying traditional associations of national identity and alcohol type, Jamaica now is known for an excellent beer, Red Stripe, and Australia is fast becoming one of the world's major wine producers. (*See also* **Terroir**.)

Further Reading

Anderson, Benedict. *Imagined Communities: Reflections on the Origin and Spread of Nationalism*. Rev. ed. London: Verso, 1991.

Douglas, Mary, ed. *Constructive Drinking: Perspectives on Drink from Anthropology*. Cambridge: Cambridge University Press, 1987.

Engs, Ruth C. "Protestants and Catholics: Drunken Barbarians and Mellow Romans?" 2000. http://www.indiana.edu/~engs/articles/cathprot.htm.

Holtman, Robert B. *Napoleonic Revolution*. Baton Rouge: Louisiana State University Press, 1979.

Wilson, Thomas M., ed. *Drinking Cultures: Alcohol and Identity*. Oxford: Berg, 2005.

Pam Sezgin

NATIVE AMERICANS

Alcohol has shaped the interaction between Native Americans and European Americans since European contact in the sixteenth century, and that interaction continues to influence Native Americans' recent alcohol usage. Many have asserted that American Indians are biologically prone to alcohol abuse, but scholars challenge this assumption. They agree that alcohol abuse is prevalent among Native Americans but attribute this to rampant poverty, cultural alienation, or a desire to rebel against white dictates rather than ethnicity.

Alcohol was rare in pre-Columbian America. Native Americans in what are today Mexico and the southwestern United States distilled alcohol from the

Mescalero cactus, but very few tribes outside these regions were aware of alcohol. Europeans quickly realized that giving alcohol to Native Americans unfamiliar with intoxication provided the former with political and economic advantages. Alcohol transformed the deer trade in the southeast as Native Americans overhunted to acquire more liquor and subsequently became dependent on European traders. Tribal leaders attempted unsuccessfully to limit alcohol consumption.

Following the American Revolution, fur traders continued to furnish Native Americans with alcohol, while federal officials and religious missionaries sought to reduce alcohol consumption by southeastern American Indians in an effort to "civilize" them. The Trade and Intercourse Act of 1802 allowed the president to restrict liquor sales in federal territories, and in 1832 Congress banned alcohol sales to Indians and throughout Indian country. Despite these and similar directives to state governments, alcohol remained plentiful among Native Americans.

Native American leaders increased efforts to limit alcohol consumption. The Shawnee leader Tenkswatawa urged followers to become abstinent. Cherokee leaders passed a prohibition law in 1819. White officials opposed this assertion of Cherokee sovereignty, and federal envoys plied Native Americans with alcohol when negotiating treaties to surrender huge tracts of land to the United States. Removal devastated Native Americans, and many sought solace in alcohol. Various tribes used persuasion to reduce drinking. The Cherokee Temperance Society organized in 1829, and the Choctaws formed a similar group by 1842.

As European Americans pushed west into Indian lands, they brought alcohol with them. The federal liquor ban carried little risk of arrest as few federal marshals were assigned to enforce it. Alcohol contributed to **violence** against Native Americans, such as during the 1864 Sand Creek massacre of peaceful Cheyennes by drunken Colorado militiamen.

White religious missionaries, instead, focused on Native American consumption, accepting the stereotypical image of riotous drunken Indians as a threat to white society. Such stereotypes continued despite the sharp decline in Native American populations. While national liquor **Prohibition** ended in 1933, prohibition of alcohol sales to Native Americans remained until 1953.

In the twentieth century, Native Americans continued to consume alcohol at very high rates. Social disruption and poverty led some to drink. Others did so as an act of defiance against white proscriptions against it. Still others viewed alcohol consumption as central to their ethnic heritage. As one scholar noted, Indians drink because anthropologists told them they were caught between cultures, and people who are caught between cultures drink. However, there are also groups who have turned to abstinence as a way of preserving their communities and culture.

Further Reading

Beauvais, Fred. "American Indians and Alcohol." *Alcohol Health and Research World* 22, no. 4 (1998): 253–59.

Spicer, Paul. "Toward a (Dys)functional Anthropology of Drinking: Ambivalence and the American Indian Experience with Alcohol." *Medical Anthropology Quarterly* 11 (1997): 306–23.

James Klein

O

OKTOBERFEST

Oktoberfest originated in Munich, Germany, in 1810. It was initially a celebration of the wedding of Crown Prince Ludwig and Princess Therese of Saxe-Hildburghausen. Oktoberfest traditionally begins on the first Saturday after September 15 and ends on the first Sunday in October. Munich's Oktoberfest is the largest public party in the world, drawing millions of Germans and visitors to the original site outside the city gates to drink copious amounts of German **beer** and **wine**, join rousing sing-alongs, and eat traditional foods under giant white brewer-sponsored tents. Waitresses and some celebrants wear dirndls and many men wear lederhosen.

After World War II, Oktoberfest celebrations were held by German American societies in the United States to try to improve the image of Germany. Oktoberfest is a celebration of German culture. Events in the United States are held throughout the country at **bars, pubs,** and community centers, but they differ widely in character. In comparison to the 16-day event in Germany, Oktoberfest in the United States can last for just one day or for more than a week. Some events feature dance or music competitions, others focus on children's activities, but almost all parties include a beer garden and German food, such as bratwurst and pretzels. American Oktoberfest celebrations almost always include their own unique touches such as marketplaces and non-German cultural entertainment and competitions, such as trap shooting, the chicken dance, or eating contests.

Oktoberfest in Munich is a popular destination for American tourists and students abroad who are beer and Oktoberfest enthusiasts. Drunkenness, especially among younger patrons, is a problem.

Further Reading

Foran, Jill. *Oktoberfest: Celebrating Cultures*. Mankato, MN: Weigl Publications, 2003.

"German Oktoberfest." Everything about Germany Web site. http://www.everythingaboutgermany.com/Oktoberfest/Oktoberfest History.htm.

"Oktoberfest." http://www.germanfood guide.com/oktoberfest.htm.

Rachel Black

In North America, the yearly Oktoberfest in Kitchener-Waterloo, Ontario, Canada, holds the record for most attendees. In the United States, Oktoberfest-Zinzinnati, in Cincinnati, Ohio, attracts approximately 500,000 revelers. More than 100 smaller events reportedly take place in 36 states. California, Pennsylvania, Texas, and Wisconsin all host eight Oktoberfests.

Source: http://www.germany.info/Vertretung/usa/en/Startseite.html (accessed February 25, 2010).

Although it is a holiday that originated in Germany, Oktoberfest became popular in America after World War II. Oktoberfest is nearly synonymous with beer drinking. (Corel)

P

PEER PRESSURE

Peer pressure involves peers reinforcing the normality of particular belief patterns and behaviors and actively encouraging others to behave or act in a certain way during group-based activities. Peer pressure technically occurs when others from a same-age group influence an individual to behave in a particular way or to do something expected by the group in order to prove allegiance. Peer pressure can act as a catalyst for drinking, a behavior modeler, and it can play an important role in the creation of social norms (Borsari and Carey 2001). Peer pressure is often thought to be a primary instigator of high-risk drinking behaviors, especially when someone takes a drink for the first time or when playing **drinking games**. Peer pressure as social reinforcement can be conceived of as negative when it encourages youth and young adults to drink in a dangerous manner or to adopt beliefs about appropriate drinking behaviors that encourage high-risk drinking. Social reinforcement can also influence beliefs and behaviors more positively by encouraging safer styles of normative behavior.

Parents often think of "peer pressure" as a deadly force that causes an innocent child to do something dangerous. By believing that external forces operate on otherwise "good kids" in this manner, culpability can be shifted from the individual to a group or identifiable individual who is a "bad influence." However, studies in social norming clearly demonstrate that group beliefs influence behavior just as assuredly as do high-risk friends, especially in alcohol use. Perkins (2002) demonstrated that college students often misperceive the amount their peers drink, thinking that others drink larger amounts. This can, in turn, influence intakes upward in order to do what others are doing. Social norming campaigns often use surveys to more accurately ascertain amounts students drink and then report results back to campus communities, such as "Most students who party drink four or fewer cans of beer each evening." By providing students with a more accurate understanding of peer behavior, these programs seek to alter perceptions of normative behaviors and encourage less risky drinking activities.

The negative side of peer pressure is often highlighted by drinking games. Drinking games encourage high-risk drinking because they require participants to drink once they have entered the game; social approbation ensures compliance. In addition, many drinking games can encourage fast and hard drinking, and once a participant is intoxicated, sloppy coordination usually ensures greater intake as the player repeatedly loses. Another negative outcome of peer pressure involves modeling high-risk behaviors such as deliberately fast group drinking. Many college students "pregame," which means they drink to get drunk in a group before attending an event. One popular style of pregame drinking is called a "power hour," in which peers drink a shot of **beer** or other alcoholic drink every minute for an hour, thus ensuring that each person is drunk before the hour is finished. Because participants can be teased if they fail to keep up, this kind of peer pressure ensures high-risk drinking for all. (*See also* **Blackouts; College Drinking Culture; Underage Drinking.**)

Further Reading

Borsari, Brian, and Kate Carey. "Peer Influences on College Drinking: A Review of the Research." *Journal of Substance Abuse* 13, no. 4 (2001): 391–424.
Perkins, Wesley. "Social Norms and the Prevention of Alcohol Misuse in Collegiate Contexts." *Journal of Studies in Alcohol*, Supplement 14 (2002): 164–72.

Janet Chrzan

PERRY

Perry is an alcoholic drink made by fermenting the juice of pears (*Pyrus communis* L.). More specifically, perry is preferentially made from special pear varieties known as perry pears. These pears are high in tannins and acid, providing the complex flavors associated with perry in addition to serving as a preservative. Early American written accounts of perry state that pears unfit for eating are desirable for perry production. Once the desired pear varieties have been collected, pears are crushed into a pulp and juiced. This juice contains naturally occurring wild yeast that will ferment the juice into perry. However, industrial methods of perry production often call for pasteurization of the juice to kill any wild yeast. Later, a known yeast variety is added to produce a more consistent product from year to year. This juice is then blended with other fermented pear juice to match desired tastes.

There are early American writings that state that ingredients such as **cider,** brandy, sherry, and lemons were added to perry to create **cocktails, punch,** and toddies. There is occasional mention of bits of meat being added to the fermenting pear juice. This was thought to add protein to the mixture and give nourishment to the yeast. Perry should not be confused with pear cider, which is an alcoholic beverage made from a combination of fermented apple and pear juice.

Perry enjoys much less popularity than other fermented beverages in the United States. Despite its inclusion in early American texts, the lack of its mention in early European historical accounts reflects this status. Perry is often made by orchardists in addition to cider and is seldom produced as a sole product. Perry and the technologies for its production have their origins alongside cider production. In some cultures, perry and cider are treated equally and are produced at the same time, though processed separately. In other cultures, perry has become associated more as a feminine or children's drink, with cider maintaining a more masculine quality. To most American consumers, perry is little more than the drink added to Guinness at their local Irish **pub**, in lieu of **champagne**, to make a Black Velvet.

Britain, France, and Portugal are well known as centers of perry production. England was producing perry before the Norman invasion, and perry production was scaled up at the encouragement of the conquerors. Elements of this remain in Britain today, as local knowledge records that farmlands visible from atop May Hill, in Herefordshire, are the lands best suited for production of high-quality perry pears. It was largely from these traditions that perry production was imported to North America.

Perry has benefitted from cultural revival movements and now enjoys a home in New England and in the Pacific Northwest. Perry production remains rather limited in most areas of North America. As such, it is most often obtained from local producers at farm shops or nearby outlets.

Further Reading

Brown, J. H. *Early American Beverages*. New York: Bonanza Books, 1966.
Luckwill, L. C., and A. Pollard. *Perry Pears*. Bristol: National Fruit and Cider Institute, 1963.

Dave Reedy

POLITICS

Because of the negative effects that alcohol misuse can have on individual and public health, most nation-states today have laws that regulate the production, **distribution**, sale, and consumption of alcohol. Though alcohol laws vary across and within national boundaries, some common areas of regulatory concern include limitations on the age of purchase, possession, and consumption; licensing of producers, distributors, and sellers; acceptable blood alcohol limits for driving motor vehicles; and pricing and taxation.

In the United States, alcohol has always been a highly charged subject in political discourse. In part, this political contention is because alcohol is no ordinary commodity; in the American cultural context, alcohol is defined as a legal drug, and as such, it is highly regulated, commercially significant, and morally contentious.

Contention also stems from the high degree of citizen interest and participation in the political process that generates, implements, and regulates U.S. alcohol policy. Historically, whenever citizen interest is high, the resulting policy debates tend to be framed in terms of morality. Complex issues are presented simply, in black-and-white terms, so that the greatest possible number of citizens can participate without having to invest time or effort in learning political nuance. The consolidation of vast numbers of citizen adherents to one or the other side of a political debate translates into a great amount of political power while ensuring that such power is not lost to bureaucratic, industry, or other competing interests.

Process

The national history of **temperance**, **Prohibition**, and its ultimate repeal resulted in the institutionalization of four significant characteristics of contemporary American alcohol policy: (1) a reformulation of federalism as the basis for an overarching regulatory framework, in which the federal and state governments share control of alcohol but with state interests taking precedence; (2) a definition of the key political actors, their agendas, and strategies; (3) a definition of the political processes for interactions between actors; and (4) a definition of laws and policy issues used in the control of alcohol.

By the end of Prohibition, there were at least four clearly defined groups with interests in regulating the production, distribution, sale, and consumption of alcoholic beverages: citizens, industry, politicians, and bureaucrats. Politicians and bureaucrats collectively create, implement, and enforce alcohol laws at federal, state, and local levels. During Prohibition, federal laws took precedence; after Prohibition, state and local laws factored more. However, because alcohol is both commercially and morally salient, and also because commercial and moral concerns are often at odds with each other, industry and citizens are highly motivated to be involved in the process. Specifically, industry and citizens use those political instruments available to them to influence politicians and bureaucrats.

To influence lawmakers, industry and citizens separately create policy, agendas, and strategies. Policy instruments are used to influence state and federal law instruments, which consists generally of statutory laws (created by legislative bodies); administrative laws or regulations (created by regulatory agencies); and case law or legal opinions (created by courts). With respect to alcohol, general laws affect **beer**, **wine**, and spirits collectively. As well, there may be coexisting laws that impact specific industry segments, for example, local laws for beer keg registration, and federal wine laws for the creation of American viticultural areas.

Law

In general, the post-repeal transfer of alcohol control from the federal government to the states did not exclude the federal government from the political process, for federal executive, legislative, and judicial branches can and do impact alcohol policy. For example, Congress imposes alcohol excise taxes on distilled spirits, wine, and beer that are in addition to those imposed by the states. Congress can also impose guidelines for the advertisement of alcoholic beverages on national radio and **television**.

Key federal political actors include the Alcohol and Tobacco Tax and Trade Bureau (TTB) in the Treasury Department; the Advertising, Labeling, and Formulation Division (ALFD), also in the Treasury Department; and the independent Federal Trade Commission (FTC). Collectively, these three oversee production, distribution, importation, and use of alcohol; restrictions on alcohol production, sale, and possession; public protection related to the production of alcohol; alcohol tax revenue; alcohol product **advertising**; alcohol product labeling, packaging and health warnings; permits and licenses; and compliance violations.

Significant state and local political actors include state alcohol beverage or liquor control boards; local land use, zoning, licensing, health code, community review, and other boards; and state and local law enforcement agencies. Because there is much variability in state alcohol laws, a partial list of some typical areas of oversight includes sales taxes; licenses for on- and off-premise operations; hours and days of operation; direct-to-consumer sales; minimum age of legal purchase, possession, and consumption; **blood alcohol content** levels; drunk driving; public drinking; open containers in moving vehicles; alcohol strength by volume; alcohol serving size; and product distribution.

Policy

Citizens and industry make up a highly fluid field consisting of multiple special-interest groups of various degrees of institutional sophistication. In general, citizen activist organizations may be "pro" alcohol (wanting less restriction and more access) or "anti" alcohol (wanting more restriction and less access), and they also be aligned with consumer advocacy groups, public health advocacy groups, professional lobbyists, and others.

Industry actors may include citizens who work in the industry; alcohol producers (farmers, breweries, wineries, distilleries), distributors, on- and off-premise retailers, professional lobbyists, and others.

Categories of political actors who may be aligned with either citizens or industry include other social activists, journalists, parents, residential communities, schools, nonprofits, grassroots organizations, research organizations, other government agencies or task forces, churches and other religious organizations, health care practitioners and institutions, and political parties.

Presently, major concerns of citizens and industry include the minimum legal drinking age, **binge drinking** (in student and worker populations), underage drinking (including that facilitated by parents or other adults), drunk driving, and other youth-related issues not already specified. Of special significance to numerous political actors are health concerns, such as the long- and short-term effects of alcohol consumption, recommended maximum intake amounts; **alcoholism** as a disease, **blackouts** and alcohol-related amnesia, fetal alcohol spectrum disorder, **fetal alcohol syndrome**, and Wernicke-Korsakoff syndrome. Health care industry political actors are also interested in interactions between alcohol and cancer, cardiovascular disease, hepatitis, liver disease, and weight. As well, special attention is paid to the health benefits of wine consumption.

Other highly politicized issues include alcohol abuse (including prevention, **intervention**, and treatment), alcohol advertising (including marketing, promotion, and sponsorship), alcohol education (including responsible beverage service), law enforcement (including breath tests and new car ignition systems), nutritional labeling, and secondary effects and costs of alcohol misuse (**violence**, crime, work productivity, health insurance, injury, and death).

Finally, one particularly salient controversy concerns the potential for producers and retailers to bypass the decentralized system of state distributors that is a legacy of the Twenty-first Amendment via direct sale and shipment to consumers using the Internet. Initially brought by small winery producers who wanted the opportunity to sell product directly to consumers in those states where state law required sale to distributors, the landmark *Granholm v. Heald* (2005) case ruling has facilitated at least some form of direct shipping from wineries to consumers in most states. State alcohol regulations still vary so much that small wineries face a challenging regulatory compliance situation that is at least as complex as the post-repeal legacy. Nevertheless, the potential now exists for future changes in American alcohol policy processes.

In *Granholm v. Heald*, industry and wine consumers aligned to support a change in state law that has the potential to rewrite how alcohol is distributed in the United States. They were opposed by certain citizen interests, namely parents wanting to deny minors opportunities to purchase alcohol over the Internet. In this case, the commercial interests of industry actors eclipsed the morality concerns of parents because the citizenry was not as well organized as industry. In contests of American alcohol policy, where the agenda of either party can prevail, organization and effectiveness of strategy determine outcomes.

Industry and citizens are both interested in attracting large numbers of adherents to their cause, so both tend to use the main strategy of simple characterizations of the issues for maximum effect. Hence, "pro" alcohol agendas typically use language of "responsibility" and "moderation" to describe ideal alcohol consumption behaviors, whereas "anti" alcohol agendas typically use language that suggests prohibition of consumption via "zero tolerance" and "abstinence."

Other specific strategies used in contests of influence by either side, some of which were already well established by temperance activists at the time of Prohibition, include making alcohol more expensive or less expensive and/or difficult or easy to obtain; stigmatizing or glamorizing alcohol; creating, populating, and funding a well-organized network of related activist groups; funding research and/or organizations; funding advertising promotion; using the media and press institutions; and subtly manipulating language in speech and print (for example, "alcohol problem" versus "alcohol misuse problem"). (*See also* **Blue Laws; Drinking Age Legislation; Dry Counties; Economics; Health Effects of Alcohol; Liquor Boards; Liquor Licenses.**)

Further Reading

Babor, Thomas. *Alcohol and Public Policy: No Ordinary Commodity*. New York: Oxford University Press, 2003.

Coleman, Tyler. *Wine Politics: How Governments, Environmentalists, Mobsters, and Critics Influence the Wines We Drink*. Berkeley: University of California Press, 2009.

Jurkiewicz, Carole J., and Murphy J. Painter. *Social and Economic Control of Alcohol: The 21st Amendment in the 21st Century*. Boca Raton, FL: CRC Group, 2007.

Meier, Kenneth J. *The Politics of Sin: Drugs, Alcohol and Public Policy*. Armonk, NY: M. E. Sharpe, 1994.

Mendelson, Richard. *From Demon to Darling: A Legal History of Wine in America*. Berkeley: University of California Press, 2009.

U.S. Department of the Treasury. Alcohol and Tobacco Tax and Trade Bureau Home Page. http://www.ttb.gov.

Karen Eilene Saenz

PROHIBITION

Prohibition, which prohibited the manufacturing, transportation, and sale of alcoholic beverages in the United States, lasted nearly 14 years, from January 16, 1920, to December 5, 1933. It was the culmination of the **Temperance** Movement,

New York City deputy police commissioner John A. Leach (right) watches agents pour confiscated liquor into a sewer following a raid during the height of Prohibition. (Library of Congress)

a century-long social reform movement led by evangelical Protestant churches to sober up the United States from the tyranny of Demon **Rum**.

Individual states had tried prohibiting intoxicating beverages before. Massachusetts first attempted to control distilled spirits in 1838, though these laws were soon repealed. Maine voted to go dry in 1851, and within four years, 13 states had passed the "Maine Law." Those laws were repealed as well, as liquor flowed over the borders as contraband.

When education failed to stop Americans from drinking, temperance reformers turned to coercion. The **Anti-Saloon League** (ASL) was founded in 1893 to shut down the "liquor traffic." Saloons were popular among immigrants in urban communities. The Protestant Temperance Movement wanted to turn immigrants—many of them Catholics and Jews—into sober citizens by imposing their view of a middle-class, dry America. The ASL was successful in its campaign to turn states dry using pressure **politics**, and without ever becoming a mass movement. By the time the United States entered World War I in 1917, most states had some form of prohibition on the books.

Volstead Act

In 1919, Congress passed the Volstead Act designed to support the Eighteenth Amendment to the Constitution, which prohibited the manufacture and sale of alcohol in the United States. Representative Andrew Volstead of Minnesota sponsored the bill that was drafted by Wayne Wheeler of the Anti-Saloon League. Officially called the National Prohibition Act of 1919, the legislation gave more detailed legal definition to national prohibition and gave the federal government the authority to enforce prohibition statutes. The Volstead Act defined intoxicating liquor as a beverage containing 0.5 percent alcohol or more by volume and fixed specific penalties for illegal liquor sales. President Woodrow Wilson, who believed in temperance but not complete prohibition, vetoed the bill but the veto was overridden. In 1933 the ratification of the Twenty-first Amendment ending national prohibition rendered the Volstead Act obsolete.

The ASL seized upon the crisis of World War I as the catalyst for change. German Americans controlled the **brewing** industry, but once the country declared war on Germany, drinking **beer** was viewed as unpatriotic. The German population in the country was suspect. The ASL proposed amending the Constitution to outlaw the liquor traffic permanently. The Eighteenth Amendment sailed through Congress on a bipartisan vote, passing on to the states on December 22, 1917. It took less than 13 months for the necessary three-quarters of states to ratify the amendment. In fact, only Connecticut and Rhode Island did not ratify the amendment.

Prohibition required an enforcement law, so Congress passed the Volstead Act in 1919. President Woodrow Wilson believed that low-alcohol beverages such as beer and **wine** should still be legal, but the ASL insisted that all alcohol should be banned. Wilson vetoed the law, and Congress overrode his veto. However, the Volstead Act allowed significant loopholes for medicinal spirits and sacramental wine for religious occasions.

Prohibition went in effect on January 16, 1920. Congress appropriated little money initially to enforce Prohibition: the ASL had promised a new day in America and assumed that people would respect the law. Because Prohibition only made the manufacture, transportation, and sale of alcohol illegal, people could make homemade beer or wine as long as they did not transport it.

Prohibition was the last hurrah for a declining, white, Protestant rural America. According to the U.S. Census, 27 percent of Americans farmed in 1920. The 2000 census noted that less than 2 percent farmed, as the United States had become predominantly urban and suburban. The urban nature of drinking undermined temperance values. Prohibition also marked the end of the Progressive Era—two decades of societal reform. Progressive reforms included the income tax, food safety laws, and the vote for women. World War I was supposed to make the world safe for democracy. However, the American public had grown weary of reform. Prohibition seemed to work, initially. The public took a wait-and-see attitude about it, but soon the cracks began to appear; too many groups, both ethnic and religious, had been marginalized by the ASL's political tactics, and these same people were now determined to disobey Prohibition. A quarter-million people lost their jobs when Prohibition began. Others were offended by the loss of a civil liberty, the right to drink. The seeds of Prohibition's failure were sown at the beginning.

Prohibition attempted to impose abstinence from alcohol on the nation by regulating private behavior. In economic terms, it cut off the supply but never dealt with the demand. Americans still wanted to drink, and they found ingenious ways to buy booze. Their drinking was simply driven underground to the **speakeasies** and local bootleggers who supplied and transported alcohol. This ultimately undermined Prohibition, as millions of Americans disobeyed the law of the land, many of them setting up stills in their homes. Alcohol was too ingrained in American culture for people simply to give it up.

The nation's borders were porous, and alcohol began slipping easily into the country, from Canada, Mexico, and along the long Eastern seaboard. Ships full of alcohol began anchoring outside American territorial waters in what were known as Rum Rows. At night, speedboats brought booze from the ships to shore, offloading the bootlegged cargo on dark beaches and inlets. A rumrunner, William McCoy, became known for the quality of his goods, giving origin to the phrase "the real McCoy."

Prohibition rolled out the red carpet for organized crime, and the federal government was unprepared. It had assumed people would obey the law, but there was so much money to be made. Countless public figures and policemen were bribed. In many places like New York and Chicago, Prohibition was unenforceable. In Washington, D.C., George Cassiday bootlegged alcohol to the members of Congress and earned the sobriquet, "the man in the green hat."

Bootleggers built souped-up, supercharged cars to outrun police and Prohibition agents while they carried loads of booze. On weekends, the drivers got together to race one another. After Prohibition ended, these drivers organized the National Association for Stock Car Auto Racing (NASCAR).

Prohibition also gave rise to the best-known novel of the 1920s: *The Great Gatsby* by F. Scott Fitzgerald. It was based it on a real person, George Remus, a German immigrant and attorney who lived in Cincinnati. Remus read through the Volstead Act—the congressional act that enforced Prohibition—and found a major loophole. It allowed licensed distilleries to continue making spirits for "medicinal" purposes. Remus bought up a number of distilleries for next to nothing, applied for licenses, then bribed policemen and Prohibition Bureau agents to look the other way while he produced more spirits than the license allowed. Remus made a fortune in just a few years. But like Gatsby's Daisy, a woman brought him down. Remus's wife, Imogene, was his downfall. Remus was arrested for violating the Volstead Act and sent to jail. Imogene Remus fell in love with the man who prosecuted her husband, and the two absconded with Remus's money. When Remus got out of prison, he hunted down his wife and shot and killed her. He pleaded not guilty by reason of insanity, and the jury accepted this defense. He was set free.

The year 1923 marked a turning point as the public was becoming disenchanted with Prohibition. Governor Al Smith of New York, the country's most populous state, signed a law repealing the state's Prohibition enforcement statute. New York had washed its hands of an unenforceable law, handing back enforcement to the federal government. Smith became the de facto national leader of the "wets." He was also a Catholic.

Wayne Wheeler, who drafted the Volstead Act for the ASL, died in 1927, and the ASL had an increasingly more difficult time dealing with the public challenges to Prohibition. Its influence was waning; the public blamed the organization for getting the country into this mess. One of its influential lobbyists, William Anderson, was convicted of embezzling money from the organization. Virginia's Methodist Bishop, James Cannon, led the ASL on the organization's rapid retreat. He achieved one final victory by playing the Catholic card against the wet (anti-Prohibition) Democratic presidential candidate, Al Smith, in 1928, turning Southern Democrats against their own candidate. Republican candidate Herbert Hoover won the election instead. Prohibition had passed during World War I as a bipartisan issue. However, it became a Republican issue to defend: they controlled the presidency and both the House and Senate throughout the 1920s. They were blamed for Prohibition's subsequent failure.

Prohibition earned its nickname, the "noble experiment," from President Hoover. Hoover had declared in a speech that Prohibition was "a great social and economic experiment, noble in motive and far-reaching in purpose." The public was disenchanted, but the federal government was determined to enforce the law. It would soon be tested as organized crime **violence** peaked.

In the late 1920s, Al Capone rose to the head of the Chicago mob. Though his rule only lasted three years, he became the best-known gangster in American history. Capone relished the limelight. He made his money largely through bootlegging alcohol, and he was constantly at war with other gangs. In 1929, when a rival gang proved a thorn in his side, Capone sent in his assassins to take them out. Capone's men disguised themselves as police offers and infiltrated the rival's garage. They rounded up seven men, lined them up against a wall, and executed them. It was February 14, and the event became known as the Valentine's Day Massacre.

The public was outraged by the violence. President Hoover declared Capone as Public Enemy No. 1, and a special squad of "untouchables" under Eliot Ness was assigned to bring him down. In March 1931, the federal government finally charged Capone with income tax evasion—the only charge they could make stick. He was convicted and sent to prison.

By the late 1920s, it was clear that Prohibition was failing. Volstead Act violators overwhelmed the court system, and the prisons were overly crowded. Violence was escalating. Unscrupulous bootleggers poisoned thousands of people with denatured spirits. The wets began calling for the nation to repeal Prohibition. Pauline Morton Sabin helped organize the Women's Organization for National Prohibition Reform, and it grew to 1.1 million members in 1932, comprising almost all women and far eclipsing the **Woman's Christian Temperance Union** (WCTU). Women had a role in creating Prohibition—and in bringing it down.

Prohibition's fate was sealed when the stock market collapsed in October 1929, sending the economy into the Great Depression. During the worst of the Depression, a fourth of the workforce was unemployed, and the economy contracted by a third. A seismic shift in the political balance took place in 1930 and 1932 as American voters drove the Republicans from power, largely because of the economy.

The Democratic Party took over Congress, and Franklin D. Roosevelt was elected president in 1932. The Democrats had adopted repeal as part of its platform, being careful to frame the debate that they were not pro-alcohol, but rather in favor of restoring law and order. With the Great Depression, the Democrats argued that reopening the distilleries and breweries would create hundreds of thousands of jobs and generate revenue for the federal government. Repeal would help get the economy moving.

The Twenty-first Amendment repealing Prohibition passed Congress in February 1933, two weeks before Roosevelt was sworn in as president. The amendment declared that states would vote by convention—that way the Democrats could control the process, rather than submit it to the voters. The American public wanted an end to Prohibition, and the state conventions met expediently. Michigan became the first state to vote for repeal in March 1933, and only nine months later, Utah became the 36th state to ratify the amendment. Prohibition was over. Repeal Day (also known as "Cinco de Drinko") is now celebrated annually on December 5.

The Bard of Baltimore, muckraker journalist H. L. Mencken, called Prohibition the "Thirteen Awful Years" in his memoirs. He celebrated repeal with a glass of water, which he claimed was his first since Prohibition began. Temperance died an ugly death, and the movement was thoroughly discredited. The result is that temperance is no longer part of the American cultural landscape.

Eighteenth Amendment

Passed by Congress December 18, 1917. Ratified January 16, 1919.

Section 1.

After one year from the ratification of this article the manufacture, sale, or transportation of intoxicating liquors within, the importation thereof into, or the exportation thereof from the United States and all territory subject to the jurisdiction thereof for beverage purposes is hereby prohibited.

Section 2.

The Congress and the several States shall have concurrent power to enforce this article by appropriate legislation.

Section 3.

This article shall be inoperative unless it shall have been ratified as an amendment to the Constitution by the legislatures of the several States, as provided in the Constitution, within seven years from the date of the submission hereof to the States by the Congress.

Source: **National Archives.** http://www.archives.gov/exhibits/charters/constitution_amendments_11-27.html#18 (accessed March 10, 2010).

Further Reading

Allen, Frederick Lewis. *Only Yesterday: An Informal History of the 1920's*. New York: Perennial Classics, 2000 (original edition 1931).

Behr, Edward. *Prohibition: Thirteen Years That Changed America*. New York: Arcade Publishing, 1996.

Clark, Norman H. *Deliver Us from Evil: An Interpretation of American Prohibition*. New York: W. W. Norton & Company, 1976.

Coffey, Thomas M. *The Long Thirst: Prohibition in America 1920–1933*. New York: W. W. Norton, 1975.

Fitzgerald, F. Scott. *The Great Gatsby*. 1925; New York: Scribner, 2004.

Gately, Iain. *Drink: A Cultural History of Alcohol*. New York: Gotham Books, 2008.

Kobler, John. *Ardent Spirits: The Rise and Fall of Prohibition*. New York: Da Capo Press, 1993.

Kyvig, David E. *Repealing National Prohibition*. Chicago: University of Chicago Press, 1979.

Lerner, Michael. *Dry Manhattan: Prohibition in New York City*. Cambridge, MA: Harvard University Press, 2007.

Peck, Garrett. *The Prohibition Hangover: Alcohol in America from Demon Rum to Cult Cabernet*. New Brunswick, NJ: Rutgers University Press, 2009.

Garrett Peck

PUB CRAWLS

Pub crawls are social events where group drinking at different venues occurs throughout the course of a set period. Participants meet at designated starting points and travel from location to location, usually by foot. Pub crawls are alternatively known as bar hopping, bar crawls, bar tours, or joint hopping.

Pub crawls can be spontaneous or planned. They can be held with as few as two participants, or as many as several thousand. Themed, costume, and historical pub crawls are popular variations. Some charities also sponsor pub crawls as fundraising events. **Beer** is often drunk during a pub crawl, though other alcoholic or nonalcoholic beverages may also be consumed. Some participants choose to limit their alcohol consumption or to not drink at all during the event.

The origins of this term are British, and its practice remains in wide use. Its adoption in the United States dates to the early twentieth century. The origins of this practice are unclear. The history of **pubs** and drinking establishments in Britain is closely tied to the development of transportation. Pubs were built along major roads and carriageways, and often served as rest stops and waiting rooms. Many workers in Britain also commuted several miles to and from work by foot, and stopped in pubs along the journey home. This practice may have provided the origins for the modern pub crawl.

Further Reading

Girouard, Mark. *Victorian Pubs*. New Haven, CT: Yale University Press, 1984.

Willa Zhen

PUBS

Throughout many regions of the world, pub refers to public **bars** or taverns licensed for the sale of intoxicating beverages. The word is an informal reference to a public house, an English term that has largely now been replaced by this more informal abbreviation. "Pub" became a part of everyday language in Great Britain and the British Empire by the eighteenth century.

Public houses have a long history in the British Isles and North America as inns or hostelries where travelers could purchase food, drink, and shelter. The English throne first granted public house licenses in the twelfth century to bring control over the sale of intoxicants as well as to guarantee that shelter and accommodations would be readily available to travelers in the British Isles.

In Colonial America, the public house system closely resembled that in the British Isles. Serving multiple roles at the center of village life, public houses frequently acted as general stores, where goods of all sorts could be purchased. Other services that pubs provided at this time included postal and coach services. In fact, public houses often represented the most common terminuses in the transportation network during the eighteenth and nineteenth centuries, where travelers disembarked upon reaching their destination or waited for the arrival of another coach for further travel. In addition, publicans often rented carts, wagons, and horses to locals as well as travelers. Some of these usages persisted into the early twentieth century in rural districts.

Beyond their importance to the economy and transportation, public houses also served as important social centers for villages and neighborhoods in the eighteenth and nineteenth centuries. The pub not only served as a meeting point for travelers, but also hosted formal and informal community and civic meetings of all sorts: political speeches and rallies, funerals, and even the occasional wedding.

By the nineteenth century, "pub" had become common shorthand for public house throughout the British Empire. In North America, the terms "bar," "saloon," and "tavern" seem to have slowly supplanted "pub" as a common name for a public drinking establishment. This change in usage also mirrored changes in consumption patterns as government regulations sought to separate businesses according to the goods they sold. In the United States, as regulations increasingly separated the retail licensing of alcohol from other businesses, the term "pub" became less frequently used, reserved for those houses that reflected the more traditional pub or an Irish pub. In the late nineteenth and early twentieth centuries, regulations aimed at fighting drunkenness required public bars to be separated from lodgings, grocery stores, and other businesses. Unlike the traditional pub, the modern tavern or bar has become almost exclusively a place for the public consumption of alcoholic drinks.

As the role of the pub increasingly centered around the consumption of alcohol, the barroom also became more male-dominated. By the late nineteenth century, respectability dictated that women not enter a pub unaccompanied by a man.

There is today in the United States very little distinction between even the use of the words pub, tavern, or bar—all of them refer to a business where alcoholic drinks can be purchased and consumed on the premises. The traditional pub, with its variety of services beyond the sale of alcohol, has long disappeared from American towns and cities.

In many regions of the world, pubs often are associated with Ireland and Irish culture. This development primarily stems from the large numbers of Irish immigrants who took up the trade of publican during the nineteenth century in places like Canada, the United States, and Australia. By the late twentieth century, the commercial success of many Irish pubs relied upon a promotion of Irish drinking culture—Irish beers such as Guinness and Jameson's **whiskey**, Irish music, and a convivial atmosphere of lighthearted revelry. Today, most businesses in North America that use the name "pub" can be found in large cities such as Chicago, New York, and San Francisco. This is mostly due to the continued connection between Irish American publicans and this traditional label for a bar or tavern. The interior of these pubs generally reflects Victorian tastes: dark paneling and woodwork, a large, often harsher-shaped bar, large gilded mirrors, and tables for drinking, eating, and socializing. Pubs often provide entertainment such as live **music**, darts, and pool. Some Irish pubs in the United States even feature multiple televisions, including large-screen, high-definition TVs, and thus resemble the American sports bar far more than a traditional pub.

Other terms associated with pubs include "**pub crawl**" and "**pub grub**." The former refers to a drinking party that visits a string of bars on foot, consuming drinks at each stop along the way. The latter referrers to food served in a pub, such as fish and chips, sandwiches, and other modern foods commonly found in bars or cafes.

Further Reading

Bailey, Peter. *Leisure and Class in Victorian England: Rational Recreation and the Contest for Control.* New York: Routledge and Paul, 1978.

Boyer, Paul. *Urban Masses and Moral Order in America.* Cambridge, MA: Harvard University Press, 1978.

Conroy, David. *In Public Houses: Drink and the Revolution of Authority in Colonial Massachusetts.* Chapel Hill: University of North Carolina Press, 1995.

Harrisson, Brian. *Drink and the Victorians.* Staffordshire, UK: Keele University Press, 1991.

Powers, Madelon. *Faces along the Bar: Lore and Order in the Workingman's Saloon 1870–1920.* Chicago: University of Chicago Press, 1998.

Thompson, Peter. *Rum, Punch and Revolution: Tavern Going and Public Life in Philadelphia.* Philadelphia: University of Pennsylvania Press, 1998.

Bradley Kadel

PUNCH

The word "punch" comes from the Sanskrit word *panca,* which means "five." It seems that the name of this drink, which can be served cold or hot, alludes to the fact that several ingredients were combined. Today, a punch may include alcohol

In American history, punch became famous during a near riot upon the inauguration of President Andrew Jackson in 1829. Jackson's supporters, the working and lower classes, were invited en masse to the White House to celebrate his victory. So many people came that the elegant furniture was overturned and men who did not know better stood on brocade chairs in their muddy boots to get a better look at their president. To end the chaos, the staff quickly moved the buckets of punch outside to the lawn, and the crowd followed. Jackson's inaugural punch was an Orange Punch, according to nineteenth-century cookbooks, made of simple sugar syrup, orange peel, orange and lemon juices, rum, and brandy.

with fruit juices, sparkling water, or soft drinks, or nonalcoholic combinations of those beverages. The drink is always presented in a large bowl or pitcher. A block of ice featuring frozen fruits may float in a cold punch, or fruit sherbets may be added to provide color, texture, and taste. Punches are often served on holidays. Examples of holiday punches include eggnog and syllabub. Punch also has a political association: in the early nineteenth century, milk punches were the rage during elections. This punch was made from sugar, **bourbon** or blended **whiskey**, milk, and nutmeg.

Further Reading

Collins, Dennis. *Mixing and Serving Drinks: A Complete Guide*. New York: Dell Purse Book, 1963.

Dabney, Joseph E. *Smokehouse Ham, Spoon Bread, and Scuppernong Wine: The Folklore and Art of Southern Appalachian Cooking*. Nashville, TN: Cumberland House, 1998.

Farmer, Fannie Merritt. *The Boston Cooking-School Cook Book*. 6th ed. Boston: Little, Brown, and Company, 1937.

Felton, Eric. "Having a Ball at the Inauguration." *Wall Street Journal*, January 16, 2009. http://online.wsj.com/article/SB123215760361192597.html.

Pam Sezgin

R

RACE AND ETHNICITY

There are various differences in the causes and patterns of alcohol use, consequences of such use, and addiction treatment of the various racial and ethnic groups. The earliest attempts to understand the effects of alcohol were limited to Caucasian samples, but more recent research has included groups of other racial and ethnic backgrounds.

Race refers to the grouping together of people with certain physical distinctions that society has deemed important; therefore, although it has its roots in genetics, the concept of race is socially constructed. Ethnicity refers to the learned traits of a cultural group, which includes a common language, religious and other cultural beliefs, and normative behaviors, but is often used to denote race due to similarities within these racial groups. Because there are numerous factors to consider regarding the connection between racial and ethnic groups and alcohol, such as biological factors, cultural factors, specific environmental factors related to community, and family influences, it is not possible to definitively ascertain specific correlations. However, a general analysis of the behaviors from a comparative perspective can be useful in understanding alcohol-related behavior.

Major racial minority groups in the United States are Latinos, **African Americans**, Asian Americans and **Native Americans**. Latinos, or Hispanics, although heterogeneous, have typically been grouped together by researchers. The different subgroups have various traits regarding alcohol consumption, consequences, and treatment. Previous anthropological and sociological research on Latino drinking was conducted on subjects in the American Southwest and dealt primarily with problem drinking. More current studies have focused on Mexican Americans, who are a much larger group, and have suggested that this group has more severe problems with alcohol than other Latino groups. Some observations to be made regarding Hispanics include an examination of the traditional explanation that Latino males drink large amounts of alcohol to inflate "machismo," or the masculine ideal. There has been no reliable evidence to support this claim, however, and it appears to be based more on stereotype than science.

Early research on African Americans, similar to that on Latinos, focused more on problem drinking behaviors and less on lighter patterns of drinking or abstinence. Again, stereotypical explanations suggested this group consumed alcohol heavily as a result of social disorganization. This limited view did not allow for other factors such as migration, as occurred in large numbers as African Americans traveled to the north in search of employment in the early twentieth century; studies have suggested that this change resulted in an increase of alcohol consumption among this group. However, recent research reveals that African Americans in large numbers tend to be rather conservative in their drinking behavior. Studies have also reported higher abstention rates of alcohol use among black women than among white women. Many factors, such as individual characteristics, social change, historical events, and cultural practices, have shaped alcohol behavior with this group.

Asian Americans have often been referred to as the "model minority," a term viewed with derision by many people, including those of Asian descent. Studies have shown lower rates of alcohol-related problems than with some other racial groups; however, there are variations within this racial group as some subgroups tend to abstain or drink less than their counterparts. Regarding gender, Asian females abstain to a higher degree than males. Due to the lower rates of alcohol consumption of Asian Americans, some researchers have proposed a "flushing response" to alcohol, which refers to a physiological response that results in a flushing of the skin, an increase in skin temperature, nausea, lightheadedness, anxiety, and other unpleasant responses; it has been posited that this response thwarts the drinker's overuse of alcohol. Other possible reasons of the low rate of alcohol use and abuse among this racial group include cultural characteristics that value abstinence and conformity to norms.

Studying Native Americans produces some of the same problems as the other racial groups: there is much racial heterogeneity and too many different cultural factors to produce a definitive explanation for drinking behavior. Early assumptions about alcohol use among this population involved the "Firewater Myth," which supposed that native peoples were unable to control themselves when under the influence of alcohol. Some studies have attributed the high rates of alcohol use and abuse of some native tribes to environmental factors such as discrimination, poverty, and unemployment. (*See also* **Men and Boys Drinking.**)

Further Reading

Caetano, Raul, Catherine L. Clark, and Tammy Tam. "Alcohol Consumption among Racial/Ethnic Minorities, Theory and Research." *Alcohol Health and Research World* 22 (1998): 233–41.

Jung, John. *Psychology of Alcohol and Other Drugs: A Research Perspective.* Thousand Oaks, CA: Sage Publications, 2001.

Leonard A. Steverson

REHAB

In American culture, "rehab" (short for "rehabilitation") is commonly used to refer to the inpatient treatment experiences of entertainment personalities who have had a drug- or alcohol-use crisis of some public proportion. The term is embedded in popular culture but is never used among professionals working in addiction treatment.

There are several popular rock band names such as Rehab and rock **music** song titles, such as Amy Winehouse's popular pop song "Rehab," that include this term. Most prominent in 2009 is the U.S. **television** program, *Rehab: The Party at the Hard Rock Hotel*. While never directly stated, this all-out, alcohol-laden series of events loaded with sexual innuendo is apparently intended to play on the term "rehab" in a manner that suggests some kind of rejection of that concept, or perhaps borderline thrill-seeking that defies "rehab."

The gap between popular and professional usage is not easily explained. While "rehab" is an abbreviation, its narrow popular reference to addiction treatment does not match the established professional term, rehabilitation. Popular culture tends to celebrate excess and celebrates the rejection of attempts to reform excessive alcohol and drug intake—there seems little hope or desire for rehabilitation. Curiously, the term "rehab" has gained almost exclusive application to addiction in the early years of the twenty-first century. It is to be distinguished from "rehabilitation," which continues to have an exclusive application to those suffering from physical consequences of injury and accidents. In this sense, alcoholics can also be framed as victims of some sort of crash or final turn toward disaster as they are unable to manage daily life as alcohol takes over.

"Rehab" almost always implies an inpatient experience, typically suggesting a multi-week duration. It is common for the media to focus intensely on the entry and exit from these treatment experiences, with a suggested anticipation of relapse. Perhaps the most famous rehab center in the United States is the Betty Ford Center. Founded in 1982 in Rancho Mirage, California, this addiction treatment center quickly became noted as the rehab clinic of choice for celebrities. Cited in popular television shows such as *The Simpsons* and *Two and a Half Men*, Betty Ford has become synonymous with addiction and rehab, transforming this former first lady's name into a popular culture icon.

Further Reading

Ford, Betty. *Healing and Hope: Six Women from the Betty Ford Center Share their Powerful Journeys of Addiction and Recovery*. New York: Putnam, 2003.

Shavelson, Lonny. *Hooked: Five Addicts Challenge Our Misguided Drug Rehab System*. New York: New Press, 2002.

Paul M. Roman and Rachel Black

RELIGION

Overview

The world's major religions are represented in the United States. The Bill of Rights guarantees freedom of religion. These world religions, though, have different perspectives on the use and abuse of alcohol. Some religions like Islam have an outright ban on the consumption of alcoholic beverages. Drinking is forbidden, and drunkenness is a sin. Other religions, like Judaism, allow alcohol in moderation and incorporate its use at holiday meals and celebrations. Yet other religions in their original form in the Old World ban alcohol, but some of their contemporary practitioners in the United States allow very controlled use of alcohol. For example, the drinking of alcohol is allowed among the Buddhist followers of Chŏgyan Trungpa Rinpoche, who brought the Vajrayana school of Tibetan belief to North America.

Still other religions do not deal in absolutes. For example, in Hinduism, alcohol is recognized as a powerful and dangerous substance, but there is no outright ban. In the Hindu social hierarchy, alcohol's use was restricted to certain categories of people, such as particular castes and types of monks. Christianity in the United States has diverse sects and no single platform regarding alcohol. Each denomination makes its own ruling. Some Christian groups incorporate **wine** in their religious rituals. Some allow social drinking, while other Christian groups consider that practice a sin.

Islam: Formal Prohibition of Alcohol

There is no ambiguity in the prohibition of alcohol, today, among observant Muslims in North America or elsewhere. Its consumption, manufacture, and sale are prohibited. Formal Islam bans the use of alcohol as well as the use of other narcotics because these substances interfere with clear thinking. They are seen to cloud the judgment, numb the senses, and prevent people from making distinctions between shame and responsibility (Bleher 2000, 1).

There are numerous passages in the Qur'an and the Hadith, the sacred texts of Islam, that illustrate problems associated with alcohol and discourage its use (Inter-Islam, 1998–2001; Kasem, 2005). Yet, other passages give examples of drinking. The purpose of these passages is to cause the reader to think about the harmful effects and problems associated with alcohol consumption. For example, a prayer recited while drunk is invalid. Or, the reading of a sacred text may be in error if the reader is inebriated. Whether Sunni or Shi'a, the two major divisions of Islamic belief, Muslims agree that alcohol is against the religion. Yet, in the United States and even in some Muslim countries, many Muslims drink. The most observant do not, but Muslims, like other postcolonial peoples, have an association of alcohol consumption with middle-class and upper middle-class material culture. Businessmen drink because it is a social activity where business is transacted.

Sufism is a mystical tradition of Islam. In its poetry and practice, both of which are popular in contemporary North America, devoted worshippers are often said to be "drunk" and wine imagery abounds. Drunkenness is a metaphor for the overwhelming ecstasy of the Sufi religious experience, the closeness to the divine, rather than having a literal meaning (Ernst 1997, 115). Sufis pray not only in the traditional way, but also using dance and **music**, a non-fundamentalist path.

Thus, for Muslims in the United States and for their relatives in other countries, it is the ideal culture that has a religious prohibition against alcohol consumption. This ideal is often at odds with the real culture of the middle class, who have adopted the drinking traditions not only of their pre-fundamentalist past, but also of bourgeois European business culture.

Judaism: Moderation in Drinking

Judaism and Islam are both Abrahamic religions that spring from the same Middle Eastern roots. Like Islam, Judaism generally condemns drunkenness, and its sacred texts provide examples of the danger and power of this substance. But unlike Islam, Judaism sanctions the moderate use of alcoholic beverages and even incorporates them into the formal, ritual practices associated with holy days and weekly Sabbath observances. The *Kiddush* is a prayer made over wine that is recited on the Sabbath before meals and on holy days. Wine symbolizes the joy of these observances. Moderate use of wine is sanctioned. A shot glass serving of spirits such as **whiskey** may be used to make the *Kiddush* on Sabbath after the morning service before a snack of bread and drink is shared by the congregants or may be served to guests with food in the *Sukkah*, a ceremonial booth for the fall harvest holiday of *Sukkoth*. Alcoholic beverages convey hospitality in these situations and build a sense of shared experience, *communitas*.

Four cups of wine are consumed by each guest at the Passover *Seder*, a ceremonial meal consumed on the first two nights of that religious festival with family and friends. The narrative of the Jews' escape from Egypt is retold each year at this meal, which goes on for several hours.

In each of the previous examples, alcoholic beverages enhance the experience and enable Jews to fulfill the *mitzvah* (commandment) of properly observing the Sabbath or the holiday. But one holiday is different: Purim is thought to be the one holiday where drunkenness is permitted. However, that may be an erroneous assumption (Siegel 2009, 4). Purim commemorates the events from the Book of Esther, where Jews in ancient Persia escape an extermination plot hatched by an evil advisor to the king. The use of alcoholic beverages, as well as the masking that goes on during this celebration, express joy and thanksgiving that the Jewish people survived what might have been a terrible tragedy were it not for the bravery of Esther and her uncle Mordecai. Jewish religious law, though, is clear regarding drunkenness: people are held responsible for their actions, even if they are drunk.

Buddhism: Mind-Body Connection

Drinking alcohol, smoking cigarettes, and taking narcotics are inconsistent with Buddhist beliefs because they distort the mind. Like Islam, Buddhism emphasizes the importance of clear-mindedness. Buddhists emphasize meditation, a discipline that improves the mind. One of the five precepts of Buddhism clearly prohibits the use of alcohol and other intoxicants. Alcohol use prevents people from dealing with life and, instead, provides a false sense of contentment.

Some American Buddhists, though, find it difficult to give up alcoholic beverages today. A practice of *mindful drinking* has ensued, although it is at odds with mainstream Buddhist practices in Asia. In this practice, small amounts of alcoholic beverages are consumed at ritual feasts, where participants are supposed to focus on alcohol's effect on one's mind. The idea is that small amounts of alcohol can be "illuminating." *Mindful drinking* was introduced in America by Chögan Trungpa Rinpoche who fled the Chinese communists. He was from the Kagyu-pa lineage of Tibetan Vajrayana Buddhism (whose monks used alcohol "to loosen the ego").

Hindusism: No Absolutes, but Abstinence Is Best

The Hindu religion does not deal in absolutes. Rather, it is a path of spirituality that helps its followers discover *dharma*, the natural laws of the universe. Different groups of people in the Hindu social hierarchy approach alcohol in different ways. The rule is that Hindus should understand the potential harm inherent in intoxicants and approach them with restraint, caution, and moderation (Frawley, 2006–2008, 4). Some groups are sanctioned to use alcohol. Doctors of Ayurvedic medicine can give herbal wines in moderation to patients for particular maladies such as indigestion, stress, and circulatory problems. Monks generally do not use alcohol, except for members of Hindu Tantric orders who use alcohol in their rituals. Aristocrats and merchants, historically, also drank alcohol. But for most people, abstinence was regarded as the best path.

Hindu immigrants to North America have had different experiences. India, the country of origin for the majority, has a love-hate relationship with alcohol. On the one hand, alcoholic beverages are associated with modernity, and on the other, prohibition is alive and well. Some intellectuals link the use of alcohol among elites in the society to colonial influences, a holdover from the British Empire.

Christianity: Each Denomination to Its Own

Among Orthodox Christians, Catholics, and Episcopalians, wine is used in the communion service, as it was by the first Christians. In contrast, Methodists, Presbyterians, and Baptists in the United States substitute grape juice for wine, even though the New Testament is full of references to wine. Christians have some important narratives regarding wine. For example, one of Jesus's miracles is turning water into wine at a wedding of one of his mother's relatives. Wine is a critical element of the communion service as it symbolically transforms into the blood of Christ in which the believers partake. Methodists, Presbyterians, and Baptists, while having a formal ban on the consumption of alcohol both in church and, for some, in their daily lives, nonetheless exist in a world where real and ideal culture clash. Bans on drinking in these Protestant sects of Christianity vis-à-vis worship and religious ritual substitute grape juice for wine. Historically, Baptists in the Southern United States also were strict about not drinking at home, but that may be different today. Some members of these congregations drink at home, in **bars**, at parties, and most importantly, at sporting events. But for others, the use of alcohol at public functions, even though they may be secular in nature, is problematic. The religious prohibition of alcohol, thus, is no guarantee that alcohol use will be prevented.

Further Reading

Blackburn, Sanja. "Buddhism and Alcohol." American National Standard Institute (ANSI). 2009. http://www.purifymind.com/BuddhismAlcohol.htm.

Bleher, Sahib Mustaqim. "One Glass Too Many: The Islamic View on the Prohibition of Alcohol." *Mustaqim Islamic Art and Literature*. 2000. http://www.mustaqim.co.uk/printalcohol.htm.

"Buddhist Ethics." Buddhanet. http://www.buddhanet.net/e-learning/budethics.htm.

Ernst, Carl W. *The Shambhala Guide to Sufism*. Boston: Shambhala, 1997.

Frawley, David. "A Hindu View on the Use of Alcohol." *Dharmic Naujawaan*, 2006, http://www.dharmicnaujawaan.org.gy/?q=node/51.
Inter-Islam. "The Harms of Alcohol." 1998–2001. http://www.inter-islam.org/Prohibitions/alcohol2.htm.
Kassem, Abul. "Wine Drinking in Islam." *Freethinker*, April 11, 2005. http://www.mukto-mona.com/Articles/kasem/wine_drinking.htm.
Ranganathan, Shanthi. "The Most Sensible Thing Is Not to Drink." *World Health Forum: Alcohol in the Third World*. World Health Organization, September, 1994, http://www.unhooked.com/sep/thirdworl.htm.
Siegel, Rabbi Daniel. "Alcohol and Judaism: One View." *Dartmouth College: Dartmouth Center on Addiction, Recovery and Education*. August 18, 2003. http://www.dartmouth.edu/~dcare/topics/jewish.html.

Pam Sezgin

RUM

Rum is a distinctly New World spirit. Though it is today associated especially with the Caribbean, where most of it is made, in pre-**Prohibition** and especially Colonial America, rum was one of the quintessential American spirits. It was not only consumed in the United States, but made here in great quantities, and until the nineteenth century was significantly more common than **whiskey**—there is a reason why the **Temperance** Movement of the nineteenth and twentieth centuries protested the ills of "demon rum," not "devilish **bourbon**."

In the seventeenth century, a visiting Englishman wrote that rum was "adored by the American English . . . held as the comfort of their souls, the preserver of their bodies, the remover of their cares, and promoter of their mirth; and is a sovereign remedy against . . . the epidemical distempers that afflict the country." The name may have come from the Romani word rum, meaning "strong," and like other liquor in the seventeenth century, rum was sometimes called simply "strong water." The Romani rum had been incorporated in the names for rumboozle and rumfustian, seventeenth-century English drinks made with **wine** and ale, and as rum became a slang word for "uproar" or "rumble," the liquor may have taken its name from its association with bar fights. Up through the eighteenth century, it could still be found as "kill-devil" in much of New England, "screech" in Newfoundland, "tafia" in the West Indies and the Carolinas, and "brandy-wine" among the Dutch of New York.

Rum itself had been an entrepreneurial solution to the discovery that tobacco grew poorly on Barbados, an uninhabited island that the English had acquired in the West Indies in 1625. The Portuguese settlers in Brazil had been distilling the juice of sugar cane—now called cachaca, or cane rum—but the English of Barbados unearthed a gold mine when they discovered that one could also distill the molasses that was left over after refining sugar. This provided two commodities, rum and refined sugar, from the same sugar cane crop. Fortunes were made quickly. Most of the Barbados molasses was shipped to New England for distillation, and the resulting rum was sold both within the colonies and overseas, especially to Africa.

A number of factors contributed to rum's popularity. Not only was it cheap—the by-product of a crop that was being harvested anyway—it had a longer shelf life than **beer**, which in those days was poorly filtered or unfiltered and could turn, especially in hot summer months. Though New Englanders and Virginians were avid **cider** and **applejack** drinkers, apples had to be introduced to newly settled land and took years to grow; as the country expanded, it was rum and not cider that filled frontiersmen's flasks.

Though **cocktails** did not develop until the nineteenth century, they came out of an older tradition of "tavern drinks," popular throughout America from its earliest days. While the oldest tavern drinks were concoctions of wine or beer, spiced or thickened with egg (the precursor to eggnog), as they drank in England, the arrival of rum led to the toddy (hot sweetened tea with rum and often lemon) and the sling (diluted sweetened rum with various flavorings). Politicians running for office—including George Washington—were known to treat voters to rum drinks.

The naval association with rum goes further than piracy and the ditty "yo ho ho and a bottle of rum." The British navy, made vulnerable to scurvy by their long voyages, made grog from their rum by adding spices and lemon juice; "bumbo," drunk by American sailors and pirates, left the lemon juice out. From the seventeenth century until 1970, every member of the British Royal Navy was entitled to a daily ration of rum called a "tot," and some rum producers still make a separate "Naval Strength" bottling of their product available.

Over time, whiskey surpassed rum in popularity. Prohibition put the remaining American rum producers out of business. In recent years, there has been a revival of American-made rums, as part of the "microdistillery" movement that followed on the heels of the microbrewing/craftbrewing movement. Breweries like Dogfish Head in Delaware and Rogue in Oregon have begun producing small-batch rums and other liquors, while small dedicated distilleries—often using pot stills rather than the column stills used by large producers—have begun operation, notably including Prichard's of Tennessee, which makes a whiskey-like rum similar in character to the best of the colonial-era rums.

Even as rum faded in popularity, it left its mark on the American palate. The "butter rum" flavor of candy, used by Lifesavers among others, is inspired by hot buttered rum, a drink of hot water and rum poured into a mug with butter, spices, and sugar, a cold-weather drink still served in some northern cities and ski lodges. Similarly, rum raisin ice cream, though not as common as it once was, uses rum flavoring and raisins, where raisins soaked in rum were once used—a practice for rejuvenating dried fruit that is also the basis for traditional Christmas fruitcakes. (*See also* **Distilling; Microbreweries.**)

Further Reading

Curtis, Wayne. *And a Bottle of Rum: A History of the New World in Ten Cocktails.* New York: Three Rivers Press, 2007.

Pegram, Thomas. *Battling Demon Rum.* Chicago: Ivan R. Dee, 1999.

Williams, Ian. *Rum: A Social and Sociable History of the Real Spirit of 1776.* New York: Nation Books, 2006.

Bill Kte'pi

S

SAKE

Sake is a traditional Japanese beverage made from fermented rice. It came to the United States with sushi, making its initial entry much like the Japanese Air Force, in Hawaii, in the early part of the twentieth century, but far exceeding Japan's military successes by subsequently invading Los Angeles and New York in the 1970s. By the 1980s sushi had spread to the heartland of America and Japanese restaurants, often owned by Korean and Chinese immigrants, and these restaurants began exposing mainstream Americans to sake.

Initially, sake in the United States was invariably a poor-quality, mass-production product served overly hot, but as many American businesspeople as well as Japanese expatriates had experienced quality chilled sakes in Japan, there soon became a small but steady market for them here.

Though Japanese food is now ubiquitous in American cities, finding a good sake list in the early twenty-first century is still difficult. Just as with novice **wine** cultures, most Americans initially prefer sweeter forms of sake, particularly nigori ("cloudy") sake, which is uncommon in Japan but a top seller here. Paradoxically, daiginjo sakes—the most expensive type, because most of the rice is shaved away for greater purity and delicacy—are proportionally more popular here than in Japan, where sake is more of an everyday beverage.

In the early twenty-first century, cutting-edge Western restaurants began stocking sake on their beverage lists, though despite its food-friendliness it is still generally paired only with raw fish appetizers. In 2003, entrepreneur Beau Timken opened True Sake, the country's first sake-only store, in San Francisco. By 2010 he was considering opening a branch in Los Angeles, but his store is still unique.

Sake is a delicate, fresh product that generally must be kept cool and consumed within 12 months of bottling. Problems with **distribution** and storage of sake

Sake, a traditional Japanese alcoholic drink made from rice, can be served either cold of hot. Along with sushi, sake made its debut in America in the early twentieth century. (Dreamstime.com)

continue to hinder its widespread acceptance. Perhaps a larger problem is the high markup in U.S. restaurants on sake because, unlike with wine, few customers know the retail price. A few companies, notably including Japan's Gekkeikan, have opened sake breweries in the United States, but while they have gained market share through low prices, none has achieved the quality of sake brewed in Japan.

Further Reading

Harper, Philip. *The Insider's Guide to Sake*. Tokyo: Kodansha International, 1998.

W. Blake Gray

SHOOTERS

Shooters are a type of cocktail served in small amounts that are meant to be drunk quickly, often in one gulp. These drinks are known for their interesting names and **drinking rituals**. Shooters were especially popular in the 1980s, when sweet **cocktails** were fashionable.

Shooters are served in shot glasses containing one to four ounces of liquid. They are sometimes referred to as shots, though they are different. Shooters contain a combination of spirits, liquors, and nonalcoholic mixers, whereas shots are purely alcohol. Like other cocktails, the ingredients used will vary between bartenders and across regions.

There are two possible origins of this drink. One theory cites roots in the Baltic and Northern Europe, where it is customary to take shots before a meal. Another theory traces the origins to the Pousse Café, or push coffee, a French cocktail with layers of colored liquors.

Shooter names are drawn from a variety of sources, including places, celebrities, and popular culture, including Scooby snack, liquid Viagra, and Alabama slammer. Many names also have an element of shock value and vulgarity, for example, slippery nipple, horny bull, and brain damage. Many shooters also have special

drinking games and rituals, such as drinking without the use of hands or taking body shots by sipping the drink off another person's body.

Further Reading

Biggs, David. *Sharp Shooters*. London: New Holland, 2004.

Charming, Cheryl. *Miss Charming's Guide for Hip Bartenders and Wayout Wannabes: Your Ultimate One-Stop Bar and Cocktail Resource*. Naperville, IL: Sourcebooks, 2007.

Graham, Colleen. "Shooter Recipes." http://cocktails.about.com/od/cocktailrecipes/a/shtr _recipes.htm.

Willa Zhen

SKID ROW AND THE BOWERY

Skid Row and the Bowery are synonymous with drunkards. Skid Row is any part of a city or town that is rundown and the home of alcoholics and others down on their luck. The term originated in the Pacific Northwest in the early twentieth century. Thought to derive partly from a logging phrase that referred to the roads along which logs were dragged from the forests to rivers and sawmills, "skid row" was first documented in a 1931 book on American slang that defined it as a place where tramps, social misfits, **winos**, and the unemployed congregate. Mark Matthews, a popular Seattle minister and **Prohibition** advocate in the early twentieth century, is believed to have used the term in reference to a former logging area of the city that had become a "skid road" to hell for those who abused alcohol. The phrase spread rapidly during the Great Depression, particularly to cities such as Vancouver, San Francisco, and Los Angeles on the West Coast to indicate slums of alcoholics and transients who slept in doorways, alleys, or flophouses.

During the Depression, the Bowery neighborhood of Lower Manhattan became a haven for the homeless and those down on their luck. The Bowery is the East Coast equivalent of skid row. The Bowery has an important place in American popular culture in **literature** and **music** and is almost always associated with drinking and vice. Although the Bowery neighborhood has been gentrifying since the 1990s, it is still remembered as a place for those down on their luck.By the 1950s, skid row referred to those city districts where the homeless gathered and where church missions, soup kitchens, and social service agencies established refuges to residents battling alcoholism, unemployment, and poverty.

Further Reading

Bahr, Howard M. *Skid Row: An Introduction to Disaffiliation*. New York: Oxford University Press, 1973.

Irwin, Godfrey. *American Tramp and Underworld Slang: Words and Phrases Used by Hoboes, Tramps, Migratory Workers and Those on the Fringe of Society*. New York: Sears, 1931.

Santé, Luc. *Low Life: Lures and Snares of Old New York*. New York: Farrar, Straus and Giroux, 1991.

Spradley, James P. *You Owe Yourself a Drunk: An Ethnography of Urban Nomads*. Boston: Little, Brown, 1970; Long Grove, IL: Waveland Press, 1999.

Kevin Grace

SOMMELIERS

Sommeliers are professionals trained in the various aspects of **wine** service as well as, to a lesser degree, the service of other alcoholic beverages. They generally work in restaurants, especially gastronomical establishments, although the presence of staff with at least some formal sommelier training has become more common in North American restaurants since the 1980s. This rise in sommelier training can be seen as concurrent with the general rise in wine consumption and wine culture in North America.

In a restaurant, the main task of a sommelier is to ensure that wines are served correctly (for example, at the right temperature, in proper glassware, decanted if necessary, without faults such as corkage) and that they match with the food. For this purpose, sommeliers must be able to provide information and advice on all wines included in the establishment's wine list, which often goes hand in hand with the task of establishing and maintaining the wine list. Sommeliers are thus often responsible for ordering and storing the wines, and doing so in collaboration with the chef, to ensure that the wine list matches the type of cuisine served in an establishment. This task is especially important in higher-end restaurants that hold a significant number of bottles in a cellar and offer more complex foods. In the world's top restaurants, sommeliers often are full partners in designing and defining the overall gastronomical experience.

Professionally trained sommeliers are required to have significant knowledge of wine regions, grape varieties, winemaking, and organoleptic characteristics of wines. Among other things, this leads some to write about wines professionally or offer **wine-tasting** courses to general audiences, providing their expertise to an audience beyond restaurant patrons. This extensive knowledge is also tested in a competitive context, with a number of "best sommelier" competitions taking place at the regional, national, and international level, and requiring participants to achieve remarkably precise feats of blind tasting (identifying region, varieties, vintage, and specific estates) and wine pairing, among other tests of knowledge and sensory abilities. There are many contests at every level, with the national and international titles being touted proudly by the sommeliers who win them— and the restaurants or other establishments who employ them.

There are a number of different training programs, certifications, and associations for sommeliers in America. The highest level of training and certification is probably the Master Sommelier, a diploma held by fewer than 200 people worldwide; it is granted by the Court of Master Sommeliers, an organization originating in England and established in the United States since 1977. Other sommelier organizations that provide education and training include the Sommelier Society of America, the United States Sommelier Association, the Guild of Sommeliers, and the American Sommelier Association. Universities, colleges, professional schools, and other hostelry or culinary institutes also provide sommelier training at various levels. Most of these educational programs are taught by sommeliers.

Further Reading

Court of Master Sommeliers Web site. http://www.mastersommeliers.org.

Rémy Charest

SPEAKEASIES

A speakeasy is a clandestine, illegal bar that often required patrons to whisper the password to enter. An untold thousands, perhaps hundreds of thousands, popped up during **Prohibition** in the 1920s to replace the nation's saloons. Bootleggers supplied the alcoholic beverages, which were often of poor quality, like bathtub **gin** made from denatured alcohol.

Speakeasies were often hidden in plain sight behind false doors or in basements. Liquor was served in teacups to deceive Prohibition Bureau agents or police who tried to infiltrate a location. Speakeasy owners went to elaborate lengths to protect their stocks of liquor in case of raids, hiding their liquor in false cabinets or even in separate locations. Any alcoholic beverages caught by agents were confiscated as evidence to try the bartender or owner for violating the Volstead Act, the law that enforced Prohibition.

Speakeasies could range from a neighboring dive bar or watering hole to the glitzy Cotton Club in Harlem, a mafia-controlled nightclub. The 1920s were known as the Jazz Age for good reason, as clubs hosted live **music** that brought in the crowds. Speakeasies defined an emerging urban nightlife, as **bars** lit by electricity meant people could stay out into the wee hours.

Prohibition failed to stop people from drinking alcohol; it simply drove drinking underground. Thousands of speakeasies proliferated across cities like New York. The police and Prohibition Bureau agents might raid one, but then it could easily reopen down the street or even in the same location. Speakeasies fostered corruption, as police were often willing to be bribed so they would look the other way or tip off a speakeasy owner about a pending raid.

Frequenting speakeasies during Prohibition became a cat-and-mouse game with the authorities that turned drinking into an appealing and sophisticated activity. Getting arrested for flaunting the law only increased one's social stature. It was also considered "smart" (highly fashionable) and modern to be seen flaunting the law with a cocktail glass, and patrons had to be "in the know" to frequent a speakeasy.

Patrons at a speakeasy in the 1920s. A secret password often had to be recited in order to gain access to these hidden drinking establishments. (Bettmann/Corbis)

Though known for its corruption and ineptness, the Prohibition Bureau also hired two remarkable agents who captured the public's attention: Izzy and Moe (Isadore Einstein and Moe Smith). These two men donned infinite disguises and infiltrated hundreds of speakeasies around the country, often locating a speakeasy within minutes of arriving in a city.

Since speakeasies were illegal, they leveled **class**, cultural, and sexual differences, as they were open to everyone. The tavern and saloon were male-only bastions during their pre-Prohibition glory days; however, once women got the right to vote in 1920, they decided they had earned a place at the speakeasy as well. In New York, some of the best-known speakeasies were run by women such as Belle Livingstone, Helen Morgan, and Texas Guinan—a colorful woman who greeted her well-paying guests with, "Hello, sucker!"

After Prohibition, many speakeasies applied for **liquor licenses** and opened as legal bars. In recent years, the speakeasy theme has popped up again among high-end cocktail bars. These became so rampant that some referred to them as "speakcheesies." (*See also* **Bootleg Alcohol.**)

Further Reading

Allen, Frederick Lewis. *Only Yesterday: An Informal History of the 1920's*. New York: Perennial Classics, 2000 (original edition, 1931).

Clark, Norman H. *Deliver Us from Evil: An Interpretation of American Prohibition*. New York: W. W. Norton & Company, 1976.

Lerner, Michael. *Dry Manhattan: Prohibition in New York City*. Cambridge, MA: Harvard University Press, 2007.

Garrett Peck

SPORTS

From earliest recorded histories, athletic pursuits and alcohol consumption have a detailed and complex relationship with each other. Like all cultural relations, sport and alcohol's connections have evolved over history, where alcohol has been used as a performance-enhancing drug, a social drug for athletes, and a social drug or ritual preparation for spectators.

The ancient Olympics were one of the earliest venues for the use of alcohol as a performance-enhancing drug. Milo of Croton, one of the most famous of the ancient Olympians, was an advocate of massive feedings of raw lamb washed down with 8 to 10 gallons of red wine as the secret to his massive strength and power. The use of alcohol as "doping" persisted into the nineteenth century, a time of great feats of stamina that were attributed in part to alcohol consumption. In England, the widely celebrated walkers of the early 1800s celebrated the role that alcohol use played in their performances. Lieutenant Fairman of the Royal Lancashire Militia walked 60 miles in 13 hours, 33 minutes, in 1804 while consuming bread macerated in Madeira wine. Foster Powell was famous for his round-trip walks between London and York, which took less than six days thanks to his mid-race supplements of wine or brandy dashed with water.

Many people in the nineteenth and early twentieth centuries used alcoholic drinks as thirst quenchers and to enhance physical stamina. Alcoholic drinks were seen as less contaminated than water. Alcoholic drinks were often made with water drawn from deep wells or boiled in their bottling processes. It was common belief that intoxicants imparted stamina, so in a manner of speaking, alcohol was the "energy drink" of that time. In North America, it was commonplace for agricultural employers to provide alcohol both to recruit a labor force and to fuel exertion during harvest or barn- or home-raising "bees."

For athletes, it made perfect sense to fortify themselves for endurance sports by the use of the stamina-inducing substance of choice—alcohol. The use of alcohol was even considered the latest in scientific coaching, as British physical educator H. L. Curtis suggested in his *Principles of Training for Amateur Athletics* (1892). Curtis suggested moderate alcohol consumption as part of an athlete's regimen, but warned athletes to resist the temptations of coffee or tobacco. In the context of sport, this time period also serves as a point of transition, wherein the demand of, and by, athletes was not merely victory, but a linear improvement in athletic performances. In the early to middle part of the century, it was common in Britain and North America to use alcohol to enhance the fighting spirit of boxers, while endurance sports—particularly marathons and cycling races such as the Tour de France—were the laboratories in which experiments involving alcohol in combination with other drugs were deployed to increase athletic performance. Champagne, cognac, and other liquors were used as part of a detailed doping program for athletes who competed in cycling, canal swimming, and indoor "shuffle" footraces. Alcohol was commonly combined with ether, heroin, cocaine, caffeine, digitalis, strychnine, or opium to create an ideal performance-enhancing polypharmacy. As one might expect, such chemistry experiments were not risk-free, and fatalities ensued when British cyclist Arthur Linton died of an overdose during the Bourdeaux-to-Paris race of 1886. Further notoriety emerged from the 1904 Olympic Games in St. Louis, when American Thomas Hicks claimed the gold medal in the marathon after collapsing at the finish line. Hicks was fortified during the race by injected doses of brandy, albumen, and strychnine, all administered by trainers who injected him while leaning out of a moving automobile while Hicks kept his championship pace.

Alcohol fell out of favor as a performance-enhancing drug in the twentieth century, and as a necessary element for the manual laborer, alcohol use had fallen out of favor with employers in the industrial economy of the early twentieth century. They implemented competitive sporting teams and leagues as a way to prevent alcohol abuse by employees. With the advent of the hour-restricted work week, employers became concerned that workers with newfound "leisure time" would spend it in the pubs and taverns, engaging in gambling and drunkenness. The employers' concern was that such behavior would lead to moral corruption of their workforces, and economic issues such as absenteeism would affect workplace discipline and productivity. The late nineteenth and early twentieth centuries also saw the rise of "muscular Christianity," a Protestant movement that emphasized the conceptions of masculinity as represented by Christ and required of God-fearing males. Sports were a way to purify the spirit and keep men on the righteous path and as such served as a diversion project to keep workers from the taverns and public houses. The modern term "recreation" emerges from this movement as "re-creation"—a regenerating of the body and soul from vigorous physical activity and abstention from liquor and beer.

While alcohol's value as performance-enhancing drug was minimal after the early twentieth century, it remains an essential element of the social aspect of membership of sports teams as an essential lubricant for a sense of camaraderie. Alcohol consumption among athletes is often seen as part of the team-bonding process, wherein athletes socialize and develop interest in their teammates as people outside of the competitive context. Rugby Union, originating within but not restricted to the British Commonwealth countries, has had a long tradition of post-game "beer-ups" wherein two teams meet after a match to consume alcohol, usually beer, and socialize. The role of alcohol can be seen at the conclusion of some major North American team sports' seasons, when one cherished tradition is to drink alcohol from the "cup," in the case where the trophy is in the form of a cup (for example, the National Hockey League's Stanley Cup). For football, alcohol consumption is a staple of the post-game celebration.

Although alcoholism is a known risk factor among athletes as well as the nonathlete population, there has not been sufficient evidence to suggest that addiction is a bigger problem among athletes than the general population. The research also has shown that athletes do not drink less, or in significantly different ways, than their otherwise similar colleagues in the larger populations. A 2001 study reiterated existing studies showing that athletes—in this particular study, the athletes were competitors in the National Collegiate Athletic Association (NCAA)—were at high risk for binge drinking (more than five standard drinks at a sitting). But in the context of a binge-drinking culture on North American campuses, comparative studies found that athletes do not drink more or more often than any other student population.

Athletes throughout the twentieth century endorsed, used, and celebrated alcohol consumption, not for its performance-enhancing qualities, but as a demonstration of masculinity and a projection of identity. High-level and professional sports became closely tied to brewers and distillers, through corporate sponsorships and endorsements of alcohol products by famous athletes.

Alcohol producers clearly believe in sports as a vehicle for greater alcohol sales. The year 2003 saw more than $540 million spent on 90,000 advertisements for American television. Sixty percent of all advertisements for alcoholic products are placed during televised sporting events.

Both Canadian and American brewers dedicate a large portion of their advertising expenditures on professional and collegiate sports. That concentration results in a relatively small number of brewers (four) that place 58 percent of the alcohol advertisements during televised NCAA sporting events. For example, between 2001 and 2003, Anheuser-Busch (who brews Budweiser), spent more than 80 percent of the total advertsing budget on sports programming.

While beer is the dominant form of alcohol associated with sports, distillers and other producers are trying to expand that market by introducing sports viewers to other alcohol products. Companies that produce malt beverages ("malt liquor") are now the most prominent non-beer advertisers. Producers of alcoholic products that are not traditional staples of the sport-alcohol-advertising triad are gradually working their way into the market. One example is the makers of Captain Morgan's Spiced Rum, who went from largely ignoring televised sport in 2001 to spending nearly $900,000 (USD) on it by 2003.

In many countries, there has been a great deal of study and public outcry about associations between alcohol advertising and problematic drinking among sports fans. Certainly, some fans of American football and NCAA sports as well as Football Association fans in the United Kingdom have a well-documented propensity to binge drink on game day, and such problem drinking has associated social costs, such as strains of medical or judicial structures.

Although there is validity to the current studies of the effects of alcohol advertising on consumption by sports fans, a historical understanding suggests that a removal of advertising will not limit the drinking of alcohol spectators. The ancient Greeks banned alcohol during the Olympic Games. Within the ruins of Olympia, an inscription dating back to 450–420 BCE forbidding wine in the stadium is inscribed on a block of the retaining wall of the stadium track. In translation, it reads:

> Wine is prohibited in the vicinity of the track. If anyone breaks this rule, he shall make amends to Apollo by pouring a libation, making a sacrifice, and paying a fine, half to Apollo and half to the informer.

Alcohol use has been suggested as a contributing factor to rowdy spectator behavior in sporting events in ancient Egypt (Nubian wrestling), Rome (the Ludi circenses), and medieval jousts in Europe. One possible explanation for use of alcohol use among sporting spectators through history could be the place of sports in many societies. Sports serve as a distraction from everyday life, wherein sobriety is socially expected to allow for productivity in daily work lives. Sports are done on personal time, and the consumption of alcohol denotes freedom from weekday responsibilities.

Further Reading

Centre for Alcohol Marketing and Youth, "Alcohol Advertising on Sports Television, 2001 to 2003." http://camy.org/factsheets/index.php?FactsheetID=20.

Collins, T., and M. Vamplew. *Mud, Sweat and Beers: A Cultural History of Sport and Alcohol*. New York: Berg, 2002.

Nelson, T. F., and H. Wechsler. "Alcohol and College Athletes." *Medicine & Science in Sports & Exercise* 33, no. 1 (2001): 43–47.

Wenner, L., and Jackson, S. J. *Sport, Beer, and Gender: Promotional Culture and Contemporary Social Life*. Zurich: Peter Lang Publishers, 2009.

Ken Kirkwood

ST. PATRICK'S DAY

From the early seventeenth century, St. Patrick's Day has played an important role as a celebration honoring St. Patrick, the patron saint of Ireland. Falling on March 17, St. Patrick's Day became an officially recognized feast day according to the Catholic liturgical calendar in the early seventeenth century, though more informal celebrations of St. Patrick's Day date back to the early medieval period in Ireland. Throughout much of its history, St. Patrick's Day celebrations have often revolved around formal informal drinking ceremonies.

Accelerated with the onset of the Great Potato Famine in the 1840s and mass Irish migration, the commemoration of St. Patrick's Day moved beyond Irish shores with immigration to England, Canada, the United States, and Australia. With the spread of St. Patrick's Day celebrations into new regions, the character of observances began to shift away from religious ritual toward a celebration of Irish culture and identity. In the United States, St. Patrick's Day became an important celebration in Boston and New York in the early 1840s, when the first St. Patrick's Day parades were planned by Irish-American communities there. These early celebrations in the United States offered the rapidly expanding Irish immigrant communities an opportunity to assert their claim to participation in the new society.

St. Patrick's Day has been observed in different ways over time in the United States through church services, dances, banquets, sporting events, and drinking sessions. The most widely recognized public face of the celebration remains, however, the St. Patrick's Day parade. These parades display a myriad of emblems and expressions, including banners, **music**, dancing, singing, and ubiquitous shades of green.

Public intoxication is writ large in many of these public displays of Irishness in the United States. In fact, drunkenness, a stigma long associated with the Irish-American community, remains a powerful corollary to the St. Patrick's Day celebration. **Temperance** reformers and civic authorities have worked together periodically since the early twentieth century to try to reduce public intoxication on St. Patrick's Day. For example, **pubs** have sometimes been ordered to shut their businesses down while parades passed nearby. In other cases, Irish temperance organization sought to close all pubs on St. Patrick's Day in an effort to purify the Irish holiday from the stigma of drunkenness. Despite these efforts, drinking remains part of the fabric of St. Patrick's Day in many communities.

One of the most important gathering points for St. Patrick's Day revelers is the Irish pub. Pubs on St. Patrick's Day typically serve traditional Irish fare such as corned beef and cabbage, Irish stew, and fish and chips. Some pubs even serve green **beer** to mark the occasion.

Further Reading

Cronin, Mike, and Daryl Addair. *The Wearing of the Green: A History of St. Patrick's Day.* New York: Routledge, 2002.

Bradley Kadel

T

TELEVISION

The relationship between television and alcohol is multifaceted, ranging from promoting alcoholic beverages, whether through overt advertising or in the form of "product placement," to using the medium to convey anti-drinking messages; to offering documentary series on addiction; to providing a vehicle to support self-help programs for alcohol abusers. By far the greatest attention by academic and popular **literature** has been on the role of television depictions of alcohol in affecting (or not) ideas and behavior concerning alcohol consumption, including considerable research on changing representations of alcohol on television over time.

In the United States, advertisement of alcoholic beverages on television is legal. The alcoholic beverage industry voluntarily imposed several restrictions on its own **advertising** efforts over the years, including a ban in the 1950s on all television ads for distilled spirits and a restriction on showing active consumption of alcohol products; however, the latter was suspended in the mid-1980s and the former entirely lifted in 1996. Commercials for **beer** outnumber those for **wine** and liquor, and most ads include a human associated with the beverage, actively drinking or not. Commercials often depict pre-drinking contexts that suggest difficult work, exotic locations, or recreation, implying appropriate situations or precursors to alcohol consumption and reinforcing mythology and stereotypes about social use patterns, for example, related to gender (men drink more beer related to working in strenuous occupations or engaging in sports events; women drink sweeter beverages like "**alcopops**"—flavored alcoholic drinks—and are shown in subservient or sexualized roles). It has been suggested that in recent years, commercials have increasingly portrayed beer as valuable and rare, suggesting that it is worth great effort to obtain, with ads showing a variety of stunts and outrageous behavior to procure the beverage. This shift parallels the societal movement to set increasing barriers to **underage drinking** and to ramp up anti-drinking messages, some of which are broadcast via television. Drunk-driving campaigns, legal purchase age enforcement, and other measures have become much more common since the 1970s. Indeed, the area of greatest research focus on the impact of television portrayals of alcohol is the targeting toward and effect on youths (defined as ages 12 to 20). Youth exposure to alcohol advertising rose significantly during the 1990s. Many of these ads were placed on shows that youths were more likely to watch, and the great majority was shown on cable television, where commercials for distilled spirits have increased significantly in recent years.

Depictions of alcohol use in television programming, as portrayals of drinking or as product placements, have increased steadily since the 1950s. Analyses done in the late 1990s demonstrated that about three-quarters of prime time episodes depicted alcohol use and/or made some reference to alcohol, mostly in a positive way. In-depth analysis has shown that frequency of alcoholic beverage choice by television characters is disproportionate to the real-life consumption of alcohol compared with other beverages. In reality, milk, coffee or tea, water, and soft drinks are consumed much more frequently than alcohol, but the reverse is true on television. Also, the circumstances of consumption on television are skewed away from the casual and toward drinking in circumstances of tension or crisis and to enhance social interactions. It is unusual to see **alcoholism** or alcohol abuse in a main character, and characters who are alcoholic tend to be presented as very different from social drinkers. Drinks offered are seldom refused, and people who are intoxicated or hung over are often portrayed in a humorous light.

In recent decades, there have been efforts to introduce greater realism in the television portrayal of alcohol consumption in shows and advertising, with more representation of harmful effects of alcohol consumption. Some of this responds to research on problematic features of alcohol and pressures from external bodies in Hollywood and the public health community. Public health messages about appropriate alcohol-related behavior have also gained airtime. For example, the **designated driver** concept is now depicted in some programming contexts, and special shows addressing substance abuse have been broadcast to children and youth. At the same time, ads continue to present images of alcohol and the "good life."

There is research suggesting that exposure to alcohol advertising on television bears some relationship to underage drinking and ideas about drinking. However, in general, the data are inconclusive about the role of television advertising in shaping alcohol use and abuse. Despite this lack of firm linkage, there are periodic calls to ban alcohol advertising on television. It has been pointed out that this would mean having to also discontinue anti-alcohol ads, as this is what occurred when smoking advertisements were prohibited in 1971. Smokeless tobacco ads persisted until 1986.

Many in the research and public health communities are highly skeptical about purported industry-sponsored efforts to alter alcohol advertising and use contexts on television toward greater realism and to provide anti-drinking messages to young people. They have pointed out that even with the increase in "responsibility ads," the industry spends far more money on alcohol-promotion ads, and the number of these dwarfs the responsibility messages. Furthermore, alcohol ads appear regularly on shows where underage viewers are proportionately greater in number than their representation in the general population.

A few intervention studies have gauged the utility of television as a medium to provide self-help programs to problem drinkers and self-regulatory tips or messages to a broader drinking public and have demonstrated some success. In a couple of instances, self-regulatory spots have even featured bartenders or bar managers and scenes from drinking establishments to convey the desired message. Certainly the ubiquity of televisions in **bars**, taverns, and **pubs** should be recognized as yet another association between television and alcohol, one that both attracts viewers to drinking contexts but may also serve, albeit ironically, to convey responsible or even anti-drinking messages to those customers.

Further Reading

Bonnie, Richard J., and Mary Ellen O'Connell, eds. *Reducing Underage Drinking: A Collective Responsibility*. Washington, DC: National Academies Press, 2004.

Center for Science in the Public Interest. Alcohol Policies Project Web site. http://www.cspinet.org/alcohol/index.html (accessed May 31, 2010).

Georgetown University. Center on Alcohol Monitoring and Youth Web site. http://camy.org.

Horner, Jennifer, Patrick E. Jamieson, and Daniel Romer. "The Changing Portrayal of Alcohol Use in Television Advertising." In *The Changing Portrayal of Adolescents in the Media since 1950*, ed. Patrick E. Jamieson and Daniel Romer, 284–312. New York: Oxford University Press, 2008.

Signorielli, Nancy. *Mass Media Images and Impact on Health*. Westport, CT: Greenwood, 1993.

Susan L. Johnston

TEMPERANCE

Temperance was a policy or stance adopted by many Americans in the nineteenth century that counseled moderation in alcohol consumption. Some temperance supporters went so far as to adopt total abstinence. Late-nineteenth-century critics of liquor consumption, convinced that persuasion was incapable of curing the social ills attributed to alcohol consumption, abandoned it for coercive prohibition at the state and eventually the national level. Following failed prohibition experiments in the United States and numerous other western nations in the early twentieth century, critics of alcohol returned to earlier policies of persuasion through groups such as **Alcoholics Anonymous (AA)**.

Widespread consumption of alcohol became a social concern in early modern Europe as distilled spirits—containing a higher percentage of alcohol than long-serving intoxicants such as **beer** and **wine**—became plentiful in the seventeenth century. The English Parliament outlawed excessive drinking but subsequently encouraged the distillation of corn liquor. Colonial America similarly frowned on immoderate drinking but welcomed temperate consumption. Many learned people believed that alcohol possessed healthful properties. James Madison drank a pint of **whiskey** daily, though he and Thomas Jefferson urged moderation. Benjamin Rush, physician to the Continental Army, was one of the first Americans to warn against the detrimental health effects of excessive drinking.

Thomas Nast illustration from March 21, 1874, edition of *Harper's Weekly* shows Death as a bartender serving rum to a patron while two small children beckon from the doorway. Popular illustrations in this period often played on the social disorder and evil that could be brought about by drink. (Library of Congress)

In the early nineteenth century, liquor production in the United States soared as western farmers distilled large corn harvests into whiskey to enhance the crop's value. The generous alcohol supply depressed prices, making it available to common laborers as well as the wealthy. This concerned the emerging middle class and their religious leaders, particularly those associated with the Second Great Awakening. In 1826, evangelical clergymen formed the American Temperance Society in Boston, urging members to become totally abstinent. Within a few years, the society spread to 19 states, mostly in the north, and similar groups formed in southern states. Most temperance supporters came from the Baptist, Methodist, Congregational, and Presbyterian faiths. Women from these denominations became active in the Temperance Movement as they were in other antebellum social reform movements.

In the 1840s, a different Temperance Movement formed. The Washington Temperance Society attracted former drunkards who pledged to abstain from drink and support fellow Washingtonians in their abstinence efforts. Launched by Baltimore artisans, its members came from the burgeoning working class. Though this group floundered within a few years, it sparked the development of the Sons of Temperance, which also stressed moral suasion to reduce alcohol consumption. Reformers, dissatisfied with persuasion efforts, turned to coercion in the 1850s as 13 states banned alcohol completely. This strategy also proved unsuccessful in eliminating drunkenness.

Following the Civil War, women came to the forefront of the Temperance Movement. Ohio women, in 1873, formed the **Woman's Christian Temperance Union** (WCTU), which soon spread to states and counties throughout the nation. Members marched on saloons and lobbied public officials for liquor restrictions, gaining influence in a political system that barred them from voting. Frances Willard, WCTU president from 1879 to 1898, pushed a broad agenda of social reform and adopted the Socialist Party's position that poverty caused drunkenness rather than the reverse. Following her sudden death, the WCTU moved in a more conservative direction and increasingly deferred to male temperance leaders.

The Roman Catholic population of the United States also organized against alcohol consumption. Early efforts led to the formation in 1872 of the Catholic Total Abstinence Union (CTAU), particularly popular with Irish-American Catholics in the Northeast and Midwest. Membership—never a large portion of the American Catholic population—peaked in the 1890s, when the union worked with other temperance groups. This connection was short-lived as the CTAU distanced itself from coercive prohibition efforts in the early twentieth century.

As the new century began, the recently formed **Anti-Saloon League** (ASL) quickly took control of the Temperance Movement. Reverend Howard Hyde Russell organized the ASL as an umbrella organization to represent all temperance groups in **politics**. While the Prohibition Party had formed in 1869, it never seriously challenged the two major parties for political power. The middle-class leadership of the ASL systematically pressured local, state, and ultimately national office holders to abolish the saloon. These reformers held the saloon—patronized by working-class men—to be without social merit. Eliminating public drinking houses would reduce violence, vices such as gambling and prostitution, poverty, and insanity.

Ernest Cherrington and others within the ASL emphasized education and moral suasion as well, but Wayne Wheeler and his supporters stressed coercive prohibition and gained the upper hand in the ASL. Their efforts resulted in 26 states banning alcohol by 1918. Flexing its political muscle, the ASL pressured Congress for nationwide prohibition. It succeeded in 1919 as the Eighteenth Amendment became part of the U.S. Constitution. Wheeler wrote the enforcement legislation for the amendment and interpreted it for enforcement officers until his death in 1928.

The rise of violent crime under **Prohibition**, the persistence of vice crimes, and the Depression that began in 1929 undercut the arguments that prohibition would end crime and usher in a golden age of prosperity in America. The Franklin D. Roosevelt administration lifted the ban on beer with 3.2 percent alcohol in 1933 and the Twenty-first Amendment, repealing the Eighteenth, was ratified by the end of that year.

Following the end of Prohibition, temperance groups remained active and returned to moral suasion to limit drinking. The ASL, identified with Prohibition, lost its political influence. The WCTU returned to a broad agenda of social reforms. In 1935, Bill Watson and Robert Smith founded Alcoholics Anonymous in Ohio. AA asserted that drunkenness resulted from **alcoholism**—a physiological and psychological condition that predisposed some to excessive alcohol consumption. The only way to escape its destructive effects was to abstain entirely. Hearkening back to the Washingtonian movement, AA set up support groups of reformed alcoholics to help one another avoid relapses into drunkenness. In 1940, AA spread from Ohio to the rest of the United States. By 1951, it had 100,000 members. As the Prohibition experience receded into the past, recent temperance efforts again have turned increasingly from persuasion to coercion.

Further Reading

Cashman, Sean D. *Prohibition: The Lie of the Land.* New York: Free Press, 1981.

James Klein

Carry Nation (1846–1911)

"Good morning, destroyer of men's souls," was the phrase Carry Nation would announce when she entered a saloon. Remembered as the radical hatchet-wielding member of the Woman's Christian Temperance Union, Nation carried out acts of vandalism against saloons in Kansas that served alcohol despite the state's prohibition vote in 1880. Motivated by her own experience of having been married to an alcoholic, Nation was also driven by her religious beliefs. Nearly six feet tall, this formidable woman initially attacked establishments using stones and bricks—later she started using a hatchet. Nation managed to shut down a number of saloons, but she also started attacking establishments selling alcohol in states where it was legal. This landed her in jail a number of times, but it also raised awareness about the Temperance Movement.

TEQUILA

Made from blue agave (*Agave tequilana*), tequila is one of few distilled beverages that does not come from a grain, vegetable, or fruit. Made in Mexico, it is quite popular in the United States. It can be consumed on its own, most often as a shot, or mixed in drinks such as margaritas (tequila mixed with Triple Sec and lime or lemon juice). Usually 76–80 proof, there are two basic categories of tequila: *mixto* (up to 49% sugar in **fermentation**) and 100 percent agave. Tequila can also be aged (*reposado, añejo*, and *extra añejo*) in wood barrels or casks to produce a much more refined and complex spirit.

Blue agave is a large succulent plant that is native to Jalisco, Mexico, and is also grown in the states of Tamaulipas, Nayart, Guanajuato, and Michoacàn. Although agave is often mistaken for a cactus, it is actually a member of the lily family. Originally the sap from this plant was fermented to produce pulque, a mildly alcoholic beverage, which was consumed by the Aztecs in highly ritualized religious rites, in feasts, and as a medicine. It was not until the arrival of Spaniards that agave nectar was distilled to produce a much more potent drink. The scarcity of other forms of alcohol led to the development and popularization of tequila during the colonial period. Tequila is a type of mezcal that is made from the sap that comes from the heart (*piñas*) of the agave plant. During the U.S. Civil War, there was a shortage of **whiskey**, and Mexican tequila producers saw the opportunity for a new and thirsty market. This was possibly the first introduction of tequila into the United States and certainly the beginning of its popularity. In 1873, this agave beverage became officially known as tequila. Mezcal producers wanted to distinguish the beverage they were making from the types of mezcal produced in other regions of Mexico. For this reason, they named their mezcal after the town of Tequila. In the same year, the first barrels of tequila were legally shipped to the United States.

During **Prohibition**, Americans crossed the border to buy tequila, which they referred to as "Mexican whiskey." However, tequila could be a bit of a rough drink that did not always appeal to American palates. For this reason, in 1930, producers started adding cane sugar to tequila during the fermentation process, making a much sweeter, smoother beverage that appealed to Americans. It was not until the 1960s and 1970s that tequila became a popular spirit in the United States, and a better-quality tequila became available in the US. Stars like Bob Hope and Bing Crosby promoted this exotic beverage and helped bring tequila-based **cocktails** into the mainstream of popular American drinking culture.

Tequila is often drunk as a shot, but it is estimated that nearly 70 percent of all tequila consumed in America ends up in margaritas. Another current trend in the tequila sales is the rise of the premium brand. Don Julio Blanco and Patron Silver are examples of premium tequilas that are made from 100 percent blue agave. Frequently associated with rowdy bar drinking or vacations south of the border, tequila producers are trying to cultivate a more refined tequila drinking culture in the United States in which aged tequila is sipped like a fine single malt whisky. (*See also* **Distillation.**)

Further Reading

Chadwick, Ian. "Tequila: In Search of the Blue Agave." http://www.ianchadwick.com/tequila/.
Weir, Joanne. *Tequila: A Guide to Types, Flights, Cocktails and Bites.* Berkeley, CA: Ten Speed Press, 2009.

Rachel Black

TERROIR

In the world of **wine**, terroir is much-debated. A French word, it refers to the combination of soil- and climate-related factors that define a particular wine-growing site and give its wines a specific taste, or "*goût de terroir.*" Temperature, rainfall, sunlight, wind, altitude, slope, orientation, soil type, soil biochemistry, and geology, as well as drainage and hydrology, are all components of what can define a particular terroir. Some research even suggests that ecosystemic factors, such as the presence of various types of wild yeasts or soil microbial life in a particular location, could play a role in distinguishing one winegrowing site from the next. The reality and importance of these factors in determining the quality and character of a wine are a matter of constant debate, with New World wine-makers often minimizing its importance, in contrast with the hyperdefinition of terroir taking place, sometimes at an almost microscopic level, in places like Burgundy or Piedmont. Modern winemaking techniques such as the use of cultured yeasts instead of wild yeasts found on location, acidification, or tannin addition are seen as well as reducing local differences. Whatever the case may be, efforts to distinguish one location from the next are constantly at work, as demonstrated in the United States by the growing number of American Viticultural Areas (AVAs), normally defined according to variations geography and climate. Within Napa Valley, for instance, there are 14 different AVAs, each presenting its own variation in soil, geology and climate.

Further Reading

Alcohol and Tobacco Tax and Trade Bureau. http://ttb.gov/appellation/

Rémy Charest

> **American Viticultural Areas (AVAs)**
>
> An AVA is a designated wine grape–growing region. Distinguished by geographic features, approximately 190 AVAs have been designated by the U.S. Bureau of Alcohol, Tobacco and Firearms (more than 90 of these areas are in California). When a wine label displays a specific AVA, this means that 85 percent of the grapes used come from that geographic location. Unlike most European appellations of origin, an AVA is not a quality designation. AVAs do not limit or regulate the varieties of grapes grown, yield, or vinification methods.

TOASTING

Toasting refers to the deeply rooted tradition of raising a glass of an alcoholic beverage in honor of others or to celebrate an event or an ideal, accompanied by a few words about the occasion. That sense of the word has also been broadened to apply to other contexts of expressing recognition or honor ("toast of the town"). This may even include, somewhat ironically, recognition of improvements in alcohol-related behavior ("a toast to sobriety"). And in recent popular culture, "toasting" has come to represent partying with **music** and/or alcohol as well as the music that is created or recorded in such a context. The alcohol may be imbibed in a ritualized way in these settings. This development appears related to a long-standing tradition in African American culture of "toasting" as a form of lengthy, rhyming, humorous, and highly skilled oratory that may include audience participation. This predecessor to rap sometimes involved pairing a drink of alcohol with each clever verse.

Toasting in the original sense of the word is customary in the United States today in formal (a wedding, a business dinner) and informal (a few friends celebrating a success) settings. While toasts are often spur of the moment, there are rules of etiquette governing the timing, order (who goes first), content, and length of toasts given under more formal circumstances. Toasts typically involve alcohol, often wine, but in modern contexts it is also acceptable to join a toast with a nonalcoholic beverage, or even an empty glass, as the emphasis is usually on the honoring, not on imbibing alcohol *per se*.

This custom of toasting may have originated in medieval Britain in a practice of mutual beverage tasting that protected people against deliberate poisoning; this eventually, among trusted friends, was replaced by simply clinking drinking vessels together to indicate shared good health. Or it may have developed from the practice of pledging one's loyalty to others, including a willingness to fight on another's behalf. A man could not draw his sword while drinking, so a comrade would have to protect him while he drank. In Elizabethan ale houses, a piece of spiced toast was often placed in the bottom of a cup of wine or ale. Eventually, the word "toast" came to be applied to the act of honoring a person with a drink and to the words spoken just beforehand. In a larger context, the custom of drinking to gods, to honor, or to health has been part of a variety of cultural traditions over millennia of recorded history.

While toasting was also prevalent in colonial America, the practice appears to have declined somewhat by the early twentieth century, a target both in Britain and America of the **Temperance** Movement. However, in the United States today, toasting has regained prevalence and a measure of prominence. A variety of sources, both textual and electronic, provide examples of toasts for special occasions and instructions on all facets of toasting. (*See also* **Drinking Rituals.**)

Further Reading

French, Richard Valpy. *The History of Toasting.* London: National Temperance Publication Depot, 1882.
Lomax, Alan. *Land Where the Blues Began.* New York: Pantheon, 1993.
Post, Peggy. *Emily Post's Etiquette.* 17th ed. New York: HarperCollins, 2004.

Susan L. Johnston

U

UNDERAGE DRINKING

Underage drinking occurs when youths younger than the legal age for purchase and possession imbibe alcohol; in the United States, that age is 21. Many people believe that underage drinking causes both immediate and long-term problems for youths, because intake is linked with increased car accidents and alcohol-related morbidity and mortality. However, most U.S. citizens, both adults and teens, regard underage drinking as a rite of passage or a normal social activity rather than a crime, and most youths try alcohol before they are of legal age.

The National Minimum Drinking Age Act of 1984 regulated the national legal age to purchase and possess alcoholic beverages by requiring all states to comply with age restrictions or to forfeit a portion of their highway development funds. Between the repeal of **Prohibition** in 1933 and the passage of the 1984 Act, the legal age for purchase was determined at the state level and varied from 18 to 21. By 1986, all states had complied with the act and raised the legal age to 21, but Puerto Rico and the U.S. Virgin Islands allow purchase/possession at 18. The act does not specifically restrict drinking but rather the purchase and public possession of alcohol; possession (and presumed consumption) with permission of a parent, in the context of religious or medical practice, and in certain private venues is permitted on the federal level. Technically, the act disallows selling to and purchase by minors and public possession by minors.

However, the phrase "underage drinking" means far more in public parlance. Following the general rise of awareness about **alcoholism** in the 1980s that accompanied that decade's neo-prohibitionary cultural shift, many people began to equate underage use with increased rates of alcoholism, alcohol abuse, and death. Certainly there is evidence that early-onset hard or **binge drinking** correlates with higher rates of early-adult social problems among at-risk youths

(Ellickson et al. 2003), but these studies used onset of use prior to 16 years of age and binge drinking as the metric for alcohol use. Reputable studies have not demonstrated a clear connection between late-adolescent moderate use and later alcohol abuse or cognitive problems, which suggests that concern about moderate drinking among those 18 and over (or even 16 and over) might be overblown. However, studies of high-end use in at-risk younger adolescents have fostered apprehension about all drinking under the age of 21, even though little evidence suggests that late-adolescent moderate drinking causes problems.

Underage drinking remains a public concern, because it is associated in public discourse with binge drinking and there is no consensus on an age of safe use. While rates of use as well as binge drinking have decreased among youths ages 12 to 17 (U.S. Department of Health and Human Services 2009), the public believes that youths have a significant alcohol abuse problem. It is very likely that the implementation of laws designed to curb youth drinking have created a belief in a problem by criminalizing normal social behavior, a belief then supported through statistics generated by arrests for possession and public drunkenness. In effect, the concept of "underage drinking" may be a cultural artifact created by a criminalization process.

Youths under 21 do use alcohol to socialize, and drinking is a rite of passage signaling the onset of adulthood for many teens. For those who go to college, alcohol is readily available at parties given by older students, and a valued experience at university is attending parties where alcohol is served. Colleges are well aware of this and struggle to balance respect for student social needs with a desire to promote safety. Many colleges have instituted medical amnesty programs to ensure that inebriated students are brought to medical attention without fear of legal consequences. Harm Reduction programs designed to teach safe drinking awareness and habits are also popular on campuses, as are programs to alter behaviors without labeling drinkers as abusers or addicted, such as Brief Alcohol Screening and Intervention of College Students (BASICS). Perhaps the most ambitious of the university programs is the Amethyst Initiative, which seeks to promote responsible drinking by encouraging the adoption of a drinking "learners permit" for students at age 18—the age at which adults are allowed to vote, sign contracts, serve on juries, and enlist in the military. The organization hopes to start a public discussion about changing a law that criminalizes behavior that is culturally condoned. (*See also* **College Drinking Culture.**)

Further Reading

Chassin, Laurie, Steven C. Pitts, and Justin Prost. "Binge Drinking Trajectories from Adolescence to Emerging Adulthood in a High-risk Sample: Predictors and Substance Abuse Outcomes." *Journal of Consulting and Clinical Psychology* 70, no. 1 (February 2002): 67–78.

Ellickson, Phyllis L., Joan S. Tucker, and David J. Klein. "Ten-year Prospective Study of Public Health Problems Associated with Early Drinking." *Pediatrics* 111, no. 5 (2003): 949–55.

Hingson, Ralph W., Timothy Heeren, and Michael R. Winter. "Age at Drinking Onset and Alcohol Dependence: Age at Onset, Duration, and Severity." *Archives of Pediatric and Adolescent Medicine* 160 (2006): 739–46.

Pitkänen, Tuuli, Anna-Liisa Lyyra, and Lea Pulkkinen. "Age of Onset of Drinking and the Use of Alcohol in Adulthood: A Follow-up Study from Age 8–42 for Females and Males." *Addiction* 100 (2005): 652–61.

U.S. Department of Health and Human Services. National Survey on Drug Use and Health. Washington, DC: United States Department of Health and Human Services, Substance Abuse & Mental Health Services Administration, Office of Applied Statistics, September 2009.

Viner, R. M., and B. Taylor. "Adult Outcomes of Binge Drinking in Adolescence: Findings from a UK National Birth Cohort." *Journal of Epidemiology and Community Health* 61 (2007): 902–7.

Janet Chrzan

V

VIOLENCE, ALCOHOL-RELATED

American society has long had a concern about the two-way relationship of alcohol use and negative consequences to the social order such as crime, worker productivity problems, family dissolution, physical maladies, and aggressive behavior. Specifically, violence has been a major concern to society in this regard. A standard definition regards violence as a type of social behavior that deliberately causes or attempts to cause physical harm to another person. Although violence is closely related to the broader construct of aggression, the latter term includes threats, intimidation, hostility, and nonphysical actions.

Sociohistorical Perspective

Viewing the issue from a sociohistorical vantage point, many of the early colonists in America used alcohol daily, partially in response to the fact that the water was often unfit for consumption. The Puritans frowned on drunkenness but not on the moderate use of alcohol in the form of **beer**, ale, and other alcoholic drinks. In fact, drunkenness was viewed as a personal character defect rather than a major social problem at the time. Factors such as religion and other forms of ethnic diversity, a sharper separation between socioeconomic status, and the actions of reformers such as the physician Benjamin Rush created a change in the opinions of ale consumption as being a harmless activity to the notion that it is the cause of many social ills, including violence.

Changes in drinking behavior occurred in the nineteenth century when ale consumption moved from the homes into the taverns and saloons. The bar environment became primarily a male-dominated one that created situations conducive for fist fighting, dueling, beating, and the "barroom brawl." The alcohol-related violence developed differently in the various regions of the country: the frontier

American West, with its legendary though often embellished image of a lawless setting where money from precious metals allowed newcomers to afford large amounts of saloon alcohol; and the Antebellum South, with its tensions related to race and **class** distinctions often resulting in alcohol-induced episodes of violent activity.

Other types of alcohol-related violence of this period include mob violence, vigilantism, lynching, and violent confrontations between government officials known as "revenuers" and the bootleggers who attempted to illegally transport and sell moonshine, alcohol distilled and sold with homemade stills, which avoided government regulation and taxation. A violent period in American history occurred before the Civil War between not only the bootleggers and revenuers, but between competing bootleggers as well.

The **Temperance** Movement became a major force in the nineteenth century, and a belief arose that alcohol use, even in nonintoxicating amounts, was a major contributor to violence, poverty, family dissolution, and other problems. **Race and ethnicity** figured into this ideology as well, as whites became fearful of other racial and ethnic groups who might become violent as a result of alcohol use. Breweries and saloons became popular fixtures in the late nineteenth and early twentieth centuries and a concern for groups such as the **Anti-Saloon League**. In 1919, with the passage of the Eighteenth Amendment to the Constitution, which prohibited the manufacture, sale, or transport of alcohol, America's policy experiment illuminated the question of whether alcohol was a contributor to major social ills such as violence. It has been suggested that alcohol use did decrease during the era of national **Prohibition**, but only because prices of illicit alcohol made it difficult to afford rather than being a reflection of a national trend of abstinence. Many people turned to making homemade **wine** to cope with the decrease in available alcohol. The Prohibition era was plagued with violence between the members of the organized crime units that engaged in illegal activity, including alcohol manufacture, transport, and sales, and the authorities who tried to bring them to justice. Chicago became a major hub of this conflict, and to illustrate this point, nearly 400 gangsters were killed due to both gang rivalries and confrontations with the police. With the repeal of Prohibition in 1933, many organized crime organizations had to turn to other means of earning money.

As other drugs entered the cultural landscape, the focus on the alcohol and violence connection became somewhat less salient.

Continuing Debate

The debate over the alcohol-violence connection has continued throughout the years, and several areas of research have received considerable attention. For example, the connection between alcohol and acts of violence such as interpersonal violence, sexual assault, child abuse, and others have been closely followed by social scientists. Research findings have not been definitive due to the complexity of factors involved, but some general information can be gleaned from the data. For example, there are some potential physiological links between alcohol and violence. The well-researched "disinhibition hypothesis" posits that alcohol can weaken mechanisms in the brain that, under normal circumstances, control impulsivity. Also, it could be that alcohol contributes to violence by causing people to misread nonthreatening actions as threatening ones. In addition, alcohol might cause users to fail to consider the consequences of potential violent behavior.

The "expectancy hypothesis" maintains that alcohol users act violently because they are expected to do so when under the influence. Expectancies promote the idea of male aggressiveness and female defensiveness and can be a contributor to rape and interpersonal violence situations. There is also the possibility that perpetrators of violence consume alcohol to defend themselves legally by claiming the alcohol was the primary cause of the action, thereby evading punishment from the judicial system.

Another consideration is the connection between alcohol consumption and mental health issues, of which violence is normally a characteristic. For example, antisocial personality disorder, a condition in which people infringe upon the rights of others, has been closely connected with early-onset (type II) alcoholism. (*See also* **Alcoholism; Health Effects of Alcohol.**)

Further Reading

Brain, Paul F. *Alcohol and Aggression*. London: Croom Helm, 1986.
Cashman, Sean D. *Prohibition: The Lie of the Land*. New York: Free Press, 1981.
National Institute on Alcohol Abuse and Alcoholism. "Alcohol Alert" 38 (October 1997). http://www.pubs.niaaa.nih.gov/publications/aa38.htm.
Parker, Robert N. *Alcohol and Homicide: A Deadly Combination of Two American Traditions*. Albany: State University of New York Press, 1995.

Leonard A. Steverson

VODKA

Vodka is a clear alcoholic beverage consisting mostly of water and ethanol purified by distillation from fermented foodstuffs such as rye, wheat, potatoes, or sugar beets. It may also contain small amount of other substances used for flavoring. The word "vodka" is a diminutive of the Russian "voda," meaning water. Vodka is the most popular spirit in Eastern Europe, with the best Russian vodkas being made from wheat. In Poland, vodka is made mostly from a rye. In the United States, distillers use a wide variety of base ingredients to create vodka of varying quality. Today most commercially available vodka in America has an alcohol content of around 40 percent (80 proof).

While the definitive origins of vodka cannot be traced, Russians firmly believe that the spirit originated in their country. Sources recognize that a form of the spirit was commercially produced in Russia as early as the fourteenth century, though it was then referred to in general terms as "bread wine." The making of vodka soon became part of the Russian way of life. Stills on estates of the gentry produced excellent vodka, and flavorings were imaginative, including acorns, horseradish, and mint. Vodka could have been made as early as the 1300s in Krakow, Poland. Originally known in Poland as *okowita*, meaning "water of life," early Polish vodka had a variety of medicinal uses and was even prized as an effective aftershave lotion. Still others trace the origins of the spirit to what is now Belarus, Lithuania, Ukraine, and even Scandinavia.

Until the mid-eighteenth century, vodka was sold mostly in taverns. Eventually, taxes placed on the spirit became a key element of government finances in Russia, providing at times more than a third of state revenues. Due primarily to government policies promoting the consumption of state-manufactured vodka, the spirit became the drink of choice for many Russians. By the turn of the twentieth century, vodka was a significant Russian export though it was still primarily consumed by Europeans until the 1950s. Vodka was introduced into the United States around 1900, when an American company bought the rights to distribute the Smirnoff brand. Initially the spirit was not widely accepted, but vodka later became very popular after marketing claims that it left no noticeable odor of liquor on the consumer's breath. America's drinking public also discovered that vodka's neutral flavor allowed it to be mixed into a wide variety of drinks, often replacing other liquors such as **gin**. Most notably, the vodka martini became very popular with drinkers around the country. By 1975, vodka sales in the United States were greater than those of **bourbon**, previously the nation's most popular hard liquor, and today vodka remains one of the world's most popular distilled spirits. (*See also* **Martinis.**)

Further Reading

Begg, Desmond. *The Vodka Companion: A Vodka Lovers Guide*. Philadelphia: Running Press, 1998.

Emmons, Bob. *The Book of Gins and Vodkas: A Complete Guide*. Chicago: Open Court Publishing, 1999.

Ben Wynne

W

WHISKEY

Whiskey is one of the primary liquors produced and consumed in the United States. Essentially, whiskey is made from cereal grains that are mashed and distilled to obtain an alcohol content of approximately 40 percent, though many distillers have released whiskeys with a significantly higher percentage of alcohol. Numerous potential combinations of grain have made for a wide variety of whiskeys. The proportion of various ingredients such as wheat, corn, and barley along with unique aging and filtering processes are the defining characteristics of different whiskeys. Among American distillers, these types include rye whiskey, bourbon, corn whiskey, and Tennessee whiskey, all of which are required by law to meet certain standards specific to each. These types developed and became legally recognized over the course of the larger history of alcohol production and **advertising** regulation in the United States.

The history of whiskey in America is long and complex. American whiskey is derived from European immigrants who brought the skills and experience needed to distill strong liquor safely. Since the recipe for whiskey, by its most basic definition, may vary widely and grains were available in large quantity, whiskey became a popular drink and commercial product. Attempts by the newly formed federal government of the United States to place an excise tax on whiskey in 1791 prompted the Whiskey Rebellion in 1794. As a popular spirit high in alcohol, whiskey was often featured in depictions of drunkards and attacks by the **Temperance** Movement. Due to cultural heritage and the availability of ingredients, the moonshine produced in illegal stills in the United States is most often an attempt to create some form of whiskey.

While whiskey is a major part of alcohol's general history in the United States, the variants of whiskey produced highlight the unique history of American

---

Whiskey Rebellion

The Whiskey Rebellion was the violent response to a 1791 tax on whiskey by the new federal government that broke out in 1794 and smoldered for several years after. This was an important historical event because it showed the government's will to enforce laws and was the first time in the history of the new republic that force was used by the government against its citizens. George Washington's government decided to raise this tax in an attempt to pay off the national debt. Secretary of the Treasury Alexander Hamilton called the 25 percent excise tax on liquor sold more a measure of "social discipline than a source of revenue."

This tax angered small distillers who ended up being taxed more heavily than larger operations. In addition, it was a burden on western farmers who had previously turned their excess grain into liquor, because they were far from markets and liquor was easier to transport than grain. One of the consequences was that many small whiskey producers moved south into Kentucky and Tennessee, which were still outside of the federal government's control. Ultimately, the federal government asserted its power, but in the process, it made the states wary of that power.

---

distilling. Corn, native to the Americas, quickly became a significant element in American whiskey production. Distilling turned cheap corn into a much more valuable commodity that was easy to transport. Rye whiskey, with a long history in Europe, is still made in the United States; however, whiskeys containing a higher percentage of corn or other ingredients are the main products of the major recognized brand names such as Jim Beam and Jack Daniel's. Bourbon, distilled from a mash of at least half corn and aged in charred oak barrels, possesses a unique history centered in Bardstown, Kentucky.

Like numerous **beer** breweries with a long history, producers of American whiskey often advertise their products with stories of their distilleries and the trial and error that led to their specific recipe. Several distilleries offer samples and guided tours, sharing their history through alcohol tourism. The two major Tennessee whiskeys, Jack Daniel's and George Dickel, are strong examples of the many distilleries that showcase their histories while remaining high-volume producers. Tennessee whiskey is identical to bourbon in ingredients and undergoes a similar process of oak barrel aging. However, Tennessee whiskey is also filtered through sugar maple charcoal in a procedure called the Lincoln County Process, named after the original county encompassing the location of the Jack Daniel's distillery at its founding in 1866. Despite the presence of the Jack Daniel's distillery in Lynchburg, Moore County, its home since the redrawing of Tennessee county lines in the mid-twentieth century, has remained a dry county since **Prohibition**.

Whiskey is also one of the more prominent alcoholic beverages in American popular culture. As a standard strong drink, it appears in the **bars** of American Westerns and the flasks of Prohibition-era gangsters. In addition, a number of American songs mention whiskey, including Johnny Cash's "Cocaine Blues."

Also, "Rye Whiskey," originally recorded by Tex Ritter in the 1930s and covered by numerous artists including Woody Guthrie, is one of America's more prominent contributions to alcohol-related songs in the English language.

Whiskey in all its variations holds a unique place in American culture. Between the introduction of corn to the distillation and the several unique styles pioneered by American distillers, whiskey has proven an enduring and popular spirit. Rough and strong, its history goes hand in hand with the larger history of alcohol in America. (*See also* **Dry Counties; Hooch.**)

Further Reading

Gately, Iain. *Drink: A Cultural History of Alcohol.* New York: Gotham, 2008

Gilmore, Thomas B. *Equivocal Spirits: Alcoholism and Drinking in 20th Century Literature.* Chapel Hill: University of North Carolina Press, 1987.

Hogeland, William. *The Whiskey Rebellion: George Washington, Alexander Hamilton, and the Frontier Rebels Who Challenged America's Newfound Sovereignty.* New York: Scribner, 2006.

Lender, Mark Edward. *Drinking in America: A History.* New York: The Free Press, 1987.

Rorabaugh, W. J. *The Alcoholic Republic: An American Tradition.* New York: Oxford University Press, 1979.

Michael Lejman

WINE

Wine is an alcoholic beverage obtained from the fermentation of a plant product, generally a fruit. In the stricter sense, it is generally taken to mean an alcoholic beverage fermented from grapes—so much so that other types of wine are generally described with another qualifier (fruit wine, blueberry wine, rhubarb wine, or rice wine, for example).

The more general definition allows the United States to claim that there are wineries in all 50 states. Referring to grape wine only would restrict the number of wine-producing states, if only because of the impossibility of growing wine grapes in the Alaska climate.

Early History

Much like **beer**, wine's origins go back to the very beginnings of civilization. Archeological traces of winemaking have been found in sites dating back some 8,000 years, in places like Georgia and Iraq. Wine was a common drink in ancient Greece and Rome and remained important in the Middle Ages as a central part of the Christian ritual and as a daily drink considered safer than the water supply.

Wine—or at least, vines—were linked to European exploration of North America from the very beginning, as Norse explorers following the East Coast of North America gave the name of Vinland (land of vines) to regions historians now generally consider to be located just south of the Gulf of St. Lawrence. All early European explorers commented on the abundance of native grapes, including Verrazzano in 1524, along the East Coast of today's United States, Jacques Cartier along the shores of the St. Lawrence River a decade later, Walter Raleigh during his attempt at colonizing Virginia in the 1580s, and other explorers and first settlers throughout the sixteenth century.

Unsuccessful attempts at growing European *vitis vinifera* grapes took place at almost every English settlement in the seventeenth and eighteenth centuries, starting with Jamestown in 1607. Although attempts at making wine from local wild grapes were regularly reported in American colonial times, consumption on the East Coast remained essentially limited to imported wines until the nineteenth century. Wines from **Madeira** were particularly popular in colonies like Virginia, Carolina, and Georgia, as this Portuguese island was very conveniently located on the sailing routes to these colonies.

At the other end of the continent, the Spanish met with more success with *vitis vinifera*, which were brought up from Mexico and planted in settlements in New Mexico and Texas, near the Rio Grande, in the mid-seventeenth century. Franciscan monks are credited with the first such plantings in California, near the missions of Northern California, around 1779.

Birth of an Industry

The first license for a commercial winery in the United States was granted to Jean Jacques (John James) Dufour, originally from Vevey, Switzerland, who established the aptly named First Vineyard in Jessamine County, Kentucky, in 1799. The first vintage was made in 1803, and two barrels were reportedly sent to the president of the United States, Thomas Jefferson, whose love of wine and collection of famous *crus* from France are well known. The Kentucky enterprise was cut short in 1809, however, when the vineyards were largely destroyed by frost. The family relocated to Indiana, where Dufour pursued vinegrowing in the newly founded town of Vevay. He went on to publish the *American Vine Dresser's Guide* in 1826, very likely the first book on American viticulture, and his experiments inspired another pioneer of American winemaking, Nicolas Longworth.

A man of considerable means, Longworth established a commercial winery in Ohio that became significantly successful by the 1840s, with still and sparkling white wines made from the native Catawba grape. In the 1850s, however, infestations of black rot delivered considerable blows to local winegrowing.

Other winegrowing enterprises took hold elsewhere in the United States, notably in Missouri and New York State, but it was really with the Gold Rush of 1849, which brought numerous immigrants to the newly conquered California, that a U.S. wine industry really began to take shape.

Growth in the second half of the nineteenth century in California was quick and unstable, with harsh boom and bust cycles. Yet those turbulent times saw the founding of many wineries that are still in operation today, like Charles Krug, Sebastiani, Inglenook, Beringer, Chateau Montelena, Simi, Concannon, and Korbel. The period also saw the planting of a great variety of European grapes, including zinfandel, now seen by many as an emblematic grape for the state. By the 1880s, production had become significant enough for wineries to be noticed internationally—Inglenook, notably, won medals at the 1889 Exposition Universelle in Paris—and for wine to be exported, particularly to Great Britain. By the turn of the twentieth century, California wine production reached over 30 million gallons per year, from a few hundred thousand gallons four decades earlier.

Prohibition

The California wine industry was dealt a severe blow in 1920 with the enforcement of **Prohibition**. Numerous California growers abandoned mountain vineyards (some of which were famously recovered in the 1970s and 1980s, creating some exceptional "old vines" cuvées), and the banning of alcoholic drinks essentially wiped out the wine industry in many other states. California winemakers managed to survive, to a certain extent, because of certain allowed uses of alcohol (medicinal, industrial, or religious), and in particular, thanks to the growth of home winemaking during that period. Indeed, section 29 of the Volstead Act, the law that enforced Prohibition, specifically allowed production of "non-intoxicating" fruit drinks at home, a provision that the courts somehow interpreted as including cider and wine. Winegrowers like the Gallo family made a significant business of selling wine grapes to individuals all over the United States. Grape shipments often including detailed instructions as to the steps that should be "avoided," lest the grapes turn into wine. Paradoxically, it is considered that Prohibition may have made many Americans more familiar with wine, as consumption increased during the 1920s. In 1930, the Bureau of Prohibition calculated that 100 million gallons of wine were made in private homes each year.

With the repeal of Prohibition in 1933, the wine industry picked up quickly, leading to another cycle of boom and bust, as increased production led to a sizable wine glut by the end of the decade. Production was largely confined to bulk wines and generic brands bearing the names of famous European appellations like Champagne, Chablis, Burgundy, and Sherry, a commercial practice that would eventually lead to conflicts with European countries whose appellations were thus being unceremoniously borrowed.

There were other shifts during that period as well, with some producers aiming for higher-quality production. Along with Santa Cruz maverick winemaker Martin Ray, the most famous was certainly André Tchélistcheff, a Russian-born, French-trained winemaker and researcher who arrived in California in 1938, at the invitation of Georges de Latour, owner of Beaulieu Vineyards. This is where Tchélistcheff worked to create a distinctive style of California wine, particularly cabernet sauvignon, while also introducing local producers to a number of technical improvements such as cold **fermentation**, malolactic fermentation, and the aging of wines in small French oak barrels. His technical expertise and example were highly influential to a whole generation of California winemakers, including several of those who came to international attention in 1976, following a tasting now universally known as "the Judgment of Paris."

Organized by British wine merchant and wine critic Steven Spurrier, the famous competition was a comparative blind tasting of American and French chardonnays and cabernets sauvignons that resulted in a surprise win by the Californian upstarts. This event is now seen as a watershed in the world of wine, as it shook the European claim of superiority in the production of quality wine and opened the way to the rapid growth of New World winemaking. In many ways, the shockwaves from this realization of the potential of places like California spurred a realignment of the market that continues to this day. It also served as a jolt to winegrowing and winemaking in California and the rest of the United States and

Canada, as the possibility of making world-class wines in locations other than the classic appellations seemed more realistic than ever.

Wine in the United States Today

Since the 1970s, U.S. wine production has grown exponentially, in California as well as in other states that had no winegrowing tradition. In 1970, the total acreage devoted to wine grapes in California was 157,000 acres. In 2000, it had increased to 480,000 acres, and this figure has since remained fairly stable. In the 1970s and 1980s, wine production also began to grow significantly in other states, in particular Washington, Oregon, New York, Virginia, Texas, Michigan, Pennsylvania, and Ohio. A significant portion of production in Eastern states shifted from hybrid grapes, which had dominated production until then, to *vinifera*, with increasing success as viticultural and winemaking techniques improved and more professionally trained oenologists became available.

Growth in wine production has been sustained and steady up to this day. Though there are significant variations between vintages, for reasons having to do chiefly with the growing season, it can be estimated that total U.S. wine production has gone up nearly 50 percent since the mid-1990s, from around 450 million gallons to over 600 million gallons in the mid-2000s. Between 2004 and 2008, the value of wine produced in the United States—over 90 percent of which comes from California—grew from $23.7 billion in 2004 to $26.8 billion in 2008, an average annual growth of 3.1 percent.

Production has grown in tune with the growth of U.S. wine consumption, which has gone from 1.31 gallons (4.9 liters) per year, per capita, in 1970, to some 2.48 gallons (7.6 liters) in 2008. While this remains well below European averages, the rise has been steady and constant since the 1970s.

The United States has also become a major producer and exporter of wine on the international stage, competing internationally at every quality level, with some cult wines fetching prices comparable to those of Bordeaux first growths. The United States is the fourth-largest wine-producing country in the world, behind France, Italy, and Spain. Exports have been growing, with some 130 million gallons of wine worth over $1 billion shipping abroad in 2008, placing the United States in the top five wine-exporting countries in the world. Almost half of exports go to the European Union (Great Britain, mainly), and a quarter to Canada.

Wine has become a central part of the drinking culture in the United States. It is the only alcoholic drink that has seen an increase in consumption since the 1980s, as beer consumption decreases and spirits consumption remains essentially unchanged. It is significant that while the 2008 recession led to a drop in the dollar value of U.S. wine sales, the actual volume of wine sold has kept on increasing, showing how the growing number of wine lovers were unwilling to forgo their drink of choice, even in hard economic times. (*See also* **Brewing; Champagne; Fermentation; Terroir; Wine Tourism; Winemaking, Home.**)

Further Reading

Barr, Andrew. *Drink: A Social History of America*. New York: Carroll & Graf, 1999.

Pinney, Thomas. *A History of Wine in America from the Beginnings to Prohibition*. Berkeley: University of California Press, 1989. http://publishing.cdlib.org/ucpressebooks/view?docId=ft967nb63q;brand=eschol.

———. *A History of Wine in America since Prohibition*. Berkeley: University of California Press, 2005.

Wine Institute Statistics. http://www.wineinstitute.org/resources/statistics.

Rémy Charest

WINE COOLERS

A **wine** cooler is an alcoholic beverage that is usually produced from a mixture of wine and fruit juice with carbonation and sugar sometimes being added to the mix. Originally an experimental homemade beverage, wine coolers began being sold commercially during the 1980s. During that decade, the drink was widely popular and entered American popular culture when many celebrities began drinking and promoting it. The company California Cooler is credited with first bottling wine coolers for sale to the public, and their new product was so successful that larger corporations such as Gallo and Seagram's soon entered the market, with dozens of wine cooler brands in existence today. Sometimes called "soda pop for adults" or "**alcopops**," coolers are popular throughout the United States and especially in areas where their lower alcohol content allows their **distribution** with fewer legal restrictions. Early recipes usually called for the use of expensive wine in a cooler mix, but because fruit juice or other sweeteners tend to obscure most of the wine flavor in the drink, the wine used in commercial versions tends to be of a cheaper grade. Changes in American tax laws during the early 1990s led many producers to substitute malt for wine in many cooler mixes to cut costs. The result technically ended the wine cooler craze, but malt-based coolers remain very popular in the United States as well as overseas.

Further Reading

Kaufman, William I. *California Wine Drinks: Cocktails, Coolers, Punches and Hot Drinks*. San Francisco: Wine Appreciation Guild, 1982.

Ben Wynne

WINE TASTING

Wine tasting involves a conscious, qualitative assessment of the **wine**, in terms of color, flavors, and aromas, and it can be done with or without actually drinking the wine. Tastings can be informal, as a personal appreciation of a particular wine, or formal, in the regulated and quantified context of professional wine reviews or wine competitions.

Beyond taking a short moment to concentrate and carefully smell and taste whatever is in the glass, wine tasting can take place in a group, with people gathering to taste a certain number of bottles, often selected according to a theme. Wineries also provide a popular context for wine tastings, as people stopping by can usually taste a certain number of the producer's offerings, where they are made.

Formal wine tasting usually involves a form of comparison. One factor is whether the wines are tasted "blind"—in other words, whether the tasters know exactly which wine they are tasting. Blind tasting is often valued as reducing the effect of preconceived notions about the reputation, price, and supposed quality of a particular cuvée, factors that can strongly affect one's appreciation. Other possibilities include horizontal tastings (all wines from a single vintage), vertical tastings (different vintages of the same wine) and comparative tastings (a selection of similar wines—from the same region, the same grape variety, the same appellation, and so forth).

The more formal tastings involve some kind of rating system (stars, medals, or points), the most famous being Robert Parker's and the *Wine Spectator*'s 100-point scale. While providing an aura of objectivity and quantifiable value, this system has also been contested because of the importance of certain thresholds (especially the 90-point limit) that can artificially inflate or deflate the demand and price for a particular wine. A number of recent studies have also shown significant variations in the scores and classification of same wines by different tasters or even, by the same taster, thereby questioning the significance of such scores and, in particular, the value of medals awarded in competitions. The question of whether there can be an accounting for taste thus seems to remain open.

Further Reading

Robinson, Jancis. *How to Taste: A Guide to Enjoying Wine*. New York: Simon and Schuster, 2008.

Rémy Charest

WINE TOURISM

As the popularity of **wine** has grown in the United States, so has the popularity of wine-related travel, as aficionados and casual visitors alike head to the wineries to see and taste wine in the place where it is being produced.

Vineyards of Napa Valley, California are extremely popular tourist destinations. Most wineries have built special tasting rooms to accommodate their guests, and tasting tours are one of the most common tourist offers in the area. (Javarman/Dreamstime.com)

Napa Valley: A Wine Tourism Destination

Situated 50 miles north of San Francisco, Napa Valley is California's second-most popular tourist destination after Disneyland. Napa's world-class wines and hospitality draw more than 4.7 million tourists a year. Most people come to taste wine, visit wineries, dine in gourmet restaurants, or relax at one of the many spas. Tourists spend an estimated $1 billion during their visits, and this industry has generated over 17,000 jobs in the area.

Wine enthusiasts flock to the wineries for a taste of the wine country life that they associate with the famed Cabernet Sauvignon and Chardonnay of this region. Films like *Bottle Shock* (2008), which tells the stories of Napa Valley's early days and the famous "judgment of Paris," in which a Chateau Montelena wine beats out French rivals in a blind tasting, have helped increase Napa Valley's wine tourism and the fascination and romance that surrounds winemaking.

Most wineries have built tasting rooms where they receive guests and charge a fee for wine tasting. This is an excellent opportunity for tourists to taste wines and also purchase them directly from the producer. In Napa, direct-to-consumer sales make up an important segment of all sales for most wineries, and the proliferation of tasting rooms has been essential in this commercial shift. Tasting rooms in Napa are often lavish, featuring local art, and frequently have restaurants or outdoor dining areas for guests to relax and take in the vineyard and countryside.

Wine tourism in Napa has an American flavor that is all its own. A "wine train" takes visitors from the town of Napa to St. Helena. The train features a restaurant where passengers can enjoy local wine and cuisine. There are also many limousine and bus services that take tourists from winery to winery, helping reduce incidents of driving under the influence. Professional wine critics are used to spitting out the wines they sample in order to stay sober and lucid while tasting. In contrast, most wine tourists view getting a little tipsy as part of the wine tourism experience in Napa.

In rural areas, the presence of vineyards can have an important effect on the local economy, not only as an added-value agricultural activity, but also by bringing visitors to localities they might not otherwise have considered. The visits can take on various forms, from city dwellers visiting neighboring vineyards as a weekend outing to visitors including a winery stop in a larger trip to a region and travelers planning a wine-centric itinerary.

According to a 2007 study produced for the Wine Institute, which represents the California wine industry, wine tourism in the United States as a whole represents over 27 million tourist visits per year, resulting in an estimated $3 billion in expenditures. California is the main and most famous producing state, and it also gets the most visitors, with some 19 million visits. Wine tourism takes place all over the country, however, as all 50 states can now boast having wineries, if one includes the production of fruit wines. Oregon, Washington, and

New York, as the three next most important wine-producing states, also see significant travel in their wine-producing regions. Wine tourism can hold an important place in the viability of vineyards, especially for smaller operations and lesser-known regions that depend much more on a direct relationship with consumers and on sales at the cellar door. Visitors also get an added value, as they can find out more about the grape growing and winemaking and the people who create the wines, and also, very often, buy bottlings that are only available at the winery. This sense of closeness and privilege can be a powerful brand-building tool for wine producers, as they compete on a marketplace where status and exclusivity are certainly as important as value, at least to the type of consumers who are willing to travel to the source. (*See also* **Economics; Wine Tasting.**)

Further Reading

MKF Research, "The Impact of Wine, Grapes, and Grape Products on the American Economy 2007" (report on the wine industry). http://www.house.gov/radanovich/wine/documents/Economic_Impact_on_National_Economy_2007.pdf.

Rémy Charest

WINEMAKING, HOME

Home winemaking is the domestic production of wine through the **fermentation** of grape juice and, to a lesser extent, other fruit juices. Home winemaking is a 2,000-year-old craft and has been a common practice in the United States since the founding of the country. Wine is made throughout the United States but is more common in the northern and coastal states than in the southern and central states. Epicenters of home winemaking activity are often located in the prime viticultural areas. Although there is no published figure listing the quantity of home-made wine produced in the United States, some estimates exceed 10 million gallons per year.

According to federal law, an adult may produce wine without paying tax as long as it is for personal or family use. Each household with two or more adults can produce up to 200 gallons per calendar year and up to 100 gallons per calendar year in households with only one adult. Although it cannot be sold, wine can be removed from the premises for personal consumption and for use at organized fairs, exhibitions, and competitions.

Since the 1970s, wine production and consumption, as well as the demand for wine in the United States, has skyrocketed. Home winemaking has mirrored the country's growing interest in wine as a fashionable beverage. As the wine industry grows, consumers increasingly seek more information about wine and its production. Wine is now made on a domestic scale, not for a lack of high-quality wine, but rather because the process of home winemaking offers insight into the ancient craft as well as a sample of the winemaking lifestyle.

Since in the mid-nineteenth century, home winemaking has been an important activity for immigrants, predominantly Italian, throughout the United States. For many Italian immigrants, making wine at home was a key element in a culinary tradition that served not only as a reminder of a home left behind, but also helped to maintain a cultural identity, which was paramount in the face of the sometimes harsh immigrant realities.

During **Prohibition**, when one could be arrested and jailed for the commercial production and sale of alcoholic beverages, home winemaking was common since the head of household was permitted to produce up to 100 gallons of "non-intoxicating **cider** and fruit juices," that is, wine. Italian immigrants and Italian Americans dominated the viticulture industry, growing grapes for home winemakers throughout the country. Because home winemaking was so popular during Prohibition, the acreage of vines planted and tonnage of wine grapes produced was greater during Prohibition than either directly before or after repeal. In 1979, legal regulations were relaxed, permitting home winemaking without registration. In the years following Prohibition, even after commercial wineries were reestablished, it is estimated that significantly more wine was made on the small scale for personal consumption than was made for commercial sale.

Today, the quality of homemade wine is determined by the same factors as any commercial wine: the quality of raw materials and the process of production. Homemade wine is produced from fresh grapes, grape concentrate, frozen grapes, and grape juice. Although some vineyards that supply grapes to boutique wineries also sell fruit to home winemakers in smaller quantities, wine can also be made at home with home winemaking kits that provide all the necessary ingredients along with instructions and recipes. Both can be a fulfilling, enjoyable, and edifying way to successfully produce wine.

Grapes are an ideal candidate to become wine because they are unique among fruit in that they contain a ratio of sugar and acid that is appropriate to ferment sufficient alcohol so that the wine is palatable and is safe against spoilage. Although other fruits do not contain the appropriate balance of sugar, acid, and water, the production of fruit wines is also popular among many home wine-makers, especially in areas of the United States with cooler climates. Although few fruits have the sufficient quantity of fermentable sugars and the balance of acid and water to make a palatable wine, fruit wines, often called country wines, can be made by supplementing the fruit's natural sugar to provide a higher alcohol content and a more drinkable finished wine. Yeast nutrients are often added to supplement the deficiency that is often common in fruit wines.

Home winemaking clubs, which consist of both home winemakers and wine enthusiasts, have sprouted up throughout the country and serve to promote the culture of home winemaking through informational, competitive, and social meetings. Because the equipment involved in home winemaking requires a substantial economic commitment, home winemaking clubs also help make winemaking equipment available, such as crusher-destemmers, presses, corkers, and filters.

Home winemakers are attracted to the hobby in part because it is considered stylish among some, associated with what is, for many, a sophisticated beverage whose production is connected with the top economic echelon of society. Whereas **beer** drinking and home-brewing in the United States have a less positive connotation for many people, in popular culture, wine is often considered a luxury beverage drunk by the wealthy. Whereas home beer brewers consist mainly of men in their twenties and older, home winemakers often include retirees and both women and men. (*See also* **Home-Brew**.)

Further Reading

Cooke, George M., and James T. Lapsley. *Making Table Wine at Home*. San Pablo: University of California Agriculture and Natural Resources, 2004. http://wineserver.ucdavis.edu/content.php?category=Winemaking.

Pinney, Thomas. *A History of Wine in America: From Prohibition to the Present*. Berkeley: University of California Press, 2005.

Warrick, Sheridan. *The Way to Make Wine: How to Craft Superb Table Wines at Home*. Berkeley: University of California Press, 2006.

Matthew Russell

WINOS

The term "wino" is an "Americanism," following the pattern of American English to add the suffix "-o" to an existing term, often to communicate affinity or disdain. The term rose to prominence in 1915, as part of the rhetoric about drunkenness used by the **Temperance** Movement to gain public and political

---

Life on the Street

Journalist-writer Lee Stringer lived out on the streets of New York for more than 10 years in the 1980s and 1990s. He battled alcohol and drug addiction and lived to write about his experience. In Stringer's first book, the descriptions of street life are harrowing, but they also reveal the fragile humanity of this difficult life. This excerpt discusses the morality of substance abusers.

> The image of street people has always been associated with an unnatural devotion to some substance. In the old, skid-row-bum, rail-riding-hobo incarnations, the liquor bottle was an emblem as indispensable as Mulligan stew. . . .
> In the ten years I spent on the street, also abusing drugs, I've met just about every type of junkie out there. And I'll tell you this: Though some of them, myself included, might be perfectly capable of immoral acts while using—as would you and nearly anyone—I cannot say of any of them they were immoral people. . . .
> Of course not one puts a gun to anyone's head and forces him to indulge in the stuff. And a common assumption is that drinking and drugging are activities that moral people eschew by nature and immoral people readily take to. Boozers and druggers routinely concur on this point.

Source: Lee Stringer, *Grand Central Winter: Stories from the Street* (New York: Seven Stories Press, 1998), 220–21.

support prior to the creation of the Eighteenth Amendment to the U.S. Constitution and the Volstead Act.

A wino is a person—usually a man—whose consumption of **wine** had made him unemployable, criminal, or socially problematic in other ways. One major sociohistorical feature of American society was the representation of drink and loyalty. Wine drinkers were suspect in their allegiances, which manifested themselves in a social expectation that being American meant an aversion to wine. These claims were rebutted by southern and eastern European immigrants openly celebrating their love of the "fruit of the vine." This tension also extended to anti-Catholic sentiment and the question of alcoholic wine in use as a sacrament, as opposed to nonalcoholic grape juice used by Baptists, Methodists, and other Protestant sects.

The wino was a particular subtype of the drunkard, whose choice of intoxicant added additional layers of social contempt. Not only was the wino "lazy" and "parasitic," but he was resistant to American values and potentially subversive.

The wino came back into popular culture during the artistic movement of the 1950s known as the "beatnik movement." The wino and his place, known as "**skid row**," became the substance of cultural representations and academic study.

Further Reading

Barr, Andrew. *Drink: A Social History of America*. New York: Carroll & Graf, 1999.

Peterson, W. J., and Maxwell, M. A. "The Skid Road 'Wino.' " *Social Problems* 5, no. 4 (Spring 1958): 308–16.

Ken Kirkwood

WOMAN'S CHRISTIAN TEMPERANCE UNION

The Woman's Christian Temperance Union (WCTU) was founded on December 15, 1873, after a group of concerned women in Fredonia, New York, heard a lecture on the moral and physical evils of alcohol by Dio Lewis. Inspired by his words, the women took up the prohibition cause, protesting at saloons by publicly praying, singing hymns, and begging barkeepers to shut down their establishments.

This 1874 Currier and Ives lithograph, "Temperance: Women's Holy War," illustrates the aggressive mission and religious purpose of the crusaders against the sale and consumption of alcoholic beverages. The Woman's Christian Temperance Union, with Frances Willard at the helm, empowered women to act politically and forcefully within their communities to promote both abstinence and women's rights. (Library of Congress)

Frances Willard, WCTU Leader, Describes Her Crusade "Baptism"

The first saloon I ever entered was Sheffner's, on Market street, Pittsburgh, on my way home. In fact, that was the only glimpse I ever personally had of the Crusade. . . . We paused in front of the saloon that I have mentioned. The ladies ranged themselves along the curbstone, for they had been forbidden in anywise to incommode the passers-by, being dealt with much more strictly than a drunken man or a heap of dry-goods boxes would be. At a signal from our gray-haired leader, a sweet-voiced woman began to sing, "Jesus the water of life will give," all our voices soon blending in that sweet song. I think it was the most novel spectacle that I recall. There stood women of undoubted religious devotion and the highest character, most of them crowned with the glory of gray hairs. Along the stony pavement of that stoniest of cities rumbled the heavy wagons, many of them carriers of beer; between us and the saloon in front of which we were drawn up in line, passed the motley throng, almost every man lifting his hat and even the little newsboys doing the same. It was American manhood's tribute to Christianity and to womanhood, and it was significant and full of pathos. The leader had already asked the saloon-keeper if we might enter, and he had declined, else the prayer-meeting would have occurred inside his door. A sorrowful old lady whose only son had gone to ruin through that very death-trap, knelt on the cold, moist pavement and offered a broken-hearted prayer, while all our heads were bowed. At a signal we moved on and the next saloon-keeper permitted us to enter. I had no more idea of the inward appearance of a saloon than if there had been no such place on earth. I knew nothing of its high, heavily corniced bar, its barrels with the ends all pointed towards the looker-on, each barrel being furnished with a faucet; its shelves glittering with decanters and cut glass, its floors thickly strewn with saw-dust, and here and there a round table with chairs—nor of its abundant fumes, sickening to healthful nostrils. The tall, stately lady who led us, placed her Bible on the bar and read a psalm, whether hortatory or imprecatory, I do not remember, but the spirit of these crusaders was so gentle, I think it must have been the former. Then we sang "Rock of Ages" as I thought I had never heard it sung before, with a tender confidence to the height of which one does not rise in the easy-going, regulation prayer-meeting, and then one of the older women whispered to me softly that the leader wished to know if I would pray. It was strange, perhaps, but I felt not the least reluctance, and kneeling on that saw-dust floor, with a group of earnest hearts around me, and behind them, filling every corner and extending out into the street, a crowd of unwashed, unkempt, hard-looking drinking men, I was conscious that perhaps never in my life. . . . This was my Crusade baptism. The next day I went on to the West and within a week had been made president of the Chicago W. C. T. U.

Source: Frances E. Willard, *Glimpses of Fifty Years: The Autobiography of an American Woman* (Chicago: H. J. Smith and Company, 1889), 339–41.

The organization became known formally as the National Woman's Christian Temperance Union in 1874 and held its first national conference that year in Cleveland, Ohio. The strength of the WCTU from 1880 to 1920 could not be matched, with membership numbers exceeding 150,000 in 1890. Its voice was heard on a national political level; the WCTU was instrumental in lobbying for the passage of the Eighteenth Amendment to the Constitution in 1919 that criminalized alcohol manufacture, transportation, and sale. In 1932, repeal of the **Prohibition** amendment dealt a serious blow to the organization's collective ego, and for the next 30 years, the WCTU began to decline in numbers as general popularity for the cause waned. Since the 1960s, the WCTU has been populated by older, rural, working-class, conservative religious women. Its membership has declined significantly since its heyday, and its focus has necessarily transformed as a return to Prohibition in the United States is unrealistic. Instead, today's WCTU members focus on issues such as **fetal alcohol syndrome**, gambling, Sunday alcohol sales, and public smoking bans. In 2009, they celebrated their 135th national convention in Wichita, Kansas. (*See also* **Temperance**.)

Further Reading

Gusfield, Joseph. *Symbolic Crusade: Status Politics and the American Temperance Movement*. 2nd ed. Chicago: University of Illinois Press, 1986.

Rollins, Cristin Eleanor. "Have You Heard the Tramping of the New Crusade? Survival and the Woman's Christian Temperance Union." PhD diss., University of Georgia, 2005.

Woman's Christian Temperance Union Web site. http://www.wctu.org.

Cristin Rollins

WOMEN AND GIRLS DRINKING

American women tend to abstain from drinking alcohol more frequently then do men, with slight versions depending on **race and ethnicity** (Galvan and Caetano 2003). This tendency toward abstinence and moderation has never been fully explained, but there are a number of illuminating historical and sociological factors.

Since the foundation of the American colonies, women and girls have been drinking. Women's consumption of alcohol has not always been viewed in a positive light and was generally socially controlled. For example, women's presence in saloons and **bars** was not acceptable or encouraged. The women who spent time in these male-dominated drinking establishments were generally thought of as "loose women." Prostitution often proliferated in saloons, and the image of the "painted lady" in the saloon is still very much part of the American imagination when thinking about the Old West. At the same time, it is this type of social control that limited women's public drinking and shaped gender stereotypes concerning women's public behavior in America.

Women were active players in the **Temperance** Movement, forming groups such as the **Woman's Christian Temperance Union**, lobbying government, and mobilizing public opinion against the production and consumption of alcohol in the United States. In this movement, women were portrayed as the moral upholders of family values, fighting against the destruction of the home and civic values, which was a product of drunkenness. In this case, women were active participants in the creation of this gendered stereotype.

During **Prohibition**, American women ironically found more freedom to drink. **Speakeasies** offered private spaces where social norms could be transgressed and the liberal consumption of alcohol aided the crossing of acceptable boundaries that had previously been governed by gender norms in the public sphere. In addition, more drinking was going on in the home, where women were more likely to participate and where they were sometimes encouraged by men and husbands to have a drink.

With the repeal of Prohibition, drinking became an acceptable social activity for men. On one hand, it was an activity that even became expected of men if they were to maintain a semblance of virility. Women who drank, on the other hand, were seen as transgressing gender norms and challenging traditional female roles. In particular, the woman who drank too much was seen as abandoning her children and domestic duties (McClellan 2004). In the 1930s and 1940s, the bar was still not an acceptable place for women.

At the end of World War II, women were encouraged to leave the workplace and retreat back to the domestic sphere. In this period of affluence, suburban **cocktail parties** were events where a woman could show off her home and her sophistication based on the **cocktails** she served and the food she offered alongside it. Women were often encouraged to drink, but a woman who drank too much was once again frowned upon. Social drinking abounded in the 1950s and 1960s, but women were still expected to remain in control, and **alcoholism** was interpreted by psychologists and medical practitioners as far more abnormal in women. Alcoholism was largely seen as a failure of femininity (McClellan 2004).

With the sexual revolution of the 1960s, the public sphere increasingly opened to women drinking. In addition, more women were attending college, which was frequently the first place women and girls would experience alcohol. For many, it became a right of passage. At the same time, this "drinking oneself into adulthood" brought with it a whole set of gender-specific issues. Drunken women are far more susceptible to rape and to having unprotected sex.

Some girls think that **binge drinking** is an expected right of passage for becoming a woman. In addition, what drinks are consumed, how, and with whom have an impact on gender status and can be perceived as the difference between being a girl and being a woman. In many ways, young women's binge drinking is also a challenge to gender roles, giving women an outlet for pushing boundaries and challenging accepted male/female social stereotypes.

Alcohol plays an important part in many women's social lives, whether it is getting together for a cocktail with girlfriends, enjoying **wine** with dinner, or heading to a bar for drinks and dancing. Much of women's drinking is shaped by **advertising** and the gendered construction of certain drinks. For example, sipping Chardonnay from a wine glass is often viewed as more feminine that chugging **beer** from a big plastic cup.

Women metabolize alcohol at a slower rate than do men. For this reason, women are more likely to get drunk more quickly than are men, which can have devastating health effects when binge drinking. Alcohol consumption also has negative effects on the development of the fetus during pregnancy, which can even lead to **fetal alcohol syndrome**. This fact has shaped social norms for women drinking, even drawing into question women's social responsibility and their role as mothers. When it comes to drinking in the United States, women are now generally free to drink where they like, but they are not free from social judgment, social risks, and the health issues associated with heavy drinking. There are many double standards when it comes to men and women's drinking habits in the United States. At the same time, recent research suggests that the gender gap between women and men when it comes to alcohol abuse and dependency may be shrinking, and new targeted prevention and **intervention** efforts may be required to address the growing problem of female alcoholism (Keyes et al. 2008). (*See also* **College Drinking Culture; Men and Boys Drinking.**)

Further Reading

Galvan, Frank H., and Raul Caetano. "Alcohol Use and Related Problems among Ethnic Minorities in the U.S." National Institute on Alcohol Abuse and Alcoholism, December 2003. http://www.niaaa.nih.gov/publications/arh27-1/87-94.htm.

Keyes, Katherine M., Bridget F. Grant, and Deborah S. Hasin. "Evidence for a Closing Gender Gap in Alcohol Use, Abuse and Dependency in the United States Population." *Drug and Alcohol Dependence* 93, no. 1/2 (2008): 21–29.

McClellan, Michelle. " 'Lady Tipplers': Gendering the Modern Alcoholism Paradigm, 1933–1960." In *Altering American Consciousness: The History of Alcohol and Drug Use in the United States, 1800–2000*, ed. S. W. Tracy and C. J. Acker, 267–97. Amherst: University of Massachusetts Press, 2004.

Murdock, Catherine Gilbert. *Domesticating Drink: Women, Men and Alcohol in America, 1870–1940*. Baltimore: Johns Hopkins University Press, 1998.

Zailckas, Koren. *Smashed: A Story of a Drunken Girlhood*. New York: Penguin Press, 2005.

Rachel Black

WORKPLACE DRINKING

Workplace drinking is mainly classified as drinking while working, during a lunch break, or at a company-sponsored event, or arriving at work already intoxicated. Within each of these situations, there are different and parallel motivating factors to drink, as well as varying degrees of harmful outcomes resulting from this behavior.

Employees may have preexisting alcohol problems that continue while at work. Others may be influenced to drink by coworkers, the demanding pressures of the job, or problems in the home. The main point many studies discuss in regard to the harmful aspects of workplace drinking is the availability of alcohol, the encouragement of excessive drinking, or the lack of attention to workplace drinking by management or supervisors. Another factor is the direct correlation between the prevalence of drinking at work and heavy drinking off the clock. Studies show that a restricted drinking environment in the workplace often leads to less drinking outside of the workplace as well. Therefore, the drinking culture at work can have a direct correlation with social drinking.

Drinking at work could be instigated by many factors. There are social pressures by colleagues to relax and let loose, and the act of drinking together creates a sense of belonging and camaraderie. Business meetings can often be held over lunch breaks or during meals where drinks are used as a social lubricant and tool to gain the favor of a potential client. Any level within the corporate or general workplace structure may be exposed to these social pressures. Another situational motivation is when employees might feel as though they are in a "dead-end job" with no real responsibility or room for advancement. Drinking may help to pass the time or be an act of rebellion against a supervisor who makes them feel misunderstood, not heard, or ignored.

A study by the University of Buffalo's Research Institute on Addiction in 2003 showed that 15 percent of the workforce in the United States worked while under the influence of alcohol. The majority of the individuals who make up that figure are men. The field of work with one of the highest percentages of drinking is the hospitality industry, primarily due to the availability and accessibility of alcohol within the everyday working environment. These industries must take special care in alcohol prevention and attention to potential abuse by employees.

To aid in reducing the amount of drinking on the job and preventing future problems, the U.S. Office of Personnel Management has written handbooks for supervisors to become better aware of the prevalence of drinking on the job and how to detect and prevent it. They state that the main preventative measure is a strict enforcement of stringent alcohol policies, as well as the ability to recognize signs of possible alcohol abuse such as absenteeism, **hangovers,** poor work performance, lateness, an unkempt appearance, or lengthy lunches and breaks. Whether an employee already has a drinking problem when hired or develops a problem while working, it is important for management to be better suited to deal with the problem at the earliest stage possible, in addition to not encouraging or promoting the acceptance of getting intoxicated at any time while on the job. In general, prevention and, most importantly, awareness seem to be key.

Further Reading

Ames, Genevieve M., Joel W. Grube, and Roland S. Moore. "Social Control and Workplace Drinking Norms: A Comparison of Two Organizational Cultures." *Journal of Studies on Alcohol* 61 (March 2000): 203–19.

Marshall, Ronald. *Alcoholism: Genetic Culpability or Social Irresponsibility?* Lanham, MD: University Press of America, 2001.

Roman, Paul M., J. Aaron Johnson, and Terry C. Blum. "The Workplace, Employer and Employee." In *Alcohol Use*, ed. David B. Cooper, 121–33. Abingdon, Oxford: Radcliffe Medical Press, 2000.

University of Buffalo Research Institute on Addictions. http://www.ria.buffalo.edu. "Workplace Drinking Culture Influences Alcohol Intake Elsewhere." *Medical News Today*, May 24, 2007. http://www.medicalnewstoday.com/articles/71849.php.

Whitney Adams

Selected Bibliography

Books and Print Materials

Aaron, Paul, and David Musto. "Temperance and Prohibition in America: A Historical Overview." In *Alcohol and Public Policy: Beyond the Shadow of the Prohibition*, ed. Mark Harrison Moore and Dean. R Gerstein, 127–81. Washington, DC: National Academy Press, 1981.

Alasuutari, Pertti. *Desire and Craving: A Cultural Theory of Alcoholism*. Albany: State University of New York Press, 1992.

Allen, Frederick Lewis. *Only Yesterday: An Informal History of the 1920's*. New York: Perennial Classics, 2000.

Ames, Genevieve M. "Middle-class Protestants: Alcohol and the Family." In *The American Experience with Alcohol: Contrasting Cultural Perspectives*, ed. Linda A. Bennett and Genevieve M. Ames, 435–60. New York: Plenum Press, 2005.

Ames, Genevieve M., Joel W. Grube, and Roland S. Moore. "The Relationship of Drinking and Hangovers to Workplace Problems: An Empirical Study." *Journal of Studies on Alcohol* 58, no. 1 (1997): 37–47.

Applebaum, Ben, and Dan Disorbo. *The Book of Beer Pong*. San Francisco: Chronicle Books, 2009.

Babor, Thomas. *Alcohol: Customs and Rituals*. New York: Chelsea House, 1986.

———. *Alcohol and Public Policy: No Ordinary Commodity*. New York: Oxford University Press, 2003.

Bahr, Howard M. *Skid Row: An Introduction to Disaffiliation*. New York: Oxford University Press, 1973.

Balko, Radley. "The Government Should Not Censor Alcohol Advertising." In *Alcohol: The History of Drugs and Alcohol*, ed. Ann Manheimer. New York: Thomson Gale, 2007.

Barr, Andrew. *Drink: A Social History of America*. New York: Carroll and Graf, 1999.

Barrows, Susanna, and Robin Room, eds. *Drinking Behavior and Belief in Modern History*. Berkeley: University of California Press, 1991.

Begg, Desmond. *The Vodka Companion: A Vodka Lovers Guide*. Philadelphia: Running Press, 1998.

Behr, Edward. *Prohibition: Thirteen Years That Changed America*. New York: Arcade Publishing, 1997.

Bennett, Linda A. "Alcohol in Context: Anthropological Perspectives." In *Alcoholism Etiology and Treatment: Issues for Theory and Practice*, ed. Bernard Segal, 89–131. New York: Haworth Press, 1988.

Bennett, Linda A., and Genevieve. M. Ames, eds. *The American Experience with Alcohol: Contrasting Cultural Perspectives*. New York: Plenum Press, 2005.

Beresford, Thomas, and Edith Gomberg, eds. *Alcohol and Aging*. New York: Oxford University Press, 1995.

Biggs, David. *Sharp Shooters*. London: New Holland, 2004.

Blair, Henry William. *The Temperance Movement: Or Conflict Between Man and Alcohol*. Boston: William Smythe, 1888.

Blocker, Jack. *American Temperance Movements: Cycles of Reform*. Boston: Twayne, 1989.

Blocker, Jack S., David M. Fahey, and Ian R. Tyrrell, eds. *Alcohol and Temperance in Modern History: An International Encyclopedia*. Santa Barbara, CA: ABC-CLIO, 2003.

Bonnie, Richard J., and Mary Ellen O'Connell, eds. *Reducing Underage Drinking: A Collective Responsibility*. Washington, DC: National Academies Press, 2004.

Brady, M. "Ethnography and Understanding of Aboriginal Drinking." *Journal of Drug Issues* 22, no. 3 (1992): 699–712.

Brain, Paul F. *Alcohol and Aggression*. London: Croom Helm, 1986.

Breslow, Rosalind A., and Barbara Smothers. "Drinking Patterns of Older Americans: National Health Interview Surveys, 1997–2001." *Journal of Studies on Alcohol and Drugs* 65 (2004): 232–40.

Brown, John H. *Early American Beverages*. New York: Bonanza Books, 1966.

Burns, Eric. *The Spirits of America: A Social History of Alcohol*. Philadelphia: Temple University Press, 2004.

Butts, Edward. *Outlaws of the Lakes: Bootlegging and Smuggling from Colonial Times to Prohibition*. New York: Thunder Bay Press, 2004.

Carr, Jess. *The Second Oldest Profession: An Informal History of Moonshining in America*. Engelwood Cliffs, NJ: Prentice-Hall, 1972.

Cashman, Sean D. *Prohibition: The Lie of the Land*. New York: Free Press, 1981.

Cavan, Sherri. *Liquor License: An Ethnography of Bar Behavior*. Chicago: Aldine, 1966.

Charming, Cheryl. *Miss Charming's Guide for Hip Bartenders and Wayout Wannabes: Your Ultimate One-Stop Bar and Cocktail Resource*. Naperville, IL: Sourcebooks, 2007.

Clark, Norman H. *Deliver Us from Evil: An Interpretation of American Prohibition*. New York: W. W. Norton and Company, 1976.

Clark, Walter D., and Michael E. Hilton. *Alcohol in America: Drinking Practices and Problems*. Albany: SUNY Press, 1991.

Coffey, Thomas M. *The Long Thirst: Prohibition in America 1920–1933*. New York: W. W. Norton, 1975.

Coleman, Tyler. *Wine Politics: How Governments, Environmentalists, Mobsters, and Critics Influence the Wines We Drink*. Berkeley: University of California Press, 2009.

Conroy, David. *In Public Houses: Drink and the Revolution of Authority in Colonial Massachusetts*. Chapel Hill: University of North Carolina Press, 1995.

Cornes, Judy. *Alcohol in the Movies, 1898–1962*. Jefferson, NC: McFarland, 2006.

Cray, Ed. *The Erotic Muse: American Bawdy Songs*. Urbana: University of Illinois Press, 1992.

Dade, Penny. *Drink Talking: 100 Years of Alcohol Advertising*. London: Middlesex University Press, 2008.

de Garine, Igor, and Valerie de Garine, eds. *Drinking: Anthropological Approaches*. New York: Berghahn, 2001.

de Visser, Richard O., and Jonathan A. Smith. "Alcohol Consumption and Masculine Identity among Young Men." *Psychology and Health* 22 (2007): 595–614.

DeGroff, Dale. *The Craft of the Cocktail*. New York: Clarkson Potter, 2002.

Douglas, Mary, ed. *Constructive Drinking: Perspectives on Drink from Anthropology*. Cambridge: Cambridge University Press, 1987.

Duis, Perry. *The Saloon: Public Drinking in Chicago and Boston, 1880–1920*. Urbana: University of Illinois Press, 1983.

Edwards, Griffith. *Alcohol: The World's Favorite Drug*. New York: Thomas Dunne Books, 2002.

Emmons, Bob. *The Book of Gins and Vodkas: A Complete Guide*. Chicago: Open Court Publishing, 1999.

Engs, Ruth. "Do Traditional Western European Drinking Practices Have Origins in Antiquity?" *Addiction Research* 2, no. 3 (1995): 227–39.

Everett, Michael W., Jack O. Waddell, and Dwight B. Heath, eds. *Cross-cultural Approaches to the Study of Alcohol: An Interdisciplinary Perspective*. The Hague: Mouton, 1976.

Fell, James C., and Robert B. Voas. "Mothers Against Drunk Driving (MADD): The First Twenty-five Years." *Traffic Injury Prevention* 7 (2006): 195–212.

Felten, Eric. *How's Your Drink? Cocktails, Culture and the Art of Drinking Well*. Chicago: Surrey Books, 2007.

Fitzgerald, F. Scott. *The Great Gatsby*. New York: Scribner, 2004 (Original ed., 1925).

French, Richard Valpy. *The History of Toasting*. London: National Temperance Publication Depot, 1882.

Gately, Iain. *Drink: A Cultural History of Alcohol*. New York: Gotham, 2008.

Gefou-Madianou, Dimitra, ed. *Alcohol, Gender and Culture*. London: Routledge, 1992.

Gilbert Murdock, Catherine. *Domesticating Drink: Women, Men and Alcohol in America, 1870–1940*. Baltimore: Johns Hopkins University Press, 1998.

Gilmore, Thomas B. *Equivocal Spirits: Alcoholism and Drinking in 20th Century Literature*. Chapel Hill: University of North Carolina Press, 1987.

Girouard, Mark. *Victorian Pubs*. New Haven, CT: Yale University Press, 1984.

Greenfield, Thomas K., and John D. Rogers. "Who Drinks Most of the Alcohol in the U.S.? The Policy Implications." *Journal of Studies on Alcohol* 60, no. 1 (1999): 78–89.

Grimes, William. *Straight Up or On the Rocks: A Cultural History of American Drink*. New York: Simon and Schuster, 1993.

Gusfield, Joseph. *Symbolic Crusade: Status Politics and the American Temperance Movement*. 2nd ed. Chicago: University of Illinois Press, 1986.

Hancock, David. *Oceans of Wine: Madeira and the Emergence of American Trade and Taste*. New Haven, CT: Yale University Press, 2009.

Harrison, Brian. *Drink and the Victorians*. London: Keele University Press, 1991.

Heath, Dwight B. "Anthropology and Alcohol Studies: Current Issues." *Annual Review of Anthropology* 16 (1987): 99–120.

———. *Drinking Occasions: Comparative Perspectives on Alcohol and Culture*. Ann Arbor, MI: Sheridan Books, 2000.

———, ed. *International Handbook on Alcohol and Culture*. Westport, CT: Greenwood Press, 1995.

Heather, Nick, and Ian Robertson. *Problem Drinking*. 2nd ed. Oxford: Oxford University Press, 1989.

Hingson, Ralph W. "The Legal Drinking Age and Underage Drinking in the United States." *Archives of Pediatric and Adolescent Medicine* 163, no. 7 (2009): 598–600.

Hogeland, William. *The Whiskey Rebellion: George Washington, Alexander Hamilton, and the Frontier Rebels Who Challenged America's Newfound Sovereignty*. New York: Scribner, 2006.

Hunt, Geoffrey. "A Comparative Investigation of the Role of Alcohol in North America, 1600–1850 and in Southern Africa, 1650–1900." *New Directions in Alcohol Research* 1, no. 4 (1983): 34–52.

Hunt, Geoffrey, and Judith C. Barker. "Socio-cultural Anthropology and Alcohol and Drug Research: Towards a Unified Theory." *Social Science and Medicine* 53 (2001): 165–88.

Jacobs, James B. *Drunk Driving: An American Dilemma*. Chicago: University of Chicago Press, 1992.

Jernigan, David H. "Alcohol Advertising to Young People Should Be Limited." In *Alcohol: the History of Drugs and Alcohol*, ed. Ann Manheimer. New York: Thomson Gale, 2007.

Jurkiewicz, Carole J., and Murphy J. Painter. *Social and Economic Control of Alcohol: The 21st Amendment in the 21st Century*. Boca Raton, FL: CRC Group, 2007.

Kaufman, William I. *California Wine Drinks: Cocktails, Coolers, Punches and Hot Drinks*. San Francisco: Wine Appreciation Guild, 1982.

Kerr, Kathel. *Organized for Prohibition: A New History of the Anti-Saloon League*. New Haven, CT: Yale University Press, 1985.

———. "Organizing for Reform: The Anti-Saloon League and Innovation in Politics." *American Quarterly* 32, no. 1 (1980): 37–53.

Kinross, Patrick Balfour. *The Kindred Spirit: A History of Gin and of the House of Booth*. London: Newman Neame, 1959.

Kobler, John. *Ardent Spirits: The Rise and Fall of Prohibition*. New York: Da Capo Press, 1993.

Krout, Jack. *The Origins of Prohibition*. Chicago: University of Chicago Press, 1979.

Kyvig, David E. *Repealing National Prohibition*. Chicago: University of Chicago Press, 1979.

Laing, Robin. *The Whiskey Muse: Scotch Whiskey in Poem and Song*. Edinburgh: Luath Press, 2002.

Leland, Joy. *Firewater Myths: North American Indian Drinking and Alcohol Addiction*. New Brunswick, NJ: Rutgers Center for Alcohol Studies, 1976.

Lemle, Russell, and Marc E. Mishkind. "Alcohol and Masculinity." *Journal of Substance Abuse Treatment* 6 (1989): 213–22.

Lender, Mark Edward, and James Kirby Martin. *Drinking in America: A History*. New York: The Free Press, 1982.

Lendler, Ian. *Alcoholica Esoterica*. New York: Penguin Books, 2005.

Lerner, Michael. *Dry Manhattan: Prohibition in New York City*. Cambridge, MA: Harvard University Press, 2007.

Lyons, Antonia C., and Sara A. Willott. "Alcohol Consumption, Gender Identities and Women's Changing Social Positions." *Sex Roles* 59 (2008): 694–712.

Mancall, Peter C. *Deadly Medicine: Indians and Alcohol in Early America*. Ithaca, NY: Cornell University Press, 1995.

Manheimer, Ann, ed. *Alcohol: The History of Drugs and Alcohol*. New York: Thomson Gale, 2007.

Marcus, Anthony. "Drinking Politics: Alcohol, Drugs and the Problem of U.S. Civil Society." In *Drinking Cultures: Alcohol and Identity*, ed. Thomas M. Wilson. New York: Berg, 2005.

Martin, Jack K., Steven A. Tuch, and Paul M. Roman. "Problem Drinking Patterns among African Americans: The Impacts of Reports of Discrimination, Perceptions of

Prejudice and Risky Coping Strategies." *Journal of Health and Social Beahvior* 44, no. 3 (2003): 408–25.

Martinic, Marjana, and Fiona Measham. *Swimming with Crocodiles: The Culture of Extreme Drinking.* New York: Taylor and Francis, 2008.

McDonald, Maryon, ed. *Gender, Drink, and Drugs.* Oxford: Berg, 1994.

McGovern, Patrick E. *Uncorking the Past: The Quest for Wine, Beer, and Other Alcoholic Beverages.* Berkeley: University of California Press, 2009.

Meier, Kenneth J. *The Politics of Sin: Drugs, Alcohol, and Public Policy.* Armonk, NY: M. E. Sharpe, 1994.

Mendelson, Jack, and Nancy K. Mello. *Alcohol, Use and Abuse in America.* Boston: Little Brown, 1985.

Mendelson, Richard. *From Demon to Darling: A Legal History of Wine in America.* Berkeley: University of California Press, 2009.

Moore, Mark Harrison, and Dean R. Gerstein, eds. *Alcohol and Public Policy: Beyond the Shadow of the Prohibition.* Washington, DC: National Academy Press, 1981.

Mullen, Kenneth, Jonathon Watson, Jan Swift, and David Black. "Young Men, Masculinity and Alcohol." *Drugs: Education, Prevention and Policy* 14 (2007): 151–65.

Ogle, Maureen. *Ambitious Brew: The Story of American Beer.* Fort Washington, PA: Harvest Book Company, 2007.

Orton, Vrest. *The American Cider Book: The Story of America's Natural Beverage.* New York: Farrar, Straus and Giroux, 1973.

Parker, Robert N. *Alcohol and Homicide: A Deadly Combination of Two American Traditions.* Albany: State University of New York Press, 1995.

Peck, Garrett. *Prohibition Hangover: Alcohol in America from Demon Rum to Cult Cabernet.* New Brunswick, NJ: Rutgers University Press, 2009.

Peele, Stanton, and Marcus Grant, eds. *Alcohol and Pleasure: A Health Perspective.* Philadelphia: Brunner/Mazel, 1999.

Pegram, Thomas R. *Battling Demon Rum: The Struggle for a Dry America, 1800–1933.* Chicago: Ivan R. Dee, 1999.

———. "The Dry Machine: The Formation of the Anti-Saloon League of Illinois." *Illinois Historical Journal* 83, no. 3 (1990): 173–86.

Perkins, H. Wesley. "Social Norms and the Prevention of Alcohol Misuse in Collegiate Contexts." *Journal of Studies in Alcohol*, supplement 14 (2002): 164–72.

———. *The Social Norms Approach to Preventing School and College Age Substance Abuse.* San Francisco: Wiley, 2003.

Pinney, Thomas. *A History of Wine in America: From the Beginnings to Prohibition.* Berkeley: University of California Press, 1989. http://publishing.cdlib.org/ucpressebooks/view?docId=ft967nb63q;brand=eschol (accessed April 24, 2010).

Pinney, Thomas. *A History of Wine in America: From Prohibition to Present.* Berkeley: University of California Press, 2005.

Popham, Robert E. "The Social History of the Tavern." In *Research Advances in Alcohol and Drug Problems*, ed. Yedy Israel et al. New York: Plenum, 1978.

Powers, Madelon. *Faces along the Bar: Lore and Order in the Workingman's Saloon, 1870–1920.* Chicago: University of Chicago Press, 1988.

Quintero, Gilbert. "Nostalgia and Degeneration: The Moral Economy of Drinking in Navajo Society." *Medical Anthropology Quarterly* 16 (2002): 3–21.

Roman, Paul. *Alcohol: A Sociological Perspective.* New Brunswick, NJ: Publications Division of Rutgers Center of Alcohol Studies, 1991.

Roman, Paul M., and T. C. Blum. "Notes on the New Epidemiology of Alcoholism in the U.S.A." *Journal of Drug Issues* 17 (1987): 321–32.

Rorabaugh, W. J. *The Alcoholic Republic: An American Tradition*. New York: Oxford University Press, 1979.

Roueché, Berton. *The Neutral Spirit: A Portrait of Alcohol*. Boston: Little, Brown and Company, 1960.

Rumbarger, John J. *Profits, Power and Prohibition*. Albany: State University of New York Press, 1989.

Salinger, Sharon V. *Taverns and Drinking in Early America*. Baltimore: Johns Hopkins University Press, 2002.

Segal, Bernard, ed. *Alcoholism Etiology and Treatment: Issues for Theory and Practice*. New York: Haworth Press, 1988.

Smith, Gregg. *Beer in America: The Early Years—1587–1840: Beer's Role in the Settling of America and the Birth of a Nation*. Boulder, CO: Siris Books, Brewers Publications, 1998.

Spicer, Paul. "Toward a (Dys)functional Anthropology of Drinking: Ambivalence and the American Indian Experience with Alcohol." *Medical Anthropology Quarterly* 11 (1997): 306–23.

Spradley, James P. *You Owe Yourself a Drunk: An Ethnography of Urban Nomads*. Boston: Little, Brown and Company, 1970.

Stephens, R., et al. "A Review of the Literature on the Cognitive Effects of Alcohol Hangover." *Alcohol and Alcoholism* 43 (2008): 163–70.

Strunin, Lee. "Assessing Alcohol Consumption: Development from Qualitative Research Methods." *Social Science and Medicine* 53, no. 2 (2001): 215–26.

Taylor, Lawrence E., and Steven Oberman. *Drunk Driving Defense*. New York: Aspen Press, 2005.

Thompson, Peter. *Rum Punch and Revolution: Taverngoing and Public Life in Eighteenth-Century Philadelphia*. Philadelphia: University of Pennsylvania Press, 1999.

Valliant, George E. *The Natural History of Alcohol Revisited*. Cambridge, MA: Harvard University Press, 1995.

Wechsler, Henry, Andrea Davenport, George Dowdall, Barbara Moeykens, and Sonia Castillo. "Health and Behavioral Consequences of Binge Drinking in College: A National Survey of Students at 140 Campuses." *Journal of the American Medical Association* 272, no. 21 (1994): 1672–77.

Wechsler, Henry, and Toben Nelson. "What We Have Learned from the Harvard School of Public Health College Alcohol Study: Focusing Attention on College Student Alcohol Consumption and the Environmental Conditions That Promote It." *Journal of Studies on Alcohol and Drugs* 69, no. 4 (2008): 481–90. http://www.hsph.harvard.edu/cas/What-We-Learned-08.pdf

White, A. M. "What Happened? Alcohol, Memory Blackouts, and the Brain." *Alcohol Research and Health* 27 (2003): 186–96.

Wiese, Jeffrey G., et al. "The Alcohol Hangover." *Annals of Internal Medicine* 132 (2000): 897–902.

Wilcox, Danny M. *Alcoholic Thinking: Language, Culture and Belief in Alcoholics Anonymous*. Westport, CT: Praeger, 1998.

Wilson, Thomas M., ed. *Drinking Cultures: Alcohol and Identity*. New York: Berg, 2005.

World Health Organization. International Guide for Monitoring Alcohol Consumption and Related Harm, WHO Document No. WHO/MSD/MSB/00.4, Geneva, Switzerland, 2000.

Zailckas, Koren. *Smashed: A Story of a Drunken Girlhood*. New York: Penguin Press, 2005.

Zimmerman, Johnathan. *Distilling Democracy: Alcohol Education in America's Public Schools, 1880–1925*. Lawrence: University of Kansas Press, 1999.

Web Sites

Alcohol and Drugs History Society. http://historyofalcoholanddrugs.typepad.com (accessed February 15, 2010).

Alcohol and Tobacco Tax and Trade Bureau Home Page, U.S. Department of the Treasury. http://www.ttb.gov (accessed February 15, 2010).

Alcohol Policies Project, Center for Science in the Public Interest. http://beersoaksamerica .org/index.htm (accessed February 15, 2010).

Alcohol Policy Information System. http://www.alcoholpolicy.niaaa.nih.gov (accessed February 15, 2010).

Alcoholics Anonymous. http://www.aa.org (accessed February 15, 2010).

American Whiskey Trail. http://www.discus.org/trail/ (accessed February 15, 2010).

Center for Alcohol and Addiction Studies, Brown University. http://www.caas.brown.edu/ (accessed February 15, 2010).

Center on Alcohol Monitoring and Youth, Georgetown University. http://camy.org (accessed February 15, 2010).

College Drinking Prevention. http://www.collegedrinkingprevention.gov (accessed February 15, 2010).

Governor's Institute on Alcohol and Substance Abuse. http://www.governorsinstitute.org (accessed February 15, 2010).

Journal of Studies on Alcohol and Drugs. http://www.jsad.com (accessed February 15, 2010).

Mothers Against Drunk Driving. http://www.madd.org (accessed February 15, 2010).

National Institute on Alcohol Abuse and Alcoholism. http://www.niaaa.nih.gov (accessed February 15, 2010).

Rutgers Center for Alcohol Studies. http://alcoholstudies.rutgers.edu (accessed February 15, 2010).

Wine Business. http://www.winebusiness.com (accessed February 15, 2010).

The Wine Institute. http://www.wineinstitute.org (accessed February 15, 2010).

Index

absinthe, xxi, xxii, **1–2**, 57, 65, 76, 122, 127
abstinence, xv, 53, 85, 139, 182; in films, 92–95; Native Americans, 141; Prohibition, 149–52; and race, 159–60; and religion, 164; and temperance, 179–81
advertising, xxi, **2–3**; arts, 12; of beer, 26, 43–44, 83; and gender, 208; law, 147; and sports, 174–75; on television, 177–78
African Americans, **4–5**; 128; and class, 52; in literature, 122; race and ethnicity, 159–60
agave. *See* tequila
Alabama, 4, 119, 126
Alaska, 134, 195
Alcohol and Tobacco Tax and Trade Bureau (TTB), xxii, 69, 147
Alcoholics Anonymous (AA), **5–6**, 30, 53; and film, 93; and temperance, 179–81
alcoholism, xiv, xxi, **6–7**; arts, 11–14; disease concept, 53–54, 113, 130, 148; film depictions of, 93–95; gender, 208–9; literary depictions of, 122–23, television depictions of, 178; and underage drinking, 187
alcopops, 7, 177, 199
American Revolution, xvi, 10, 35, 37, 121, 141

Anchor Steam Brewery, 24
Anheuser-Busch, 24, 37, 83, 174
Anti-Saloon League (ASL), xxi, **7–10**, 35, 80, 150–51, 181, 190
Appalachia, 36–37, 109–11
apple brandy, 48. *See also* applejack
applejack, **10–11**, 48, 60, 65
apples, 10–11, 48–51, 66, 110, 166
Appleseed, Johnny, xvi, 10
Arizona, 49
arts, 11–14. *See also* films; literature
Atlanta Race Riot, 4

baby boomers, 82, 85
bar bets, **15–16**, 100
bar games, **16–17**
barfly, **17–18**
barley, xvi, 10, 49; beer, 25, 42, 134; bourbon, 38; barleywine, 65; whiskey, 193
bars, xvii, **18–21**, 179; music, 136–38; women, 207. *See also* pubs; speakeasies
bartending, **21–23**, 46, 112, 118, 171
beer, xvi, xxi, xxii, 4, **23–27**, 37, 65–67, 87–89, 115; advertising, 2–3, 174; ale, 42; arts, 11–12; blue laws, 34; distribution, 68, 119, 120; drinking games, 27, 29, 71–72; drinking glasses, 74; economics, 82–84;

food, 96–98; gender, 132; lager, 23–25, 37, 82, 133; lambic, 42; Native Americans, 140; pale ale, 25; porter, 25; Prohibition, 151; sports, 173–74; stout, 25; wort, 41. *See also* brewing; home-brew; microbreweries; Oktoberfest

beer belly, **27**

beer bong, **27–28**

beer garden, 34, 142

beer goggles, **28**

beer pong, **29**, 71, 112

beer runs, **29–30**

biergarten. *See* beer garden; Oktoberfest

binge drinking, 27, **30–32**, 61–62, 76–77, 97; gender, 208; national identity, 138; sports, 174; underage drinking, 184, 187

blackouts, **32–33**, 104, 148

blood alcohol content (BAC), **33**; binge drinking, 32; breathalyzer, 39–40; MADD, 135–36; politics, 146, 148

blue laws, xix, **33–35**, 137

Bond, James, 57, 129

bootleg alcohol, **35–36**, 68; Prohibition, 82, 152, 171; violence, 190

Boston, 20, 50, 83; St. Patrick's Day, 175; 180

bourbon, xvi, xviii, **36–38**; cocktails, 59–60; distilling, 65–66. *See also* whiskey

Bowery, 169. *See also* Skid Row

brandy, 10; cocktails, 56, 58, 60; distilling, 65; glasses, 73; sport, 172–73. *See also* apple brandy

breathalyzer, xxi, **39–40**; BAC, 33; MADD, 136

breweriana, **40**

brewing, xvi, xix, **41–45**; economics, 83–84; and Prohibition, 151. *See also* beer; home-brew; microbreweries

bubbly. *See* champagne

Buchner, Eduard, 87

Budweiser, 3, 25, 174

Bukowski, Charles, 17, 124

burping, **45**

cabarets, 18

California, 34, 161; beer, 133–34; blue laws in, 34; sparkling wine, 47; wine, 84, 117, 184, 195–202

calories, 27, 44

calvados. *See* applejack

Campari, 12, 59

Canada, 120; bootleg alcohol from, 35–36, 68, 152; cider, 49–50; wine, 198

Capone, Al, 36, 123, 153

carding, **46**

Caribbean, xix, 121, 140; bootleg alcohol from, 68; rum, 38, 165; sugar, 42, 121

Carter, Jimmy, 83

Catholic, 8, 75–76, 122, 126–28, 164; Catholic Total Abstinence Union (CTAU), 181; class, 52; Prohibition, 152–53, 181; St. Patrick's Day, 175–76

Centers for Disease Control (CDC), xiv, 31–32

champagne, xxii, 12, **46–48**, 117, 197; glasses, 12, 72–73

Chicago, 36, 137; Prohibition in, xx, 152–53, 190

China, 42, 52, 70, 76

cider, xvi, **48–51**, 166; ciderkin, 49; fermentation, 87–88; perry, 145–46; Prohibition, 197, 203

Civil War, xx, 3, 35, 37, 80, 83, 182

class, xvii, 18, **51–55**, 58–59, 93, 97, 123, 172, 190; middle class, 12–13, 18, 73, 150, 180–81; upper class, 96, 102; working class, 18, 90, 102, 157, 181, 207

cocktail parties, 11, **55–56**, 57, 97

cocktails, 11–13, 22, **56–61**, 74; collins, 59–60; food, 96; gender, 97, 208; gin, 102; rum, 166; tequila, 183

college drinking, 27, **61–63**, 77. *See also* drinking games

Colonies, xvi, xix, 125; applejack, 10; bars, 16, 18; beer, 23; cider, 49; laws, 34; Madeira, 125–26, 196; rum, 165

Colorado, 44, 49, 109, 141, 151

Connecticut, 54, 69

contraband. *See* bootleg alcohol

control states, 69, 82

Coors Brewing Company, 3, 24–25, 44, 83

corn, xvi, 92, 133, 179–80; fermentation, 87–88; distilling, 66, 109–10; whiskey, 193–95

craft brewers, 23, 25, 43, 50, 108, 133–34; economics, 83–84

Declaration of Independence, xvi, 20, 125
decorative arts, 11–13
de Kooning, William, 14
Democrats, 9, 95; and Prohibition, 153–54
design, 11–13; glassware, 73, 74
designated driver, xxii, 62, **64–65**, 79, 178
distilling, xvi, xix, xx, xxi, 10, **65–67**;
    applejack, 10; bathtub gin, 102;
    boilers, 111; home distilling, 56, 67;
    kettle, 41; mash, 38, 111, 193–94;
    microdistilleries, 66–67; rum, 165;
    still, 109, 111; whiskey, 194
distribution, 35, 52, **68–69**; hooch, 110;
    Internet, 112–13; politics, 146–48
Dogfish Head Craft Brewery, 66, 166
drinking age legislation, **69–70**
drinking games, 16, 18, **70–72**; drinking
    rituals, 76; peer pressure, 144–45;
    "power hour," 72; shooters, 168
drinking glasses and vessel, **72–74**; face
    jugs, 110; steins, 74; tankards, 74;
drinking habits, 50; African American, 4;
    anti-social, 99; binge drinking,
    30–32, college drinking, 61–63;
    economics, 82; women and girls,
    207–09
drinking rituals, **74–77**; bars, 18; drinking
    songs, 77; shooters, 168–69;
    toasting, 184–85
drinking songs, **77–78**
driving under the influence (DUI), xiv, 33,
    78–80; campaigns, 112, 136
drunkometer. *See* breathalyzer
dry counties, xxi, **80–81**. *See also*
    Prohibition

eau de vie. See spirits
economics, 23, **82–84**
education, 26, 53, 80, 148; brewing, 134;
    health, 106; Internet, 112; MADD,
    136; temperance, 181; wine, 168
Egypt, 42, 75, 175
Eighteenth Amendment, xxi, 9, 35–36, 55,
    154, 190; temperance, 181; Volstead
    Act, 151; Woman's Christian
    Temperance Union and, 207
elderly, **85–86**
England, 49, 103, 104; applejack, 10; beer,
    23; gin, 52, 90, 101; music, 77, 78;
    rum, 166
ethnicity, xvii, 4–5, 140–41, **159–60**;
    gender, 132, 207; violence, 190

fashion, 55–56, 132, 171, 202
Faulkner, William, 122
federal laws, 38, 147, 202
fermentation, 10, **87–89**; beer, 25, 41–43;
    cider, 49–50; hooch, 110; tequila,
    182–83; wine, 47, 195–97, 202
fetal alcohol syndrome, xxii, **89–91**, 106,
    148, 207, 208
films, 17–18, 57–59, 62, **91–96**, 129;
    Bottle Shock, 201; *Sideways*, 84
Fitzgerald, F. Scott, 123, 124, 152
fizz, 56, 127
flavored malt beverages (FMSBs). *See*
    alcopops
Florida, xix, 12
food and drink culture, **96–99**
Ford, Betty, xxii, 95, 161
France, 18, 37, 76, 83, 95; gin, 102; wine,
    46–47, 117, 196–98
Franklin, Ben, 121
free drinks, 15–16, 20, **99–100**

gay, xvii, 19
gender, xvii, 4, 19, 85, 93, 97; and
    cocktails, 58–59, 160; femininity,
    52, 132, 207–9; masculinity, 78,
    131–33, 173–74; and television, 177
Georgia, xix, 4, 81, 109–11, 137, 196
Germany, 37, 134, 140, 151; Oktoberfest,
    xx, 142–43
gin, 11, **101–2**, 129–30, 192; advertising,
    3; "bathtub gin," 55, 58, 171;
    distilling, 65–67, 102; epidemic, 52,
    90; "gin lane," 52, 101
glasses, 12–13, 58–59, 72–74, 168
Granholm v. Heald, 84, 119, 148–49
Great Depression, 2, 55, 58, 68, 110,
    153–54, 169
Greece, 102, 103, 140; brewing, 42;
    drinking games, 70; drinking
    rituals, 76; wine, 195
grenadine, 11, 57–58

hair of the dog, 96, **103**, 104
Hancock, John, 121
hangovers, 103, **104**; food, 96
happy hour, **105–6**
Harpoon Brewery, 50
Harvard School of Public Health, xxii, 31,
    62, 64–65
health effects of alcohol, xiv, xxi, 6, 85,
    89–90, **106–8**, 148, 208; binge

drinking, 31–32; education, 112;
    gin, 101; health warnings, 147;
    medicine, 130; temperance, 179
Heidseick, Charles, 47
Hemingway, Ernest, 121, 123, 129
highballs, 59–60
Holland, 101–2
home-brew, 26, 67, 83, **108–9**, 134.
    See also brewing
hooch, 57, 65–67, **109–11**, 193–95.
    See also moonshine
housewives, 59

ice cider. *See* cider
Idaho, 119
Indians. *See* Native Americans
Internet, 29, 40, 56, 78, 108–9, **112–13**,
    134; sales, 67, 148–49
interventions, **113–14**, 187
Ireland, 16, 20, 140, 156, 175–76
Italy, 95, 117, 140, 198

Jack Daniel's, 3, 140, 194
Jack Rose, 11
Japan, 16, 20, 65, 140, 167–68
Jefferson, Thomas, xx, 49, 179, 196
Jellinek, Elvin, 6
Jersey Lightning, 11
Jim Beam, 38, 194
Jim Crow laws. *See* segregation
Johnson, Vernon E., 113
julep, 56

karaoke, 16, 20
keg, 41, 115; laws, 147
keggers, **115**
Kentucky, 80; bourbon, 37–38; distilling,
    66; whiskey, 10, 194; wine, 196
kosher wine, **116–17**

Laird, Robert, 10
Laird, William, 10–11
last call, **118**
lesbian, xvii, 19
license states, 69
Lightner, Candy, xxii, 80, 135
liquor boards, **118–19**
liquor licenses, **120**
liquor stores, 26, 29, **120**
literature, ix, xiv, xviii, 177, **120–24**; Skid
    Row, 169
low-alcohol beverages, 24, 49, 151, 196

Madeira, xv, **125–26**, 140, 172
maize. *See* corn
malt, 41, 72, 109; brewing, 24, 133; liquor,
    7, 174, 199; whiskey, 66–67, 183
Mardi Gras, **126–28**
margarita, 58, 83
martini, 13, 57, **129–31**
mash, 10, 38, 41, 102, 109–11, 194
Massachusetts, xix, xx, 69, 105, 150
Matthews, Mark, 169
medical uses of alcohol, xvi, 1, 101, 110,
    130–31, 194; and Prohibition, 66,
    151–52, 197
men and boys drinking, 27, 62, **131–33**,
    173, 177, 210; advertising, 2–3;
    bars, 19; beer, 26; cocktails, 58–59
Mexico, 42, 196; and Prohibition, 35, 36,
    152; tequila, 140, 182
mezcal. *See* tequila
microbreweries, xxii, 25, 42–43, 66, 68,
    133–34
microdistillery, 67, 166
middle class, 12–13, 18, 52, 55, 73;
    Prohibition, 150; Temperance,
    180–81
Miller (brewing company), 3, 25, 44,
    83, 105
Mississippi, 81
monasteries, 42–43
moonshine, 36, 56, 67, 69, 109–11, 190,
    193. *See also* hooch
Mothers Against Drunk Driving (MADD),
    xxii, 64, 79–80, 111, **135–36**;
    Remove Intoxicated Drivers
    (RID), 135
music, 20, **136–38**, 142, 156, 176;
    country, 137; jazz, 171; folk, 78;
    rock, 161; and speakeasies, 36, 171

NASCAR, 110, 152
Nation, Carry, 19, 182
national identity, **139–40**
National Institute of Alcohol Abuse and
    Alcoholism (NIAAA), 7, 31, 53–54
National Minimum Drinking Age Act,
    xxii, 70, 186
Native Americans, xv, xvi, xx, 18, 122,
    128, **140–41**, 159–60
New Albion Brewery, 133
New Hampshire, 119
New Mexico, 12, 49, 196
New Orleans, 18, 34, 37, 80, 122, 126–28

New York, xvii, xx, xxii, 19–22, 66, 79;
    legal drinking age, 69, 79;
    Prohibition, 152–53, 171–72; wine,
    196, 198, 202
nightclubs, 13, 18, 20, 36, 58, 171; free
    drinks, 100; music, 136–37
Ninkasi, 42
noble experiment. *See* Prohibition
nonalcoholic beverages, 24, 57
North Carolina, 109, 119

oak barrels, 10, 83; bourbon, 36–38;
    whiskey, 194, 197
off-premise venues, 34, 83, 148
Ohio, 7, 69, 102; Alcoholics Anonymous,
    181; Anti-Saloon League, 7; corn,
    37; Johnny Appleseed, xvi, 10;
    wine, 198; Woman's Christian
    Temperance Union, 180, 207
Oklahoma, 5; dry counties in, 80–81
Oktoberfest, xx, **142–43**
O'Neill, Eugene, 13
on-premise venues, 34, 70, 83
orchards, xvi; applejack, 10; cider, 49–50
Oregon, 119; distilling, 66, 166; brewing,
    134; wine, 198, 201
Oxford Group, 5

passing out, 32
Pasteur, Louis, 43, 87
pasteurization, 48, 117, 145
pastis, 1, 127
peer pressure, **144–45**
Pennsylvania, xx, 119; drinking age, 69;
    wine, 198
perry, 48, **145–146**
piña colada, 59
Poe, Edgar Allan, 122
Poland, 140, 191
police, xxii, 18, 36, 120; breathalyzer, 39;
    DUI, 78–79; MADD, 136;
    Prohibition, 150; 152–53, 171, 190;
    Stonewall riots, xvii, 19
politics, xiv, 5, 49, 95, 123, **146–49**;
    Prohibition, 150, 20; Temperance,
    9, 181
Pollock, Jackson, 14
Prohibition, xvi, xx, xxi, 2–5, 68, 82, 130,
    149–55, 182; Anti-Saloon League,
    7–9; beer, 24, 43–44; bootlegging,
    35; cider, 50–51; class, 52–53;
    cocktails, 55–57, 129; film, 92–95;

gin, 102; literature, 122–23;
    politics, 147; Repeal Day, 113, 154;
    rum, 166; speakeasies, 20, 36,
    171–72; temperance, 180–81;
    violence, 190; wine, 117, 197, 203;
    Woman's Christian Temperance
    Union and, 207–8
Prohibition Party, xx, 9, 181
psychology, xiv, 28,
pub crawls, **155**, 157
pubs, xviii, 16, 18, 29, **155–57**; food, 98;
    St. Patrick's Day, 175–76;
punch, **157–58**

Quebec, 48, 119

race, xvii, 4, 76, 127–28, **159–60**, 190;
    bars, 18; gender, 207
radio, 109; advertising, 3, 91, 147
reciprocity, 15, 100
rehab, **161**
religion, **161–64**; Baptist, 80–81, 164,
    180, 205; Buddhism; Catholicism;
    Christianity, 164 163–64;
    Hinduism, 164; Islam, 162; Judaism
    116–17, 163; politics 34; rituals,
    75; role in Prohibition, 9
Republicans, 9, 153
restaurants, 42, 137; food, 97; license,
    119; wine, 168, 201
retail, 29–30, 46, 83–84, 116, 118–19,
    120, 156; Blue Laws, 34
revenuers, 109–10, 190
rice, 24, 133, 140, 195; sake, 167–68
roadblocks, 39, 136
Roe v. Wade, 90–91
Roederer, 47–48
Rogers, Roy, 57
Rogue (microbrewery), 66, 166
Roosevelt, Franklin D., 3, 122, 154, 181
Rothko, Mark, 14
rum, xix, 4, 38, **165–66**; advertising, 3;
    demon rum, 121, 150; distilling, 10,
    65; rumrunners, 35, 110, 121, 152;
    toddies, 56
Russia, 191–92
rye, 10, 101, 110, 191; bourbon, 37–38;
    brewing, 42; distilling, 66; whiskey,
    193–95

Sabbatarians, 34
sake, 41, 140, **167–68**

saloon, 17, 156, 172; gender, 207; and
        temperance, 181–82, 207; violence,
        190. *See also* bars
San Francisco, 20, 24, 129, 157, 166, 169
Scotland, 10, 140
segregation, xvii, 4, 18
session drinking, 50
sex, 26, 28, 33, 123, 132, 208;
        and bars, 20
Schlitz, 3
shooters, 112, **168–69**
Skid Row, 53, **169**, 204
slaves, 4, 18
sommeliers, 84, **170**
South Carolina, 68, 109–10
South Dakota v. Dole, 70
Southern Baptist Convention, 80
Southern Comfort, 60
Spain: absinthe, 1; cider, 49; wine,
        117, 198
sparkling wine. *See* champagne
speakeasies, 13, 20, 36, 105, 152, **171–72**;
        cocktails, 55, 58; gender, 208
spirits, xx, xxii, 35, 65–68, 179; applejack,
        10–11; Blue Law, 34; cocktails,
        56–61; economics, 80, 83–84;
        hooch, 110; law, 119–20, 147;
        vodka, 192. *See also* distilling
sports, 16, **172–75**; advertising, 2, 74, 83,
        177; bars, 19, 157; doping, 172–73;
        fans, 78; pregame drinking, 145
St. Patrick's Day, **175–76**
stemware. *See* drinking glasses and vessel
stereotypes, 26, 53, 122, 160; gender, 208
Stonewall Riots, xvii, 19
Sunday closing laws. *See* blue laws

tavern, 17, 21, 156–57, 172
taxation, xvi, xx, 29, 68–69, 190;
        distribution, 68; wine, 113
television, xxi, 16, 45, 62, **177–79**; *Cheers*
        (television sitcom), 20, 21;
        commercials, 3, 147, 174, 177–78;
        interventions, 114; politics, 146;
        rehab, 161; shows, 178;
        warnings, 91
temperance, xiv, xx, 19, **179–81**, 190,
        193; women, 207. *See also* Anti-
        Saloon League (ASL); Prohibition;
        Woman's Christian Temperance
        Union (WCTU)
Temperance Society, xx, 35, 141, 180

Temple, Shirley, 57
Tennessee, 109, 166; whiskey, 10, 66, 140,
        193–94
tequila, 11, 65, 74, 83, 140, **182–83**
terroir, **183**
Thacher, Ebby, 5
Thomas, Jerry, 21–22, 129
toasting, 76, 125, **184–85**
toddies, 56–57, 145, 166
transgendered, xvii, 19
Twain, Mark, 122
Twenty-first Amendment, xxi, 9, 24, 36,
        68, 82, 106, 113, 119, 148, 151, 154

underage drinking, 7, 26, 105, 136, **186–88**;
        college drinking, 62; politics, 148;
        television, 178
Utah, 119, 154

Van Gogh, Vincent, 1, 76
Vermont, 50, 66, 69
vermouth, 55, 129
vineyards, 12, 196, 201
violence, xiv, xvi, 6, 106, 148, **189–91**;
        men, 131; and Prohibition, 153;
        and temperance, 181
Virginia, 11, 49, 111, 119; wine, 195–98
vodka, 11, 37, 83–84, **191–92**;
        advertising, 12; cocktails, 57;
        distilling, 65–66; martinis, 129–30
Volstead Act, xxi, 24, 151–53, 171,
        197, 205

Washington, George, 10, 49, 166
Washington (D.C.), 180
Washington (State), 49, 119, 134, 198, 201
Wechsler, Henry, 31, 62
whiskey, xvi, xviii, xx, xxi, 3, **193–95**;
        advertising, 3, 193; bootleg, 35;
        distilling, 65; distribution, 68;
        Prohibition, 19. *See also* bourbon;
        hooch
Whiskey Rebellion, xx, 37, 68, 193–94
Williams, Tennessee, 13
Willard, Frances, 180, 205–6
Wilson, Bill, 5
wine, 51, **195–99**; advertising, 3;
        American Viticultural Area (AVA),
        183–84; distribution, 68, 119–20;
        economics, 84; food, 96–98;
        glasses, 72–73; homemade, 59, 108;
        Internet, 112–13; kosher, 116–17;

laws, 147–49; religion, 75–76; tannins, 73. *See also* champagne; fermentation; kosher wine; Madeira

wine coolers, 50, 199. *See also* alcopops

wine tasting, 170, **199–200**

wine tourism, 82, 84, **200–202**; Napa Valley, 38, 200–201

winemaking, xix, 73, 170, 183, 195–98, 201–3; at home, **202–4**; during Prohibition, 108. *See also* wine

winos, **204–5**

Woman's Christian Temperance Union (WCTU), xx, 9, 35, 153, 180, **205–7**. *See also* Nation, Carry

women, xvii, 17–21, 26, 86, 131, **207–9**; AA, 53; advertising, 2–4; health, 90–91; pubs, 156; speakeasies, 172; Temperance, 180. *See also* Woman's Christian Temperance Union (WCTU)

working class, 13, 52, 58, 123, 207; gin, 102; and temperance, 180–81

workplace drinking, 96, **209–10**

World Health Organization (WHO), 31

World War II, 3; brewing, 24; Oktoberfest, 142; women, 208

World Wide Web. *See* Internet

yeast: brewing, 25, 41–43, 108, 134; cider, 48; perry, 145; wine, 47, 203. *See also* fermentation

zymurgy. *See* fermentation

About the Editor and Contributors

Editor

RACHEL BLACK is Assistant Professor in the Gastronomy program at Boston University. An anthropologist and historian by training, her research has mainly focused on food distribution, urban agriculture and the culture of drink.

Contributors

WHITNEY ADAMS is a sommelier who represents an Italian wine portfolio for JK Imports. She writes a blog about wine at Brunellos Have More Fun.

KEN ALBALA is Professor of History at the University of the Pacific in Stockton, California. He has written and edited many books including *Eating Right in the Renaissance*, *Food in Early Modern Europe*, *The Banquet*, and *Beans: A History*. He is editor of *Food Cultures of the World Encyclopedia*, coeditor of the journal *Food, Culture and Society*, and coauthor of the cookbook *The Lost Art of Real Cooking*.

BEN APPLEBAUM is an advertising creative director and author of *The Book of Beer Pong*. He is also the creator of CollegeStories.com.

RÉMY CHAREST is a food and wine writer and former restaurant critic. He blogs on winecase.ca and foodcase.ca.

JANET CHRZAN is a lecturer in the Department of Anthropology and the School of Nursing at the University of Pennsylvania. Her research explores a range of medical anthropology topics including prenatal nutrition, food education and alcohol studies. She has published articles on food use, nutrition education, and health and culinary tourism.

DAVID M. FAHEY is professor emeritus of History, Miami University, Oxford, Ohio. His publications have focused on the Anglo-American temperance movement.

MICHAEL P. FERRARI is the founder and publisher of Blue Room Publishing. He is the author of the college-themed novel *Assault on the Senses*.

JOSEPH GELFER is an Adjunct Associate at the School of Political and Social Inquiry, Monash University, Australia. He is founding editor of *Journal of Men, Masculinities and Spirituality*.

W. BLAKE GRAY writes for the *Los Angeles Times*, Wine Review Online and other publications and his blog, The Gray Market Report.

KEVIN GRACE is the Head of the Archives and Rare Books Library at the University of Cincinnati where he also serves an adjunct assistant professor in the College of Education, Criminal Justice, and Human Services. His research is on urban culture and American vice.

SUSAN L. JOHNSTON is Professor of Anthropology at West Chester University, West Chester, Pennsylvania. A former bartender, she is a medical/nutritional anthropologist whose work has focused on health and nutrition transitions in fourth world populations and on food ecology.

BRADLEY KADEL is an Assistant Professor of History at Fayetteville State University in Fayetteville, North Carolina. His areas of interest include modern Irish history and the history of temperance and alcohol.

KEN KIRKWOOD teaches and researches at the University of Western Ontario in London, Ontario, Canada.

JAMES KLEIN is Assistant Professor of History at Del Mar College in Corpus Christi, Texas.

BILL KTE'PI is an independent scholar and writer.

MICHAEL LEJMAN is a PhD candidate in modern European history at the University of Memphis. His research is primarily focused on Modern France, European and American politics, imperialism, African American history, and the effects of Western politics and culture on the postcolonial world.

DEMOND MILLER is Professor of Sociology and Director of the Liberal Arts and Sciences Institute for Research and Community Service at Rowan University, Glassboro, New Jersey. He has worked as an evaluator for alcohol and tobacco social norms projects and is a certified clinical substance abuse counselor.

JOY NEWMAN is a doctoral candidate in the University at Albany (SUNY) Department of History. Her dissertation is "The Drinking Age Debates: A History of Youth Alcohol Use and Related Policy in the United States."

GARRETT PECK is an independent scholar and the author of *Prohibition Hangover: Alcohol in America from Demon Rum to Cult Cabernet*.

DAVE REEDY is an ethnobotanist exploring ways in which cultural practices maintain biodiversity, the biogeography of culturally important plants, and traditional resource management.

CRISTIN ROLLINS is an Assistant Professor of Sociology and the Director of Institutional Research at Piedmont College in Demorest, Georgia. She has focused on the Woman's Christian Temperance Union and other cultural elements of alcohol.

PAUL M. ROMAN is Distinguished Research Professor of Sociology and Director of the Center for Research on Behavioral Health and Human Service Delivery at the University of Georgia. He has published many articles on alcohol.

MATTHEW RUSSELL is a doctoral candidate in Spanish literature at the University of California, Davis. He has worked in the California wine industry and is a home-brewer and home winemaker.

KAREN EILENE SAENZ is a sommelier, beverage educator, and marketing writer for the wine industry. Her research has focused on expressive culture in Northern Territory, Australia, and American drinking cultures.

PAM SEZGIN is a Professor of Anthropology and History at Gainesville State College, Georgia. Her research interests include expressive culture (music, art, food), sustainability, and historic preservation.

LEONARD A. STEVERSON is an Associate Professor of Sociology at South Georgia College in Douglas, where he teaches sociology and criminal justice. Steverson formerly worked in community corrections and mental health/substance abuse programs and was an addictions counselor.

BARRY STIEFEL is a Visiting Assistant Professor in the joint program in Historic Preservation at the College of Charleston and Clemson University. His academic interests center on the preservation of Jewish heritage.

VANESSA TAYLOR is a Research Fellow at Greenwich Maritime Institute, Greenwich University.

BEN WYNNE is Assistant Professor of History at Gainesville State College in Georgia.

JOEL YELIN is a Research Assistant at Rowan University. He has published several works in the areas of religion and tourism, environmental justice, and environmental terrorism.

WILLA ZHEN is a PhD candidate in Anthropology at the School of Oriental and African Studies in London, England.